Total Facility Control

Total Facility Control

Don T. Cherry, CPP

Butterworths
Boston London Durban Singapore Sydney Toronto Wellington

Library of Congress Cataloging-in-Publication Data

Cherry, Don T.
  Total facility control.

  Includes index.
  1. Buildings—Protection. 2. Buildings—Security
measures. I. Title. II. Title: Facility control.
TH9705.C46 1986   658.4′7   85-19487
ISBN 0–409–95149–8

Butterworth Publishers
80 Montvale Avenue
Stoneham, MA 02180

10 9 8 7 6 5 4 3 2 1

Printed in the United States of America

This book is lovingly dedicated to my wife, Jackie, whose support, advice, patience and editing skills made it possible.

It is also dedicated to those who live in, visit, work in, or manage large facilities; and to those individuals who seek a better way to provide a safe, secure, efficient, and cost effective working environment.

Contents

Preface

Years ago when I began designing control systems for different types of buildings, I was frustrated at not being able to locate suitable resources. Thus, the idea for this book was born. *Total Facility Control* is a proven concept that provides safety, security, efficiency, and economy by integrating various building system functions into a single operating system. Nearly any facility having 100,000 square feet of occupied floor space and 100 or more occupants can benefit from an integrated control systems approach.

The key buzz words in building operational management today are **intelligent building** and **smart building**. Most of the material available about achieving such a facility falls far short of meeting the total concept of building control. *Total Facility Control* is concerned with the integration of various building systems. This concept can lead to more efficient monitoring and control of facilities.

Efficient energy management and equipment maintenance will cut operational costs. Payback for a properly designed system can be realized in tangible savings within two to four years, in most instances. Effective fire detection and patrol tour management can reduce insurance premiums while affording better protection for the building, its contents, and its occupants.

Intangibles may account for even greater savings. These intangibles include the fire that was quickly extinguished, the rape that did not occur, the pilferage that could not take place, the proprietary material that was not stolen, and skilled employees who stayed because of company concern and high morale.

The goal of this book is to provide the means to meet a variety of potentially disastrous situations and limit their effect.

The text explains the concept of total facility control and how to attain it, while the glossary is a dictionary of over 900 pertinent terms, each of which is cross referenced to the chapter in which it appears. These terms will appear in **bold face** within the text. This terminology will provide owners, managers, security directors, and students with a working vocabulary of building control.

Total Facility Control outlines in one volume how energy management, movement control, fire protection, physical security, audio, closed circuit television, preventive maintenance, and personnel protection can all be organized into a facility control scheme that will guarantee a safer and more efficient building in which to live, work, or visit.

This book can be used by architects, facility managers, and department heads such as maintenance, safety, security, and energy management. Chief executive officers will find it valuable for long range planning and executives responsible for operations and management should find the contents a key source of information. This is also an excellent book for the student and entry level junior executive desiring to explore the entire spectrum of facility control. The information presented should be of use to any individual having management responsibilities in business, industry, education, health care, banking, airports, hotels, and other fields.

Don T. Cherry
August 6, 1985

About the Author

Don Thomas Cherry is the chief executive officer of Cherry Limited, a facility control consulting firm. He specializes in designing mutually supportive facility control systems that integrate physical security, fire management, closed circuit television, access control, energy management, equipment monitoring, preventive maintenance, and patrol tour management. His expertise lies in developing innovations to meet the unique requirements for highrise office buildings, industrial plants, research centers, health care facilities, military installations, petrochemical plants, and educational institutions.

Mr. Cherry is a retired U.S. Air Force intelligence officer. Much of his practical experience in sensitive security areas was attained through the operation and management of special compartmentalized intelligence in the United States, Europe, and Asia during his military career.

His lectures and seminars on facility control have been presented at universities and technical schools and to numerous professional organizations throughout the United States and abroad. His articles on related subjects have appeared in professional journals.

His professional certifications include Certified Protection Professional (CPP) by the American Society for Industrial Security, Certified Professional Consultant (CPC) by the Consultant's Institute, and Professional Member of the Construction Specifications Institute (CSI).

He maintains additional professional affiliations with the National Fire Protection Association, Academy of Security Educators and Trainers, Association of Energy Engineers, American Consultants League, Association of Former Intelligence Officers, National Counter Intelligence Corps Association, Navy League, and Air Force Association.

Acknowledgments

Physical space precludes specific acknowledgment of each source of the total material used to develop the concept of *Total Facility Control*. I would like to mention my many professional friends and clients who afforded me access to their thoughts and facilities; they provided much in the way of hands-on experience. There are literally hundreds of manufacturers whose literature provided many of the building blocks for this text. The national code, standard, and testing groups were an excellent source of system performance requirements and guide lines.

To single out only one or a few would be unjust to the many. I would like to make special mention of Ed Pepke and Bart Long, two unwitting mentors who made this project a possibility. They provided the spark and I will be forever grateful for their faith in me.

To Jackie, Carla, and Eric, without whom I never could have survived the human trial one places upon himself when he undertakes writing such a book, I thank you from the bottom of my heart. Let's do it again!

Total Facility Control

Total Facility Control: A Proven Concept

Increased efficiency at reduced cost is the dream of all executives in the world of commerce and industry. Government agencies at every level also seek this goal, as do institutions involved in education, health care, and research. The explosion of modern technology has provided the capability to achieve these results today. The development of microprocessor-based control and monitoring technology has opened the door to building automation and energy cost control. (Figure 1.1, p. 2).

A basic automation system can perform many functions. Temperature, equipment, and alarm sensors located throughout the building can collect data constantly and transmit it to a central processing unit where it can be displayed visually. A single operator can know what is happening at any point being monitored. He or she can supervise equipment, humidity, and energy consumption as well as whether an intruder is attempting to penetrate a perimeter fence. Such a system functions to provide management with continuous monitoring, evaluation, and control of the working environment. Problems are therefore spotted before they become unmanageable.

Computer technology makes it possible to control the operation of building equipment and machinery, the consumption of energy, and the comfort level for personnel, and to provide greater levels of safety and protection. Building management can be further enhanced by integrating various building control systems (Figure 1.2, p. 3).

Total facility control entails much more than simply integrating two or three of the building's systems. For truly effective building control, all systems should be integrated into a single functional master arrangement. This includes monitoring and control of the building environment, as well as fire and security protection.

In general, an integrated facility control system will be cost-effective for facilities of 100,000 square feet or more. The larger the facility, the more complex its activities, and the greater the building population, the more beneficial a facility control system will be. Multiple buildings or several buildings at different geographic locations make the integrated systems approach essential for minimizing operating costs.

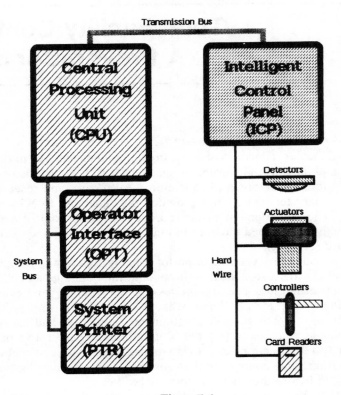

Figure 1.1

Through the development of computer-based automation systems, the control functions of multiple buildings can be consolidated into a centrally located console. This makes it feasible for one person to perform the man-machine interface effectively and efficiently. It is possible to build a "dream system" that will provide maximum safety, protection, and efficiency for industrial, commercial, and institutional facilities. This system can provide early detection of fire, in-depth security and surveillance, controlled movement of people, reliable communications, finite equipment monitoring, and cost-effective energy management, yet requires only a limited number of personnel to supervise the system. Standard equipment, fully designed and tested, is available today to provide just such a system.

Total Facility Control

Expanded Configuration

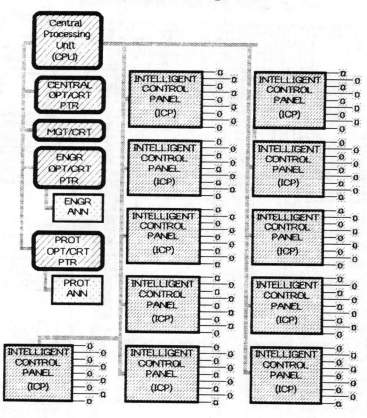

Figure 1.2

Anyone with the responsibility for managing a large high-rise office building in which the majority of space is leased knows that there is much competition in keeping the building fully occupied. Why not have a system that will give your clients something the competition does not offer? A computer-based building automation system can provide safety and comfort to tenants and minimize operational costs. Total facility control integrates fire detection and alarm, building protection services, and energy management into a centralized system—truly a dream system for the building management team (Figure 1.3, p. 4).

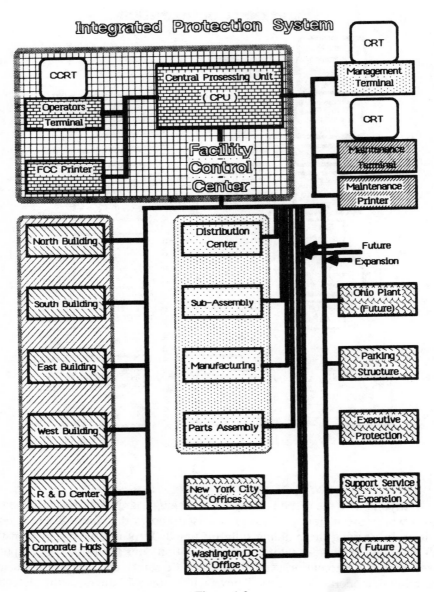

Figure 1.3

ENERGY MANAGEMENT

Controlling the energy consumption of a single facility is difficult, but computerized building automation offers this capability. With the right equipment, proper system design, and innovative management, energy consumption and costs can be reduced while maintaining optimum environmental comfort.

The cost of heating, cooling, and lighting a building is a major operating expense. Recent increases in utility charges make it mandatory that physical plant efficiency be markedly improved. High energy costs can deprive fire safety and security areas of the funds required to protect both physical plant and personnel. The maintenance department can receive the lion's share of the operational budget, yet grow more antiquated as those extra funds go to higher energy costs and more and more time is spent inspecting equipment and repairing breakdowns.

Computerized energy management systems control heating, ventilating, and air conditioning (HVAC). The computer memory can regulate energy use on the basis of the building's previous use under similar conditions. Heating a building slowly early in the morning requires less energy than turning the HVAC system up to its maximum output just before beginning the workday. The **start/stop** technique controls the building comfort level according to time and temperature readings. The building automation system can constantly monitor outside air temperature and humidity to use free air whenever possible. During unoccupied hours the facility control system can automatically set back the temperature requirements to conserve energy. Peak electrical demand periods can be monitored and anticipated with equipment programmed to cut back on metered utility requirements.

LIGHTING CONTROL

Internal and external lighting are essential to all operations, but too often lights are on for no valid reason. Incorporation of lighting control can be a huge dollar-saving effort. Even security lighting along the perimeter can be powered down most of the time and automatically brought up to full power if the security system indicates a perimeter penetration. This same technique will turn on and point closed circuit television cameras to the area of the indicated alarm.

In open office areas or a modular arrangement, a light modulating system can power down the lighting to the desired level. This not only prolongs the bulb or tube life as much as 100 percent (from three to over six years for a standard fluorescent tube), but also cuts the maintenance costs in half. With proper ambient light sensors and special ballast, safe lighting levels are automatically maintained as a function of natural illumination.

In interior offices, a system of infrared sensing can be installed to turn on the lights automatically when someone enters the office and to turn them off shortly after the area has been left untended. This technique also works in open office areas and next to outside windows. An ideal application of this type of lighting control is in emergency stairwells. The norm for stairwell lighting is lights on seven days a week twenty-four hours a day. What a waste! Why not incorporate into the facility control system a lights-off capability when the stairwell is unoccupied? What a tremendous dollar-saving technique! Automatic supervised sensors can immediately turn on the lights the instant anyone enters the stairwell and remain on as long as the stairwell is occupied. This could also serve as an additional security measure, alerting the security control center that the normally empty stairwell is occupied. This same energy-saving method can be applied to tunnels and overhead walkways, parking facilities, maintenance penthouses, supply rooms, and similar areas normally lighted but unoccupied.

FIRE MANAGEMENT

Integrating the building's fire, security, and maintenance functions offers many benefits. Of primary importance is a fire management system that automatically notifies occupants in the alarm zone. At the same time, the entire building is notified that an alarm has been sounded and is being investigated. Elevators are captured and returned to the ground floor for firefighters' use. The heating, ventilating, and air conditioning systems are directed to shut off air to the zone in alarm and supply 100 percent airflow to the surrounding areas to aid in containing the fire. These actions limit the spread of smoke beyond the fire area. Venting fans exhaust smoke and fumes from the threatened area while other fan systems are activated to put a slight overpressure of fresh air in the stairwells and designated safe havens. This precludes smoke from following people as they exit the zone in alarm. Locked doors automatically unlock. In special areas such as vaults where corporate records, computer tapes, and other valuable items may be stored, doors go to a **fail-secure** condition. This locking technique allows personnel in the vaulted area to leave, but prevents anyone else from entering the area. This also precludes possible damage by firefighters.

Building or fire officials can communicate with various areas of the building via a supervised communications system. The fire battalion chief has a means of communicating with the firefighters without the problem of building structural interference, often referred to as **steel masking**. Suppression systems for computer rooms, kitchen hoods, and sprinkler systems are automatically monitored, and all actions taken by the system are recorded.

MOVEMENT CONTROL

In controlling the movement of people, let us again take the large office building as an example. It is normally open for business from 7 AM until 6 PM Monday through Friday and from 8 AM to 12 noon on Saturday. Thus, the building doors should open and close automatically at those times. But what about the law firm that needs to meet with clients at night, another tenant's weekend crash project, or the secretary who must return after hours to finish an assignment? How does one cope with long weekends and holiday schedules?

Why not set up a standard card access system through a security staff for the tenants? With a well-designed system, individual clients can set the times at which their employees come and go. If a law firm chooses to work nights, their access control can be tied into the HVAC so that they alone are charged for the after-hours portion of electricity and air conditioning they use rather than spreading the cost among the other tenants who were not working during those odd hours. An access control system should be flexible enough to permit access for the weekend project group or a secretary who must work late.

Suppose a secretary must return to the building at 7 PM and work until 11 PM for two consecutive nights. The system being described would allow use of her access card to enter the building between those hours. It would permit the elevator to take her only to the floor where she works, open the door to her office, turn on the lights and heat, and let her work in peace knowing that she is securely locked in. When she leaves, the lights and heat would automatically go off. The elevator would return her to the ground floor where she would again use her access card to exit the building. Her employer could even request a hard-copy record of her entrance and departure times, as the system would record all her after-hours transactions.

A properly designed access control system will provide management with increased control over their facility, permit flexibility of access for the tenants, and improve overall protection. Such a system would allow building management to control the times when vendors would be permitted entry to service vending machines. The managers of data processing centers would be able to control access to computer rooms and, even more importantly, access to data file storage vaults. It could be arranged so that a programmer's card would not grant access until all operators had departed from the computer room. Doors of entry and exit would be established so that the programmers and operators would not meet inside the data processing center. This is a step to preclude possible collusion. The same access card would ensure that they could only park their cars in designated, separate areas, if such a degree of separation were required.

PROTECTION CONTROL

High crime rates across the nation dictate the need for a security element of some type at almost every moderately large facility. The key to using security personnel effectively is electronics. The minimum guard force on duty at any one time should never be less than two. One individual can monitor the facility control console and be responsible for directing activity. The second can roam the facility on patrol tours and be responsive to alarms as directed by the console operator.

Supervised electronic devices and controls allow constant and automatic monitoring of the building's fire systems. Patrol tours are automatically logged for assured building coverage as well as insurance premium reductions. Closed circuit television (CCTV), properly designed and installed, can provide the operator with multiple eyes that are constantly on guard. Current state-of-the-art technology permits the installation of CCTV cameras that also act as motion detectors. They do not normally display a picture on a monitor unless the electrons on the face of the camera tube are disturbed by movement. At that point they not only can cause an alarm and hard-copy printout, but also can cause a video cassette recorder (VCR/VTR) to begin recording the activity and activate a date-time generator (DTG). This type of system will provide evidence that is admissible in court.

Far too little use is made of audio systems in facility protection. It is an ideal way to provide protection in parking structures or overhead and underground tunnels connecting buildings. The building engineer can realize considerable savings in manpower and equipment by being able to audibly monitor air-handling units, remote equipment, and isolated penthouse machinery.

MAINTENANCE MANAGEMENT

For effective facility control, an efficient maintenance department is essential. The basic requirement is a system that not only monitors the building's systems but, more importantly, also controls those systems. To appreciate the complexity of maintenance control, one needs to understand the myriad of building control systems, only a few of which normally interact with one another.

Preventive maintenance has been practiced to varying degrees over the years, but generally it has been pegged to the calendar. A truly effective preventive maintenance system permits equipment servicing on the basis of actual use.

SPECIAL APPLICATIONS

There are many unique applications of facility control as one moves from one industry to another. For example, a large hospital might want to use the system to monitor and record all pharmacy drug transactions. Video could record every prescription issued as well as the individual picking up the drugs.

Mental institutions and correctional facilities are designed to confine the inmates. Fires are sometimes deliberately set to get the doors unlocked. Proper system design will unlock the cell doors of the zone in alarm, allowing the inmates to escape the fire area and, at the same instant, cause a fail-secure

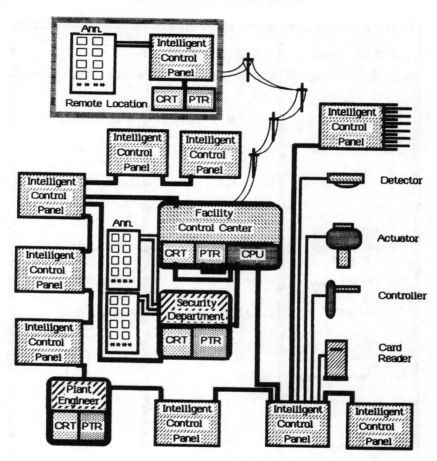

Figure 1.4

situation that will create a double ring of security away from the fire/smoke danger area, while safely containing those incarcerated.

A petrochemical plant may normally require only moderate perimeter control and limited monitoring of systems. Once a problem occurs, such as an explosion, the system may then be required to turn on pumps and cascade the flow of water through a manifold piping system to the problem area. Tank water levels would need to be monitored, pumps started, plant personnel alerted, outside agencies notified, and records kept of all actions.

Total Facility Control
System Growth

First Year	Third Year	Future
Facility Control Console/CPU	Color CRT Terminal	Operating System Save
Start/Stop Programs	Chiller Optimization	Off-Line Memory Access
Reports & Logs	Load Reset	Enthalpy Control
Event Initiated Programs	Data File Logs	Memory Diagnostics
Command Language Interpreter	Peripherals Exerciser	Perimeter Security
Optimum Start/Stop	Operating System Verify	Pump Control
Access Control	Closed Circuit TV	Remote Building Control
Duty Cycling	Compartmentalized Areas	
Power Demand Control	Equipment Monitoring	
Patrol Tour		
Building Perimeter Security		

Figure 1.5

Research and development centers using an access control system can determine who goes where and when and also make it impossible for one person to enter a sensitive area alone. The same application can be made to biohazard areas and nuclear facilities where the buddy system must be rigidly enforced. Here the door will not open until a second valid card is entered into the system for access within a given time frame.

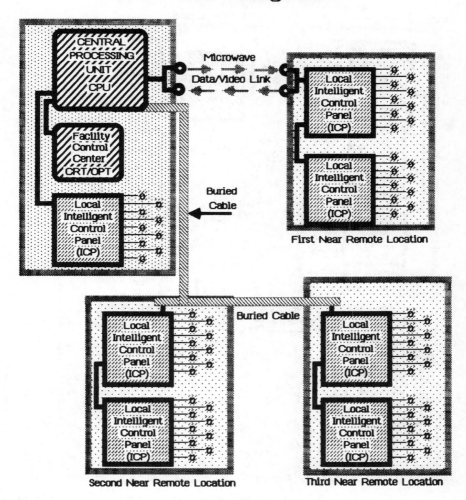

Figure 1.6

Some buildings require much closer movement control than others, and this must often be accomplished discreetly. Some facilities require certain visitors to be escorted 100 percent of the time, while others are allowed to roam freely, as they know their way about and are trusted, familiar individuals. Even in this last case, there are probably some places where they should not be, and that is where positive movement control becomes extremely effective. For

Total Facility Control

Far Remote Configuration

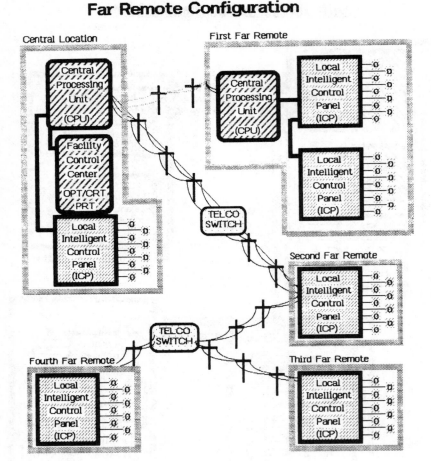

Figure 1.7

graphic representations of total facility control system applications, see Figures 1.4 (p. 9), 1.5 (p. 10), 1.6 (p. 11), 1.7 (above), and 1.8 (p. 13).

TOTAL FACILITY CONTROL—APPLICATIONS

Energy consumption control is essential to the successful management of any facility. Building and grounds lighting will provide protection and still be a source of energy savings when properly controlled. High-rise building and in-

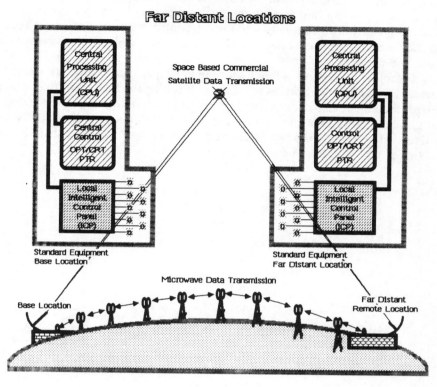

Figure 1.8

dustrial fire management techniques protect lives and property, improve employee morale, and reduce insurance premiums. Controlling the movement of personnel and vehicles in and around the facility is an effective way to improve safety, reduce property damage, and limit the potential for theft. Managing and monitoring the movement of protection officers will increase security visibility, reduce insurance premiums, improve safety, and provide increased protection for the patrolling officers. Electronic maintenance management will extend the life of equipment, provide for more effective use of personnel, and permit tighter control over issued tools and expendable supplies. Centralized control of building systems will permit special applications to be applied to a full array of unique building situations that might otherwise create major and expensive hazards.

Management is responsible for operating an efficient, safe, and secure facility. Operational expenses can be reduced by controlling energy consumption. The safety of building occupants can be enhanced by controlling the protective systems. Protection of corporate assets can be controlled by managing the movement of people within the building and by monitoring the various fire, surveillance, and internal security control measures. These control elements, when designed into a mutually supportive control system, are cost-effective and can actually reduce operational expenditures while improving overall safety and security.

Total facility control is much more than simply controlling one's place of business. **Total Facility Control** is totally controlling the facility so that it is not only protected but also managed efficiently and cost-effectively. The synergism that is total facility control provides the facility with a series of mutually supportive systems where the protection and control is much greater than the sum of all its parts. The dream system can be a reality.

2

Integrated Building Monitoring and Control

ENERGY CONSUMPTION

In years past the method for monitoring a building's **heating, ventilating, and air conditioning (HVAC)** systems was for "Charlie in the basement" to wander around the building, read dials, adjust knobs, and make notations in the boiler room log. With the advance of technology, rising labor costs, increased complexity of building environmental equipment, and growth in physical size of the overall facilities, it is no longer practical, much less cost-effective, to continue this type of building management system.

A new approach is required to provide efficient management for large facilities or buildings located throughout a large complex, across the street, across town, or across the state. Present technology applies the power of the microprocessor to the task of monitoring and controlling a facility's HVAC systems. This frees the maintenance staff to perform **preventive maintenance** functions and other more productive activities.

The technology of building management systems now permits corporate executives to do more with less, to have better control of their facilities at lower cost, and to use personnel more effectively to prevent problems. The bottom line is that building operating costs can be reduced while increasing the efficiency of the facility's systems.

ENERGY CONSUMPTION MANAGEMENT

To many building owners energy management is done automatically by some "black box" in the basement. These relatively simplistic systems can save energy, but they leave gaps in adequate building control. For example, lighting levels are frequently reduced in an effort to lower utility costs. This may make employees reluctant to enter dimly lighted areas or may produce a more inviting target for vandals. It may also negate the effects of **closed circuit television**

Factors Affecting Energy Consumption

Building Envelope

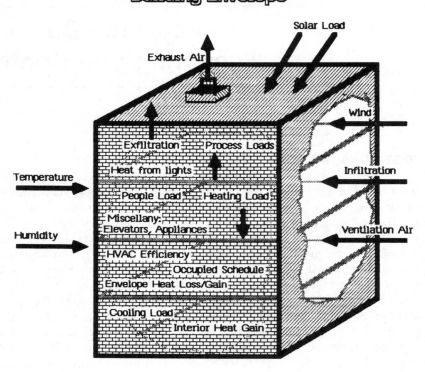

Figure 2.1

(CCTV). From a cost-saving point of view, such efforts may actually be counterproductive.

The control logic inherent in an integrated microprocessor-based facility management system can fill these gaps. The heating, ventilating, and air-conditioning (HVAC) system functions as an essential tool. Building control sensors can report a wide variety of information and current status such as on/off, open/closed, hot/cold. When a sensor indicates a normal condition, the central processing unit (CPU) is usually programmed to note the condition and continue its **polling** routine. When a sensor indicates an abnormal condition, the CPU will automatically: (1) take corrective action, (2) report/record the condition and action taken, (3) sound an alarm to initiate action. In these instances, a sensor-activated cascading program can begin that will perform an open-ended series of actions.

Such technology can even be used on a smaller scale in the home. The U.S. Department of Energy has conducted extensive tests on a device called an "energy cost indicator" for homeowners. With it the homeowner can push a button and read the cost of gas and electricity being used on an hourly, daily, or monthly basis. This provides immediate feedback on energy management techniques, without waiting for the gas or electric bill to arrive.

Such rapid response is important to any **control loop**. A delay in realizing that the energy consumption is out of bounds can be very costly to the building's operational budget. If it is obvious that sensing or measurement are the keys to building protection and control, then what must be done in a typical commercial building? When looking at all the internal and external influences affecting a building's energy consumption (Figure 2.1), the task appears formidable. It isn't enough simply to charge rising building costs off to the ever increasing cost of energy. Efficiency in building operational control is required. This efficiency can be greatly increased by adding a few sensors and monitoring the performance of energy consumers.

MONITORING ENERGY CONSUMERS

The man-machine interface of any facility control system must be simple to operate. The system's outputs must be easy to read, use standard American Society of Heating, Refrigerating and Air Conditioning Engineers (ASHRAE) equations, provide both **digital** and **analog** information and, above all, readily interface with other building control systems.

To control energy consumption effectively, the following items must be monitored and controlled.

- **Optimum Start/Stop Times.** Under this control situation, the computer compares outside weather conditions with the building CPU's memory of how long it took the building to warm up previously under similar conditions and starts the HVAC equipment at the latest possible time before occupancy. This program also shuts off HVAC equipment at the earliest possible time prior to close of the business day.
- **Duty Cycling.** The system will calculate electrical, cooling, heating, and humidity requirements and cycle through the various pieces of mechanical equipment to shut them down for a portion of each hour, thus generating considerable savings.
- **HVAC Economizers.** The CPU, through the operating system, will regulate equipment controllers to position fan system dampers so that cooling energy requirements are minimized.
- **Outside Air Control.** Additional savings are obtainable by controlling the volume of outside air taken into the HVAC systems. Modern ventilation standards permit introduction of less outside air, and this can be a major saving factor in most applications.

- **Chiller Optimization**. This program reduces the chiller plant's electrical load. It automatically selects the most favorable operating conditions for the condenser supply water temperature, chilled water supply temperature, and the best combination of available **chillers** for any system load condition. When done in conformance with the manufacturer's recommendations, the technique of automatically rotating chillers has proved to be cost-effective in reducing energy consumption. This is a difficult procedure for man to monitor, but a simple, routine operation for an energy management system's CPU.
- **Supply Air Reset**. The system can achieve additional savings resulting from automatic reset of the supply air temperature. Under this procedure, during periods of moderate building heating and cooling loads, the discharge air temperature from the fan system can be reset to minimize the amount of energy required.
- **Humidity Control**. The system will calculate humidity requirements and energy-savings potential. This will result in a lower winter relative humidity set point and reduced energy costs.
- **Demand Limiting**. Extremely large energy savings are possible by closely monitoring the electrical demand limit and automatically shutting down pre-programmed equipment during peak electrical demand periods. Should automatic shutdown not be enough to cope with peaking facility electrical demands, the system will signal the operator of excess requirements, and additional ancillary equipment may be turned off.

In addition to these items, the following factors should also be measured in energy management. They are listed in order of importance. These items are points of consideration for the **design team** in establishing requirements for a computer-based facility control system. They are constant factors affecting a building's **envelope**. An asterisk(*) indicates factors that are generally available from the local weather bureau or newspaper on a monthly basis. Figure 2.1 provides an illustration of the various factors acting upon a building's envelope.

- **Outdoor temperature** *
- **Heating load**
- **Cooling load**
- **Lighting load**, if manually controlled
- **Occupancy**, if variable
- Relative humidity*
- **Wet bulb temperature**
- Solar radiation*
- Wind velocity*
- Wind direction*

Daily building constants are those items which may, for the purposes of energy management, be presumed to remain constant for a given building. An asterisk (*) indicates items that apply during occupied times.

- Ventilation/exhaust rates*
- Infiltration/exfiltration
- Efficiency of HVAC equipment
- Lighting, if on timed schedule
- Occupancy, if on fixed schedule*
- Power for air distribution fans
- Envelope loss/gain factors

Outdoor temprature/degree days, those days above or below certain temperatures, are easy to measure and convert to degree days for energy management applications. A degree hour, the hourly mean temperature for a given degree day, can be readily calculated by the building management computer system. This is more accurate, especially for cooling degree days, since the heating or cooling load can be tallied separately into occupied and unoccupied periods. As confusing as that may sound, it is important and relatively simple to do. The distressing fact is that this is rarely done manually by the maintenance staff. It may be recorded on a time basis and entered into the maintenance log book, but seldom is this information used to cut energy consumption!

LIGHTING CONTROL APPLICATIONS

Lighting usually involves many circuits. If the lighting is not on time clocks or otherwise controlled, it is difficult to measure cost-effectively. Strangely enough, occupied hours for buildings are the most difficult to measure. This is probably why occupancy is most often neglected in the building manager's equations when he attempts to account for energy use. It is obvious that unoccupied buildings do not need full lighting after hours, except for safety and security purposes and to prevent vandalism.

A recent, cost-effective innovation in lighting control has been made with infrared (IR) sensing devices. This is an updated version of earlier radio frequency (RF) and ultrasonic devices. The infrared sensor will detect the presence of a human body and automatically turn on the lights. Based on a time-delay principle, the sensor will turn the lights off after an adjustable period of from three to twelve minutes after the IR sensor last sensed body heat. Figure 2.2, p. 20, shows a single floor in an office building where this technique is employed. The floor is divided into four major control zones. Only the lower right-hand quadrant is occupied in this example, and thus, only that quadrant's lights are on. This is very effective when there is only random occupancy during the hours of darkness.

Infrared Lighting Control
For
Occupancy Detection

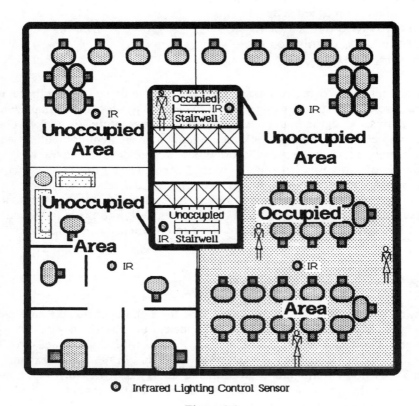

● **Infrared Lighting Control Sensor**

Figure 2.2

A more finite application of this lighting control technique is in areas that are seldom used. Figure 2.3 illustrates the infrared coverage in a small conference room. Normally the room is unoccupied and therefore the lights are automatically turned off by the IR sensor. As soon as the room is entered, the lights go on. Dimming, if required, is managed by a manual override. Once the room has been vacated, the IR sensor will detect the lack of human presence and, depending on the time period selected, turn the lights off after three to twelve minutes.

This lighting technique also has a security application. If the room in question is of a sensitive nature, the IR sensor can be zoned as a security point

Infrared Lighting Control

Single IR Sensor Space Monitoring

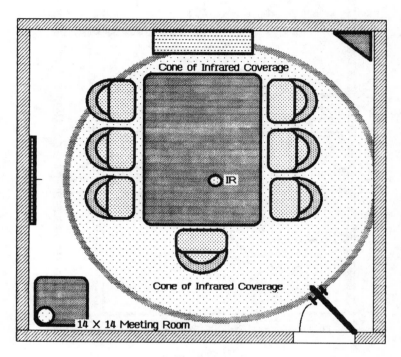

Figure 2.3

on the facility control system. Thus, in addition to being a lighting control sensor, the IR device also works as a security sensor and reports any intrusion of the room. When managed by the facility control system, the security alarm can be programmed to report only during periods when it is necessary for the room to be monitored. This is but one of many examples of the flexibility of a true facility control system.

Applications of this infrared lighting control technique include stairwells and those areas of the building that only rarely have human traffic. The IR sensors will also shut off lights during nights and weekends when the building is unoccupied. When tied to the integrated system, the control center operator can actually track a person's movement through the areas of the building monitored by the IR-controlled lighting system.

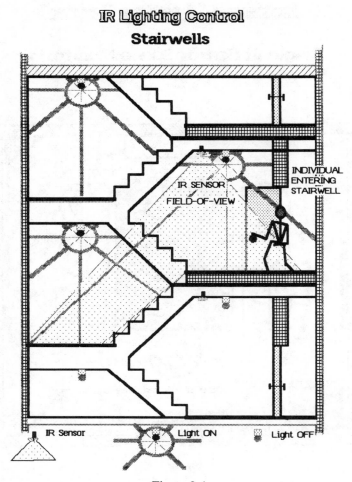

Figure 2.4

Figure 2.4 illustrates how the IR sensor picks up the body heat of an individual entering the stairwell. It automatically turns on the lights at the point of entry, the floor above, and the floor below. If the individual moves up the stairs, the lights will be turned on as each new zone is penetrated. From a security point of view, the direction of movement in the stairwell can be valuable information when an interception is necessary.

COMFORT CONTROL

Knowledge of the Btu (British thermal unit) content of fuels is essential to their proper consumption by the building's HVAC systems. If fuel or electricity is

Facility Energy Consumer

Fixed Rate Energy User

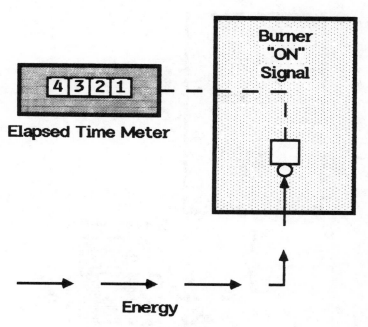

Figure 2.5

consumed by boilers, each boiler should be separately metered so that an accurate analysis of the amount of fuel used can be determined. As the Btu content of many fossil fuels varies, the vendors of such fuels should supply the Btu ratings of the various fuels.

Duty cycling is a technique used in different ways. Programmed duty cycling is used to automatically rotate the use of various major pieces of HV.'.C equipment. This is done to reduce energy consumption while maintaining the desired internal building comfort zone for the occupants. This technique allows for the equal use of these major items, reducing excessive wear from an imbalance in activity.

Cooling energy can be measured by consuming fuel at a fixed rate. A low-cost, lapsed time meter simply records the hours of on-time. The on-hours are then multiplied by the rate of Btu-hours or kilowatt-hours to arrive at the energy totals. Figure 2.5 is a simplified example of a device used to measure energy consumption at a fixed rate.

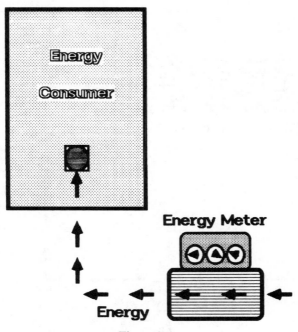

Figure 2.6

Cooling energy may also be measured by using an electric meter for the entire cooling plant or for each device. A further refinement is to measure the actual Btu's delivered by the system. Figure 2.6 illustrates the metering of energy consumers that operate at various times and volumes of fuel consumption.

LOAD SHEDDING

During unusually hot or cold days, the building's energy consumption may be excessive. This can be extremely expensive if the demand limit for the facility is exceeded for over fifteen minutes. **Load shedding** is an automatic technique to preclude these extra charges.

When the facility control system detects energy consumption approaching the demand limit, it will automatically start shutting down equipment deemed of less importance to building operations. These pieces of equipment will have been prioritized in advance and the load shedding will turn off the least important items first. If the building's energy demand continues to rise, additional energy consumers will be shut down. When the situation reverses itself, the load shedding program will bring the previously shed loads on line, taking into consideration the manufacturer's recommended off-time. If all preprogrammed energy consumers are shut down and the energy consumption continues to rise, the system is programmed to sound an audible alarm and provide a printed record of actions taken up to that point, as well as listing various candidates for manual shut down.

MONITORING AND CONTROL OF PEAK DEMAND

The monitoring and automatic control of the facility's **peak demand** is essential for a cost-effective energy management system. When the peak demand is exceeded for at least fifteen minutes, for any reason, the utility company may legally charge the customer for 90 percent of the peak for the next eleven months.

Assume that a facility has a peak demand limit of 10,000 kWh (kilowatt-hours) based on the previous eleven months' electrical demand history of the company. Along comes a hot August day and for a period of sixteen minutes the facility requires 11,500 kWh to keep functioning at a normal mode. For the next eleven months the company will be charged at the rate of 10,350 kWh demand requirement, even if only a fraction of that amount is used during subsequent months. In August of the following year a new peak demand will be calculated, based on the highest demand period subsequent to the 11,500 kWh peak the year before. Assuming that the highest fifteen-minute peak demand during this preceding eleven-month period was 9,000 kWh, the customer would then be charged at the rate for 8,100 kWh, or 90 percent of the peak demand.

If used as part of a well-designed and organized energy management effort, any building owner can well afford a one-time cost of from 2 to 5 percent of annual energy cost for a submeter to pinpoint efficient energy use or energy waste. Some of the areas where submetering is generally lacking include: campus buildings, manufacturing processes, heating in all-electric buildings, oil-fired boilers, coal-fired boilers, chillers and chiller plants, absorption chillers, steam used for manufacturing processes, and HVAC systems.

The actual measurement of the energy variables will do little for the building manager until the information collected is reduced to a meaningful form. For this data to be useful, it must be received rapidly and in an easily understood format. Signal error indicators (submeters), by themselves, will not produce the desired corrective action if they are so slow that the conditions have changed.

Energy Control Loop

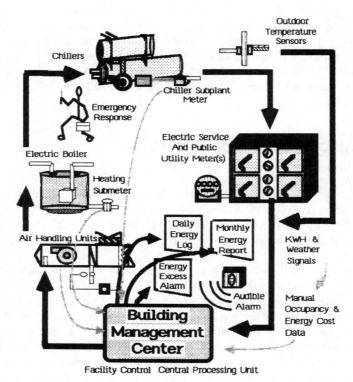

Facility Control Central Processing Unit

Figure 2.7

Any control loop must have a sensor or controller such as a thermostat capable of providing an indication that something is not normal—either too hot or too cold. This sensor or controller would generate a signal to correct the error, for instance, turning the furnace off or on.

Once energy sensors have been attached to the facility control system, it will be possible to set energy limits consistent with the outside weather conditions and the requirements of the interior occupancy. Figure 2.7 graphically illustrates how the building management center monitors and controls air handling units, electric boilers, and chillers. Various submetering devices report data directly back to the central processing unit.

By sensing outside temperature and humidity, the utility company demand meter for kilowatt-hour consumption, and other external factors that affect the building's energy consumption, and by receiving inputs on building occupancy schedules, the facility control system can do a credible job of energy management, thus saving energy and money. The monitoring and control of energy consumers will cost some money, but failure to monitor and control them will cost much more.

TOTAL FACILITY CONTROL— SYSTEMS INTEGRATION

The integration of building systems into a manageable, efficient, and cost-effective operation is not as difficult as it might seem. This is really the only way that energy consumption can be effectively controlled. This is done through a series of documented software programs that monitor energy consumers. These programs monitor the various factors bearing on the efficiency of a given piece of equipment and activate the equipment on an optimized start/stop basis to provide the service required with the most efficient on- and off-times. Duty cycling can be provided to offer the best use of equipment. There are a broad spectrum of heating, ventilating, and air-conditioning economizers that can be instituted, monitored, and controlled by an integrated system.

Standard systems offer such things as supply air reset and humidity control for improved and less costly comfort control. With an integrated system all these functions can be monitored and controlled to meet each building's demand-limiting requirements.

Lighting control can be used to greatly reduce energy consumption and still improve safety and security. Lighting can be balanced to meet area requirements while taking full advantage of available outside illumination. Night use of certain areas that consume heat and light can be billed accordingly, providing a reduction to tenants not working during night hours.

Temperature control without comfort loss can be accomplished with an ever increasing sophistication as the system senses and stores a variety of internal and external building conditions. Load shedding can be used on an automatic basis to reduce energy consumption without any loss of comfort. The monitoring and control of excessively hot or cold days can be programmed to limit the peak demand and save on future excess demand limit charges.

Building system integration will reduce energy costs, improve safety, increase fire and security protection capabilities, and permit more effective use of personnel. The integration of building management systems is a first step toward total facility control.

3

Fire Protection

FIRE DETECTION AND ALARM

Fire protection is a team effort involving those charged with planning and installing the system and those safety and security personnel who are responsible for monitoring and testing the system. Should a fire occur, the company fire brigade, local fire department, security staff, and employees are all involved.

The building owner bears the ultimate responsibility for the installation and continued effectiveness of the fire system. A building that "meets the codes" is seldom truly adequate.

Fire protection begins in the planning stage. The services of an architect are essential in the fire design for new construction, and are sometimes required for a fire system **retrofit.** Consulting engineers must ensure that all systems work in harmony and are mutually supportive. The system design team also includes the building owner, key operational chiefs, and the insurance underwriter.

The wise owner will have his underwriter check with the Insurance Services Office (ISO) for design and construction guidelines. The ISO establishes building rating criteria for underwriters' use in setting premiums on specific buildings. Construction materials, number and size of exit points, and occupancy factors are only three of the many criteria considered in establishing insurance credits for the owner.

In planning for fire protection, the design team must prepare for all possibilities. The fire system layout should consider all protective aspects of the personnel and property to be protected. The fire system hardware must include the equipment necessary to cope with potential problems. Building and fire system expansion are also key elements in long-range planning for a fire protection system. Last, review of facility fire protection requirements, continual testing, and system maintenance and updating must continue after installation.

There is no such thing as a fire-proof building. Fire codes are generally nothing more than minimum requirements. A few communities have improved their fire codes, but they should still be more stringent. There is also need for stricter enforcement of existing fire codes.

MEETING CODES AND STANDARDS

Fire protective systems must operate in a legislated arena. There are a great many codes and standards that determine what equipment can and what equipment cannot be used in connection with fire alarm systems. These codes and standards also dictate how that equipment will be installed and how it should operate. While these codes vary from locality to locality and are governed by rules laid down by the **authority having jurisdiction**, every facility management team must be aware of and conform to any number of these codes and standards.

Fire protective systems are generally subject to local building codes, state building codes, National Fire Protection Association (NFPA) codes and standards, and a requirement for **UL (Underwriters Laboratories) listing** and/or **FM (Factory Mutual) approval**.

State and local municipalities, under the *authority having jurisdiction* provision, add their requirements to the nationally accepted codes and standards. More recently, the state fire marshall's approval is being required under force of law. In some regions this approval must be granted in advance of even offering the sale of fire alarm equipment, much less installing or using it. When owners add extra requirements, a nonstandard system can result. This may call for approval by the *authority having jurisdiction* prior to construction or installation.

FIRE SAFETY TECHNIQUES

Construction techniques such as **fire walls**, **fire doors**, and ventilation system closures by **fire dampers** have done much to contain fires to limited areas. They cannot, by themselves, solve the problem. There must also be some indication that a fire door is closed and that the fire dampers on a ventilation closure order have been activated. If the system does not provide this sort of information, it is not properly protecting the facility.

No building is immune to a hot fire—a fire so intense that even steel may warp. Almost all materials used in the construction and furnishing of a building have a combustion point. There are **fire retardant materials** available, but they give off explosive vapors and toxic fumes when heated. Most synthetic materials burn twice as hot and emit fumes 500 times more toxic than natural materials. It is important to remember that smoke and gas are the real killers. Synthetic fibers give off deadly chlorine and cyanide-based gases when burned.

It is essential that fires be detected as quickly as possible so that danger can be kept to a minimum. The location of an explosive fire must rapidly be identified and brought under control to minimize the threat to life and property. If the fire alarm system is well designed with an efficient detection system and early initiation of alarm, such a rapid response is possible.

Local Fire Alarm System

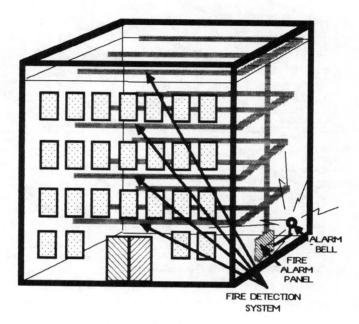

Figure 3.1

FIRE ALARM SYSTEMS

To be intelligently conversant about fire systems, one must know what the various systems are and which National Fire Protection Association **NFPA** standard applies to each.

The **Local Fire Alarm System** is a system in which the operation of an automatic or manual initiating device will cause alarm-indicating devices to alert individuals on the premises to evacuate or investigate. Generally speaking, this type of system provides no record of any activity by the alarm system. It is important to note that the **local alarm system** does not provide for alarm information to be transmitted off the premises. Figure 3.1 illustrates the simplicity of a local fire alarm system. The building has a fire system that rings a bell on an outside wall. The expectation is that someone will hear the bell and call the fire department.

Local systems offer little peace of mind, since only people present at the time of the alarm are alerted. When the building is unattended, the system is simply an alarm that sounds in the night in hopes that someone will hear and

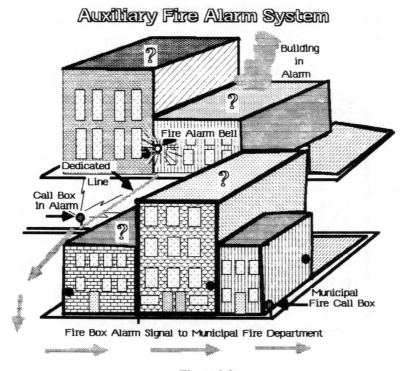

Figure 3.2

report the signal. NFPA 72A, *Local Protective Signaling Systems*, should be read closely and the system's limitations understood before recommending or installing this type of fire alarm system. An **Auxiliary Fire Alarm System** is only one rung up the alarm ladder. This is basically a local system with a connection to the municipal fire alarm system (i.e., street fire box) to transmit a fire signal to the municipal communication center. Here signals from an auxiliary fire alarm system are received on the same equipment and by the same alerting methods as alarms transmitted from the municipal fire boxes located on the streets. Permission must be obtained from the local *authority having jurisdiction* before any linkup with a municipal system can be made. NFPA 72B sets forth the criteria for this system.

Figure 3.2 graphically displays the problem. The building with smoke rising from it is in alarm. This fact is transmitted to the municipal call box on the street. The municipal communications center cannot generally distinguish between the street municipal fire box and the signal generated by the auxiliary fire alarm system. Therefore, the initial response by the municipal fire department will be to the location of the street fire box, not to the facility using the auxiliary system. Upon arrival at the street fire box, firefighters must actually look for smoke or fire to locate the source of the alarm. This task is difficult enough on a summer night, but given a cold winter night with snow, sleet, or rain, the source of the fire alarm might not be discovered until the blaze is out of control.

Auxiliary fire systems may work in some instances, but in others they are practically useless. While this type of system provides a bit more balm to the conscience than a local fire alarm system, it still fails to furnish real fire protection in a timely manner. NFPA 72B provides the standards for Auxiliary Protective Signaling Systems.

Remote–Station Fire Systems are really nothing more than local fire alarm systems connected to a twenty-four-hour operation. Typical remote stations are a sheriff's dispatcher, volunteer fire department, or even an all-night filling station. Individuals at the central location must be trained to recognize emergency signals and competent to take whatever action is required.

Figure 3.3 illustrates how the building's fire system is connected to a

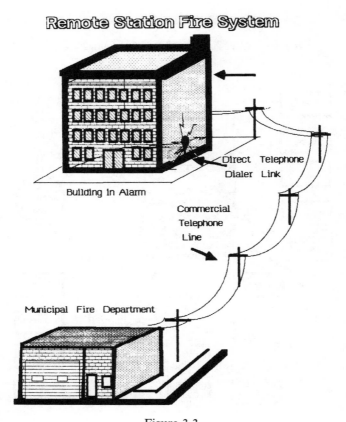

Figure 3.3

response location—a local fire department—via telephone lines. These lines may be **dedicated leased lines** or merely the standard telephone line with an automatic telephone dialer providing a prerecorded alarm message.

Remote station operations are a major step up from the local or auxiliary fire alarm systems and, short of going to the expense of a central station operation, are a viable alternative in certain circumstances. NFPA 72C describes remote station protective signaling systems. The cost-effectiveness must be rationally considered before any system is chosen.

Central Station Operation is a system, or a group of systems, in which the initiation of certain sensors and various devices at a remote location are signaled automatically to an appropriately equipped central alarm-monitoring facility. These signals are supervised, recorded, and maintained through the services of the central station operator. Figure 3.4 illustrates how various client locations can tie into the central station via dedicated telephone lines, buried cable, or radio.

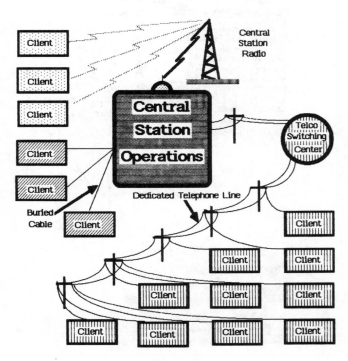

Figure 3.4

In a well-managed central station operation, trained personnel take the action required by the alarm indication. This action includes, but is not limited to, any or all of the following: (1) notifying the nearest fire department; (2) alerting the building management; (3) dispatching a "runner" who will act as the owner's agent on the scene pending the arrival of the owner's de facto representative.

As there are a wide variety of central station operations and operators, generally the *authority having jurisdiction* recommends reliance on an *Underwriters Laboratories approved* central station service only. These UL-approved central station facilities are subjected to annual no-notice inspections to ensure reasonable and timely response actions.

Good central station operators maintain a staff of skilled installation technicians as well as competent personnel at the central station around the clock. While practices vary with geographic location, it is generally preferable to have the central station operator provide a **turn-key** installation. This protects the owner by having a complete professional installation performed. The central station operator will not have to rely on an outsider's installation and sensors. Complete definition and information concerning this type of protective system in found in NFPA 71, *Central Station Signaling Systems*.

A **Proprietary Fire Alarm System** is the on-site installation of protective signaling systems which serve a single property or multiple properties under a single ownership. Ideally, this system is staffed continuously by trained and competent personnel, but it could also operate untended, if properly designed. A proprietary fire detection and alarm system is an intregal part of a total facility control protective system.

Figure 3.5 (p. 36) illustrates how the company owned and operated proprietary system can use direct **hard-wire** connection to local buildings; reach across the city or state via commercial telephone lines; use microwave transmission across freeways or rivers where dedicated telephone lines might be prohibitively costly to monitor and control nearby facilities; and even reach across oceans to monitor foreign operations.

For small, single-location operations with up to about 50,000 square feet, a hard-wired system will probably be more cost-effective. Depending upon the use of the building's space, somewhere between 50,000 and 100,000 square feet is generally the break-even point for adoption of a proprietary **multiplex** fire detection and alarm system. In a multiplex system the majority of the system data is transmitted by a single twisted pair of wires or possibly by **fiber optics**. This data **transmission bus** connects the **central processing unit (CPU)** and **intelligent control panels (ICPs)** at appropriate locations throughout the building. Short runs of typical copper wire connect the various sensors, actuators, controllers, and building control devices to the ICPs.

For most facilities in excess of 100,000 square feet, a complex of buildings, numerous remote locations, or multiple buildings at separate locations, a multiplex system will generally be the most cost-effective approach. Many options are available within the field of multiplexing. Upward mobility of the system

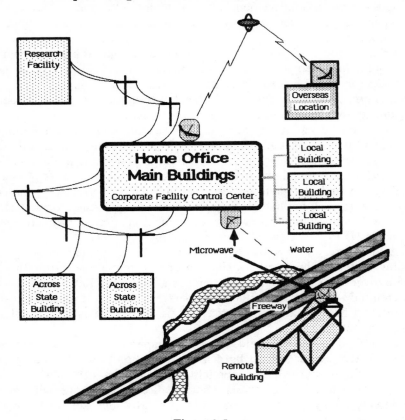

Figure 3.5

can allow for future facility expansion, yet permit management to maintain continued close control of local and remote building systems.

Proprietary systems normally require a greater initial outlay of funds. However, like most capital expenditures, they pay for themselves in a relatively short period of time, usually in three to five years.

Before selecting either a hardwire or multiplex system **NFPA 72D, Proprietary Protective Signaling Systems**, should be read. It is also helpful to visit and investigate proprietary systems already in operation at other facilities. With this knowledge, the right decisions can be made.

Proprietary Fire Alarm Systems provide complete coverage when staffed by trained operators. The operators usually work out of a supervising office located on the property to be protected. The central operating location includes equipment and a control console that permit the operators to maintain, test, and operate the system. Upon receipt of an **alarm signal** or **trouble signal**, the operators can take local action as required under the guidance provided by management, as well as the rules of response established by the insurance rating organizations having jurisdiction over the facility.

State-of-the-art proprietary systems based on a microprocessor/multiplex arrangement are capable of supervising proprietary fire alarm and security systems over a large number of buildings at multiple geographic locations. Large system applications of multibuildings and multiple locations are extremely cost-effective.

Proprietary systems are available that incorporate other systems in addition to fire detection and alarm. These include full energy management, security, access control, closed-circuit television (CCTV), and patrol tour management. They can readily pay for themselves if normal building management systems are totally integrated. By including security, access control, CCTV, energy management techniques, lighting control, equipment monitoring, and preventive maintenance schedules with a proprietary fire alarm system, operating budget savings will immediately become evident.

The threat presented by fire depends upon whether a fire develops slowly or erupts quickly. The critical first few minutes will generally determine how destructive the fire will be. There are four stages of fire: **incipient, smoldering** (smoke and gas), **visible flame,** and **intense heat**. (Figures 3.6–3.9, pp. 37–38).

The Four Stages of Fire

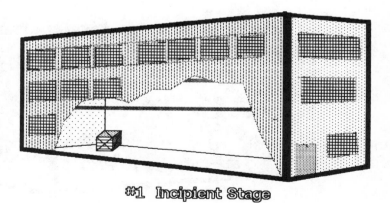

#1 Incipient Stage

Figure 3.6

The Four Stages of Fire

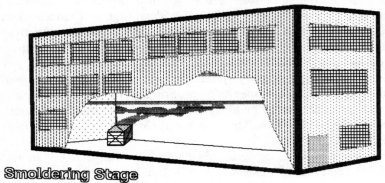

#2 Smoldering Stage

Figure 3.7

#3 Visible Flame Stage

Figure 3.8

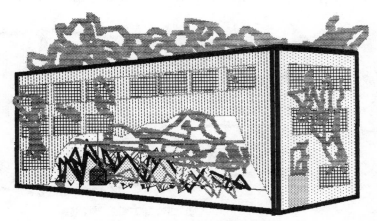

#4 Intense Heat Stage

Figure 3.9

BUILDING FIRE ZONING

The key to rapid fire detection and alarm is finite zoning. The smaller the individual zones, the quicker the actual fire location can be determined. Great care must be taken to ensure that fire zoning takes into consideration the physical construction around and within the zone, the human factor being protected, cost of material being protected, suppression systems concerned, and emergency response elements.

Zoning must be specifically designed to provide effective physical compartmentalization of the building. Provisions need to be made for use of the building's heating, ventilating, and air-conditioning (HVAC) system in containing the smoke and fire by zone. Careful planning is required for the design of venting and smoke evacuation. Selection of specialized suppression systems may call for expert consultation. Building codes determine the number and size of emergency exit points by zone, but these requirements should be viewed as minimal. Finally, the indication of a zone in alarm should be rapid and easily understood.

The selection of fire detection devices and their proper application is necessary to ensure that the zone is adequately protected. Knowledge of the various devices, where they can and cannot be used, the effects of air currents, physical placement of the devices, device reaction time, and many other variables are important considerations in the development of a zoning scheme. There are no hard and fast rules for correct zoning. There are minimum requirements as established by local fire and building codes, the National Fire Protection Association (NFPA), and the *authority having jurisdiction*. In the final analysis, proper zoning, like proper protection, is the responsibility of the owner.

CLASSES OF FIRE

Fires are classified into four groups. These groups and what these designations mean are important in the development of any fire suppression system, from fire extinguishers to large industrial, **stand-alone** systems. The type of extinguishment used is dependent upon the type, or class, of fire.

Class A fires are fires that are fueled by ordinary combustibles. These fires can normally be brought under control with water or water fog. In a Class A fire the water or water fog is used to cool the mass below the ignition point to stop the fire.

Class B fires are fueled by petroleum, oil, lubricant (POL), and volatile fluids that are present practically everywhere. Only the volume or amount of POL fuel base seems to change. Class B fires are usually smothered with carbon dioxide (CO_2) or water fog, which is excellent because it cools the fire without spreading the flame. A stream of water sprayed on a petroleum-based fire can be disastrous. This action spreads the combustible fluids and with it the flames.

Class C fires are those concerned with live electrical equipment, including transformers, generators, and electrical motors. Automatic action to shut down such equipment in the event of fire is prudent, and this possibility should be investigated.

Class D fires are fueled by combustible metals such as magnesium, sodium, and potassium. The best extinguishing agent in the case of Class D fires is usually a dry powder. In many cases this may be the only method of suppression. This type of fire only occurs when the combustibles are in use. Thus they are rare, but nevertheless dangerous. The use of water or other extinguishing agents could result in an explosive chemical reaction. Care must be exercised against storing combustible metals in areas covered by automatic sprinkler systems.

FIRE DETECTION DEVICES

All elements of a fire system are essential, but none more so than the individual detection sensors. These devices include **manual stations** (Figure 3.10). When

NON-CODED, BREAK-GLASS, GENERAL ALARM DEVICE

Figure 3.10

Fire Detection Devices
Ionization Smoke Detector

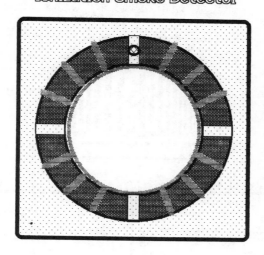

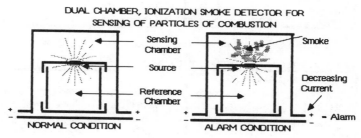

DUAL CHAMBER, IONIZATION SMOKE DETECTOR FOR
SENSING OF PARTICLES OF COMBUSTION

Figure 3.11

properly zoned, a manual pull station will indicate that a human being initiated an alarm and also the location of the alarm.

An even more efficient detection device is the **ionization smoke detector** (Figure 3.11), which is designed to detect microscopic particles of combustion too small for the eye to see. These devices are adept at providing early warning of smoldering fires, and their unit cost is relatively low. Ionization smoke detectors can readily be used indoors, but they are easily contaminated, and care must be taken concerning the environment where they are installed. They are effective at rapid detection of Class A, C, and D fires.

A similar smoke detection device is the **photoelectric smoke detector** (Figure 3.12, p. 42), which works on a principle of smoke reflectance or obscuration. It goes into alarm when smoke reflects light into a receiving element or obscures a beam of light. It provides relatively early warning of smoldering fires and has a low unit cost. This device is limited to indoor use and the smoke

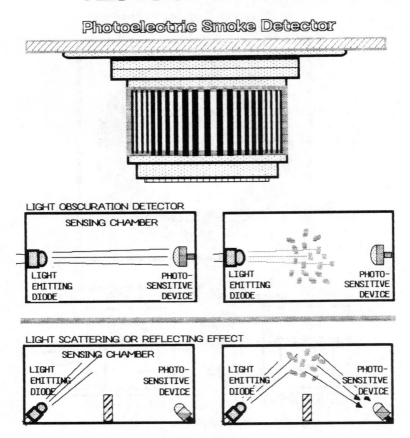

Figure 3.12

must be contained within the unit to effect an alarm. Photoelectric detectors are also effective in office space and commercial buildings. Their best response is against Class A fires.

Infrared (IR) heat detectors (Figure 3.13) are high-speed detectors sensitive to heat. They have a moderate sensitivity and cost. There is usually a manual self-test capability through the sensor's window. IR detectors are affected by temperature and subject to a false alarm due to the myriad of infrared emissions in the industrial environment. Applications for the IR detectors are indoors, in **plenums** and in air ducts. They respond best when faced with Class A or B fires.

Dual infrared (IR/IR) detectors (Figure 3.14, p. 44) provide moderate speed and sensitivity and a low false alarm rate. However, this dual device has a

Fire Detection Devices
Infrared (IR) Heat Detectors

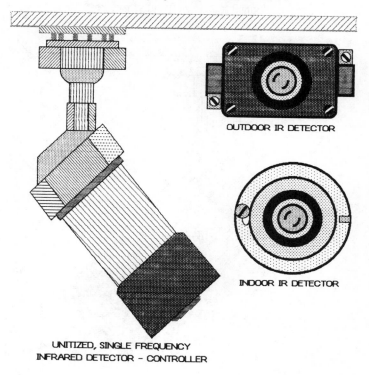

OUTDOOR IR DETECTOR

INDOOR IR DETECTOR

UNITIZED, SINGLE FREQUENCY
INFRARED DETECTOR - CONTROLLER

Figure 3.13

limited operational temperature range and self-testing capability. The dual sensor makes this a relatively expensive device. It can be used both indoors and out and is effective against Class A and B fires.

At the other end of the visible spectrum are **ultraviolet (UV) flame detectors** (Figure 3.15, p. 44). In addition to their high speed, they also have a high sensitivity and automatic self-test. Considering the moderate cost per unit, the UV flame detector is a viable sensor in many industrial situations. It is subject to false alarms, but these are generally from readily identifiable sources. This device is subject to being blinded by thick smoke and, if faced with that sort of situation, should be used in conjunction with an appropriate type of smoke detector. The ultraviolet detector can be used indoors and out and is effective against Class A, B, and D fires.

The **dual infrared and ultraviolet (IR/UV) detector** (Figure 3.16, p. 45) is a very effective device. It incorporates high speed with high sensitivity and has a

Fire Detection Devices

Dual IR and IR Detector

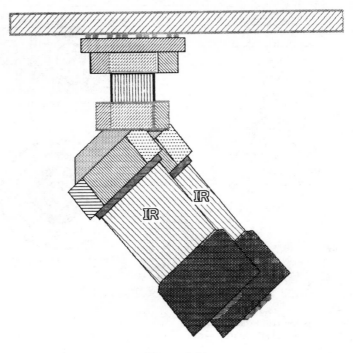

Figure 3.14

Fire Detection Devices

Ultraviolet (UV) Flame Detector

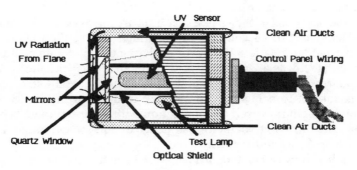

Figure 3.15

Fire Detection Devices

Dual IR and UV Detector

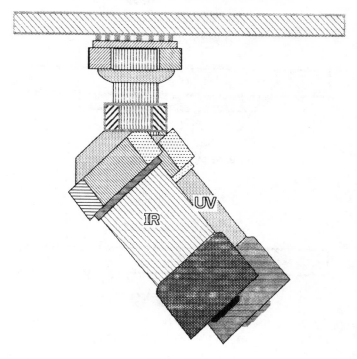

Figure 3.16

low false alarm rate. A wide operational temperature range and automatic self-testing are incorporated in this device. It is an expensive unit and thick smoke will reduce the range, but it can be used both indoors and out and is effective against Class A, B, and C fires.

Among the less expensive and sophisticated devices are **thermal detectors** (Figure 3.17, p. 46). They work on the principal of the **fusible element** and need no electricity to activate. They are low cost and highly reliable, but are very slow, as heat must impinge upon the fusible link itself. This type of device should only be used as a backup working in conjunction with a fully supervised system. Most common uses are in commercial and industrial buildings or sites subject to explosive heat situations requiring immediate deluge activation. Thermal fusible link devices are usually targeted against Class A, B, and C fires.

Another reliable and simple sensor is called a **fixed temperature, heat-activated device** (Figure 3.18, p. 46). It is effective indoors and is a low-cost unit; however, it is slow and can be affected by the wind. The normal application

Fire Detection Devices

Heat Sensors

Thermal Detector
(Self-Restoring)

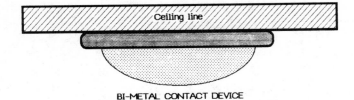

BI-METAL CONTACT DEVICE

Thermal Detector
(Non-Restoring)

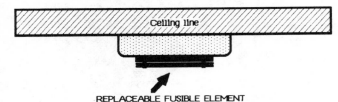

REPLACEABLE FUSIBLE ELEMENT

Figure 3.17

Fire Detection Devices

Fixed Temperature - Heat Activated

Automatic Fire Detector

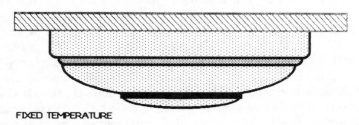

FIXED TEMPERATURE

Figure 3.18

Fire Detection Devices

Automatic Fire Detector

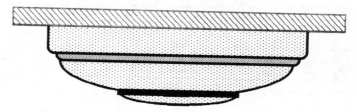

FIXED TEMPERATURE RATE-OF-RISE DETECTOR

Figure 3.19

is indoors in an enclosed area. It is used to detect Class A, B, and D fires.

The **fixed temperature, rate-of-rise detector** (Figure 3.19) is self-adjusting to temperature, day and night, summer and winter. It can detect a rapidly growing fire more rapidly than the fixed temperature device. This device is activated by heat riding on convection currents, and the heat must actually impinge on the sensor. The device is affected by the wind. Its normal application is indoors in an enclosed area. Properly installed, it is effective against Class A, B, and D fires.

A proprietary **heat-detecting cable** (Figure 3.20, p. 48) is available for a wide variety of industrial fire detection applications. According to UL tests, this heat-detecting cable responds at least thirty seconds faster than a sprinklerhead rated at the same temperature, even when the cable is installed 50 percent further away from the fire. Normally heat-detecting wire is installed in direct contact or at least in very close proximity to the equipment being protected. Its normal application is to shut down equipment and activate fire suppression systems. It is designed to be installed in close proximity to virtually any conveyor system or monorail in open manufacturing areas. It is also used to protect cable trays, power distribution apparatus, dust collectors, cooling towers, pipelines, fuel distribution terminals, piers, mine shafts, offshore platforms, tank farms, refrigerated warehouses, and a wide variety of unusual industrial equipment operations.

ALARM INITIATING TECHNIQUES

Fire detection devices, regardless of whether they are designed to sense smoke, fire, flame, or heat, can easily be hardwired to one of the intelligent control panels of a multiplex system. Fire detection is initiated by the sensors, with a signal being transmitted over the system's transmission bus to the central sys-

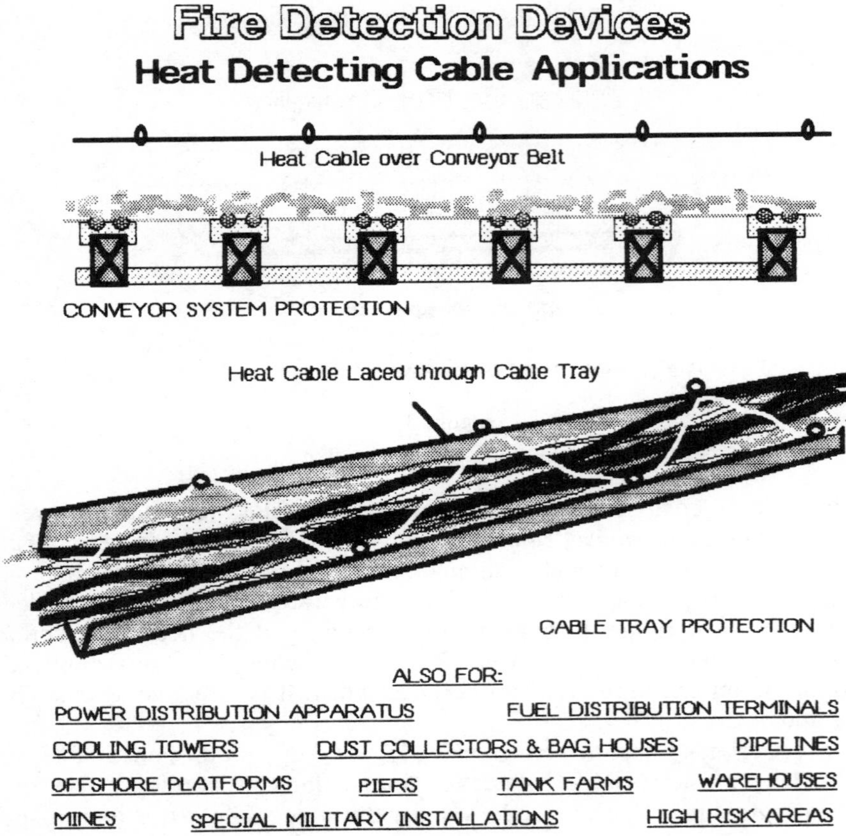

Fire Detection Devices
Heat Detecting Cable Applications

Heat Cable over Conveyor Belt

CONVEYOR SYSTEM PROTECTION

Heat Cable Laced through Cable Tray

CABLE TRAY PROTECTION

ALSO FOR:

POWER DISTRIBUTION APPARATUS   FUEL DISTRIBUTION TERMINALS

COOLING TOWERS   DUST COLLECTORS & BAG HOUSES   PIPELINES

OFFSHORE PLATFORMS   PIERS   TANK FARMS   WAREHOUSES

MINES   SPECIAL MILITARY INSTALLATIONS   HIGH RISK AREAS

Figure 3.20

tem. It is up to the central system to provide the occupants of the building with the indication of the alarm.

FIRE INDICATION AND REPORTING

All the best fire sensors in the world are worthless unless there is also some method to warn of impending fire danger. There are many devices available that provide audible signals indicating a fire.

There are fire **horns** designed for indoor and outside use. A sonalert buzzer has been designed for indoor alerting. Fire bells generally come in two versions, a rapidly vibrating alarm bell and a single-stroke alarm bell. While designed for either indoor or outdoor application, the single-stroke bell is more suitable for indoor use where a horn or vibrating bell would be undesirable (Figures 3.21 and 3.22).

Fire Warning Devices
Bells, Horns, Buzzers and Chimes

FIRE ALARM BELL

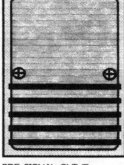

PRE-SIGNAL CHIME

AUDIBLE ALARM BUZZER

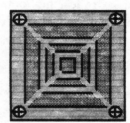

FIRE HORN

Figure 3.21

Fire Warning Devices
Fire Horns with Projectors

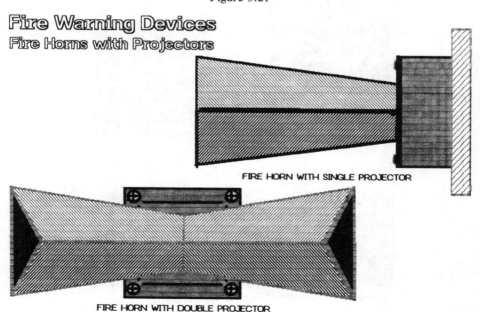

FIRE HORN WITH SINGLE PROJECTOR

FIRE HORN WITH DOUBLE PROJECTOR

Figure 3.22

Next up the line in fire annunciation devices are a series of felt-paper cone speakers, usually about 8 inches in diameter. Most of these speakers are suitable for tone or voice transmission and a wide variety of general-purpose communications and public address applications.

For use in noisy industrial areas there are some UL-listed speakers that conform to section 2531 of NFPA 72A. They are highly efficient and applicable to life safety and communications systems providing high intelligibility reproduction and transmission of audible fire alarm signals and voice messages. This type of fire annunciation device can be found under the heading of 15-watt reentrant speakers in most speaker catalogs. These loudspeakers are equipped with enclosed wiring and a vandal-deterring cover.

The newest innovations in fire signaling devices include **visual alarm signals**. These devices offer a high-intensity xenon flash tube that operates like a multiple flashing strobe light. Some of these visual alarm signals come equipped

Figure 3.23

with an audible horn or speaker. The better ones are designed to flash cycle below the threshold that might trigger latent epileptics (Figure 3.23).

Latest in the speaker line are **voice communication and alarm system speakers**. The compression driver/horn provides greater sound pressure levels than other devices of similar size. They are highly efficient in the voice and signaling range and may be equipped with a visual alarm signal (Figure 3.24).

To provide additional visual indication of the alarm, there are a wide variety of standard annunciator panels. In addition, individual custom annunciators may be locally manufactured and used as an additional visual indication of the alarm. Since annunciators are not usually electrically **supervised**, they may *not* be used as a primary source of fire annunciation and still meet NFPA and UL standards.

The most efficient and effective approach for coordinating fire-alarm indicating, initiation, and reporting is via the multiplex system. Finite zoning is the key to determining the location of the alarm in the most efficient manner.

Fire Warning Device
Combination Audible-Visual Fire Alarm

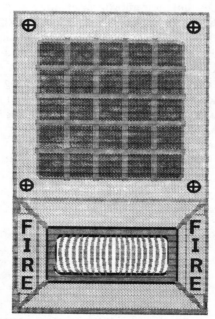

WHOOP, TEMPORAL TONE OR VOICE
COMBINED WITH FLASHING LIGHT OR STROBE

Figure 3.24

TOTAL FACILITY CONTROL AND FIRE PROTECTION

Failure to understand the interactions between the fire protection system and other building management systems can be disastrous. When the building management system has met UL fire device standards and NFPA standard 72D, you can be reasonably sure you have a quality system. But this is only the first step in fire protection.

All local fire codes and standards will have to be met by all pieces of equipment associated with the direct fire reporting system. Since the local requirements are only minimums, it is important to incorporate various fire safety techniques for real fire protection. This depends upon the type of fire system the facility uses and the condition in which it has been maintained.

Next to the actual fire detection and alarm system, the fire zoning of the building is extremely important. The more finite the fire zoning, the easier the identification of the fire area can be made. In the development of a facility control system, knowledge of the classes of fire will assist in the compartmentalization of the building into physical fire barriers. When in doubt, always check with the local *authority having jurisdiction*, but remember, codes and standards are only minimum requirements.

In developing the total facility control concept, knowledge of the types of fire detection devices and their appropriate application is essential. This will often require the services of individuals with in-depth experience in design and installation of fire systems. These individuals will be able to provide expert knowledge on fire alarm initiating techniques, fire indicating and reporting methods, and system supervision.

A facility control system that taps into all building systems can provide considerable assistance in the way of mutual support in the event of a fire. It can do much to keep panic, death, and property damage to a bare minimum if properly integrated.

4

Fire Management

LIFE SAFETY AND PROPERTY PROTECTION

The systematic control of mechanical, electrical, communication, and transmission systems within a facility can ensure optimum life safety and minimum property damage from smoke and fire. This can be achieved by integrating the operating systems of a facility so that they become mutually supportive, working in unison to protect lives and property in a fire.

Fire safety engineers generally believe that recent advances in construction methods, materials, and designs have made many fire codes ineffective. Many buildings today meet the codes, but still fall grossly short of providing adequate protection to the occupants.

HIGH-RISE FIRE MANAGEMENT

Smoke and Heat

Tall buildings are subjected to severe pressure differentials from outside winds. Once a fire starts, the building can become a giant smoke stack, quickly suffocating the occupants (Figure 4.1, p. 54).

Modern construction methods with curtain walls, elevator shafts, and **poke-through construction** between floors allow rapid spread of smoke and flame. Air-conditioning systems, designed to recirculate internal air, can recirculate lethal smoke, toxic fumes, and gases throughout the entire building.

Building Fuel Loading

Even when a building is designed to be fire resistant, typical office furnishings provide more than adequate fuel to produce fires generating tremendous volumes of toxic smoke. Housekeeping, or its lack, can also contribute to a building's susceptibility to disastrous fire.

High Rise Fire Management

Stack Effect

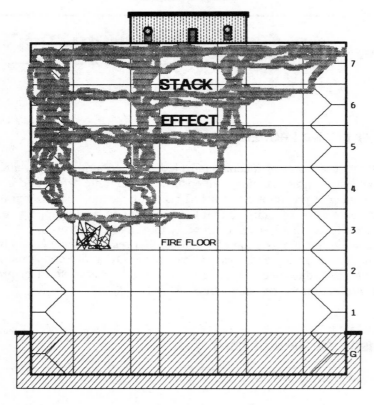

Figure 4.1

Detection and Evacuation

Many fires go unreported while a building's occupants attempt to fight the fire, warn others, or simply leave the building. People attempting to escape from a fire area often find that the stairwells are filled with smoke. In cases where elevators are called to the floor involved in the fire, people discover that they cannot leave because smoke has obscured the photoelectric beam that holds the door open. Panic and death can follow; the public is often unaware that elevators can be death traps in a fire (Figure 4.2).

Even under the best conditions, orderly evacuation of large numbers of people from high-rise buildings by way of narrow stairwells is virtually impossible. A piecemeal approach to facility control in the areas of life safety

High Rise Fire Management
Detection and Alarm

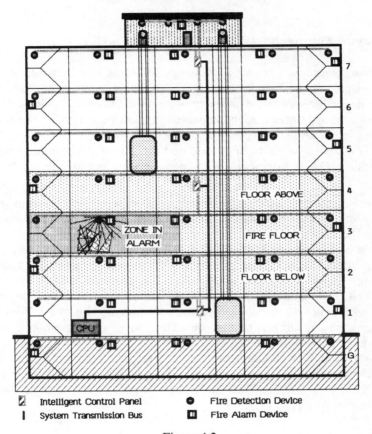

Figure 4.2

and fire management only invites disaster. For a facility to merely conform to the codes is no longer adequate.

The Fire Safety Approach

Fire safety engineers have already determined that a better approach is imperative. Agreeing that there is no such thing as a ''fireproof'' building, they have set as their primary goals the safety of the building's occupants, the building itself, and the building's contents. Also in their equation of a ''safe'' building is a system capable of doing the job required with reasonable capital expenditure. Broad investigation by many interested parties has indicated that the best solution for a safe building is an integrated systems approach.

The Systems Approach

By using an integrated systems approach, conflicting requirements can be resolved cost-efficiently. Design teams have been able to achieve trade-offs that greatly improve life safety and property protection. Owners are pleased to learn that, by eliminating unnecessary measures, this has been done with little or no increase in initial costs.

The four basic areas to be considered in a fire management system are: (1) prevention, (2) containment, (3) extinguishment, and (4) life safety.

- **Prevention** starts with the original design of the facility and the consideration of building materials, layout, furnishings, and **fuel loading**. Prevention becomes the responsibility of the owner upon occupancy.
- **Containment** uses fire barriers, vents, dampers, and the heating, venting, and air-conditioning (HVAC) system to effectively keep the fire and smoke from spreading. These actions should occur automatically in the event of fire, while still maintaining the flexibility to cope with unforeseen events.
- **Extinguishment** or suppression techniques include fire vents, hand extinguishers, hoses, kitchen hoods, sprinklers, specialty stand-alone suppression systems, and fire department equipment.
- **Life safety** includes communications, refuge areas, routes of egress, alarms, and transmission of data. Occupants must be successfully removed from the danger area and the firefighters must be able to gain safe access to the fire zone.

When each of these basic areas is confronted and successfully accommodated, the designers know that they have planned a safe building that will meet the codes and will also be a safe place to work or visit.

Building Operating Systems

Modern buildings have a number of operating systems which can work either for or against life safety goals. It is simply a function of how these systems are applied. By designing the mechanical, electrical, security, fire alarm, transportation, communications, and environmental systems to work in concert, the building can be provided with a coherent, efficient arrangement for rapid response to a fire emergency.

Today it is not unusual to see numerous systems electrically tied together to provide a safe work place. Some of these systems are:

- Manual fire alarm
- Emergency signaling
- Automatic fire and smoke detection
- Water flow monitoring and alarm
- Sprinkler supervision
- Audio communication
- Elevator control

- Radio communication
- Closed circuit television
- Security
- Mechanical equipment
- Equipment monitoring
- Lighting control
- Patrol tour management

When these systems work together, they not only perform their primary function, but also automatically respond to a fire emergency in a mutually supportive manner. The combined systems react to trigger automatic responses that will provide a head start for the occupants and the fire department in avoiding a disaster.

High-rise fire management is a part of total facility control. When designing a fire management system, one of the primary objectives is to detect the presence of particles of combustion, heat, and flame at the earliest possible time. The HVAC system is a valuable tool in fighting a high-rise fire. A tall building is very much like a ship at sea and must fight a fire from within rather than with external resources. A building's HVAC system can help to contain the fire by controlling air movement. Included in this procedure is the automatic closing of ducts, vents, and pedestrian doors to preclude the spread of smoke and toxic fumes. Safe havens are created for the occupants through use of HVAC system interaction as it automatically responds to a fire alarm. Capturing the elevators and bringing them to a predetermined ground level makes them available for firefighters' immediate use in transporting equipment (Figure 4.3, p. 58).

Emergency Communications

At the first indication of a fire alarm, the fire management system's communication equipment notifies the occupants of the floor in alarm, the floor above, and the floor below that they should evacuate their area by using the stairways and going down three floors. At the same time, other occupants are alerted that an alarm has been sounded in another part of the building and that people may be entering their area. As the system "captures" the elevators and directs them to the ground floor, the fire management communication system alerts the elevator occupants.

All this emergency communication is done automatically through a controlled and supervised alarm network via prerecorded announcements. Up to this point in the alarm, there is no requirement for human intervention since

High Rise Fire Management
Building Compartmentalization

BUILDING COMPARTMENTATION IS ACCOMPLISHED BY CONSTRUCTION
OF PHYSICAL FIRE BARRIERS AND THROUGH UTILIZATION OF HEATING,
VENTILATING, AND AIR CONDITIONING SYSTEMS TO PROVIDE SAFE-HAVENS
ON EACH FLOOR, IN THE PENTHOUSE, STAIRWELLS AND BASEMENT.

EMERGENCY COMPARTMENTALIZATION IS ACCOMPLISHED AUTOMATICALLY
BY THE FIRE MANAGEMENT SYSTEM THROUGH THE BUILDING MANAGEMENT
SYSTEM CENTRAL PROCESSING UNIT.

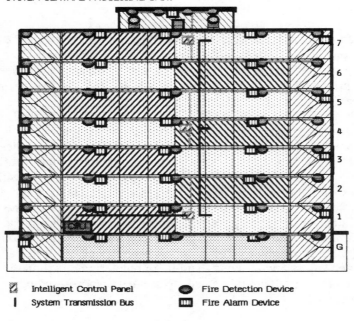

	Intelligent Control Panel		Fire Detection Device
	System Transmission Bus		Fire Alarm Device

Figure 4.3

the system is fully automatic. Building management or command firefighters can override the automatic announcement. This permits real-time information and directions to be given to the building occupants (Figure 4.4).

An integral part of any good high-rise fire management system is the firefighters' emergency communication system. Whether this is a part of the facility emergency communication system, it gives the firefighters direct communication with the fire commander without fear that **steel masking** in the building might block out their communication. From this same console that is dedicated to the fire emergency, the fire commander and building management can override the HVAC system, unlock doors, make announcements to the

High Rise Fire Management

Building Emergency Communications

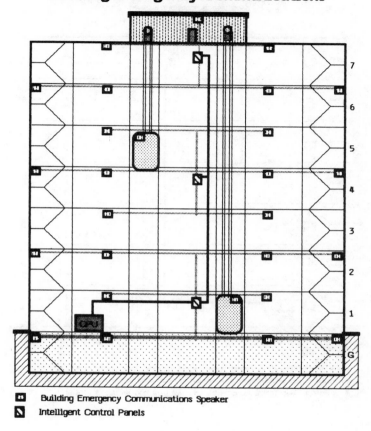

Building Emergency Communications Speaker

Intelligent Control Panels

Figure 4.4

entire building or only to selected floors, and communicate privately with firefighters on the upper floors (Figure 4.5, p. 60).

System Reporting and Logs

Computers are capable of handling all these functions, but it is also important to maintain appropriate reporting of building systems' activities. Normal logs are required, but automatic reporting and preparation of hard-copy reports are

High Rise Fire Management

Firefighter Communications

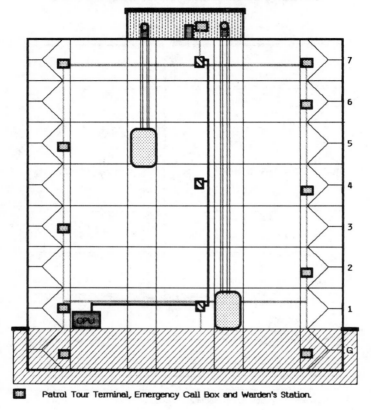

Figure 4.5

mandatory for postmortem reconstruction of monitoring devices and responding equipment actions following an incident.

In addition to the reconstruction of incidents, the development of logs will supply information concerning equipment performance. While quick reaction is essential to cope with an ongoing emergency, the ability to develop an in-depth analysis after the fact is an important tool in the prevention of a recurrence. Such information is also valuable for designing future industrial and commercial structures.

Integrated System Requirements

For a fully integrated high-rise fire management system, the following building subsystems should be incorporated:

- Fire detection and alarm system
- Sprinkler system water flow monitoring
- Supervised audio communications system
- Security system
- Heating, ventilating, and air-conditioning control
- Equipment monitoring
- Elevator control
- Suppression system monitoring

Although incomplete, this list can be used as a starting point.

A building's high-rise fire management system should automatically take the following actions when a fire is reported:

1. Assume control of the building's air-handling systems, fans, and dampers and cause them to provide negative pressure in the fire area and positive pressure in the areas that lie above, below, and adjacent. Positive pressure is also provided to enclosed stairwells and elevator shafts.
2. Initiate a **municipal trip** that will automatically notify the municipal fire department of all building fire alarms.
3. Capture all elevators and return them to predetermined floors.
4. Initiate prerecorded instructions over the emergency communications systems to alert occupants and direct them away from the fire area and toward points of safe haven or egress.
5. Lock in visual alarms and audible annunciation of all fire and emergency signals, including graphic **annunciators** and CRT information pertaining to the emergency (Figure 4.6, pp. 62–64).
6. Display the status of all mechanical system control elements including fans, dampers, and pressures.
7. Initiate tape recordings of all verbal conversations on the emergency communications system.
8. Initiate hard-copy recordings of all actions taken in all building systems, subsequent to the initiation of the first indication of an emergency situation.
9. Provide the redundant control point and digital display with all information pertaining to the emergency on a per zone basis. Redundant reporting, recording, and hard-copy reports are initiated at this remote location (Figure 4.7, pp. 65–68).

This information is provided as a guide and is built around a typical high-rise building. Similar techniques are applicable to industrial buildings, manufacturing plants, high-technology facilities, medical centers, petrochemical operations, military reservations, penal institutions, and most facilities in excess of 100,000 square feet.

Facility Control Center (FCC)
Graphic Annunciator – FIRE

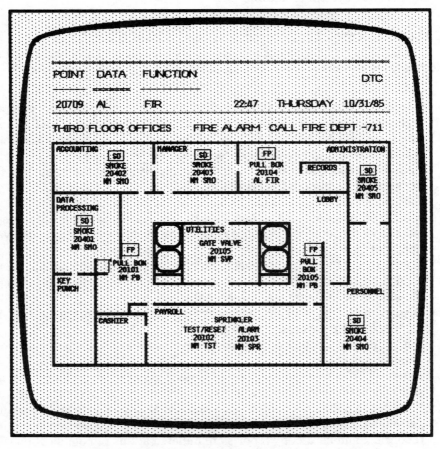

GRAPHIC DISPLAY OF A TYPICAL FIRE ALARM SYSTEM
PULL BOX, 20104, IN ADMINISTRATION SHOWN IN ALARM

Figure 4.6a

Facility Control Center (FCC)
Graphic Annunciator - SECURITY

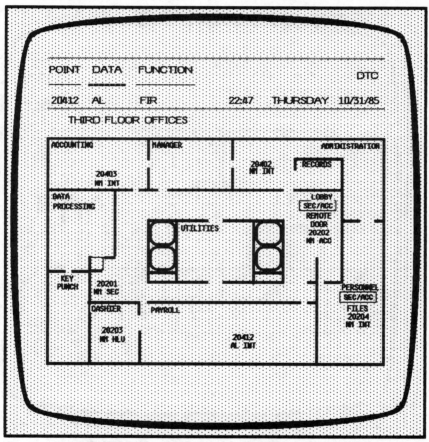

GRAPHIC DISPLAY OF A TYPICAL SECURITY ALARM SYSTEM
MOTION DETECTOR, 20412 ,IN "PAYROLL" SHOWN WITH INTRUSION ALARM.

Figure 4.6b

Facility Control Center (FCC)
Graphic Annunciator – HVAC Fan System

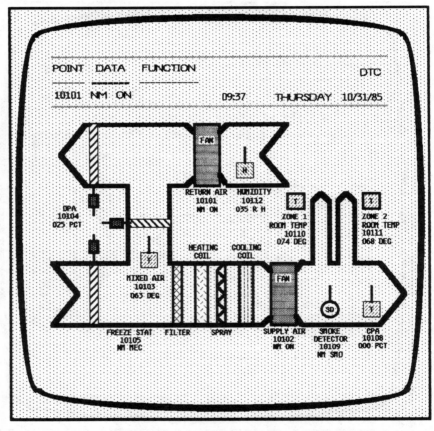

GRAPHIC DISPLAY OF A TYPICAL HVAC FAN SYSTEM
RETURN AIR, 10101, SHOWN IN THE "NORMAL" AND "ON" CONDITION

Figure 4.6c

Building Fire Command Center
Audio Communication Selection

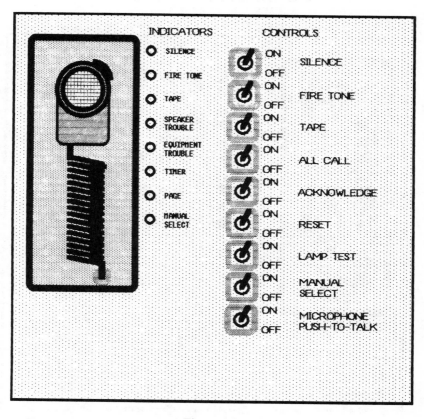

Figure 4.7a

Building Fire Command Center

Warden Station Selection

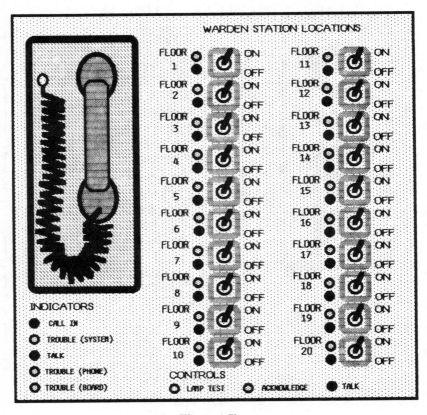

Figure 4.7b

Building Fire Command Center
Building Systems Override Console

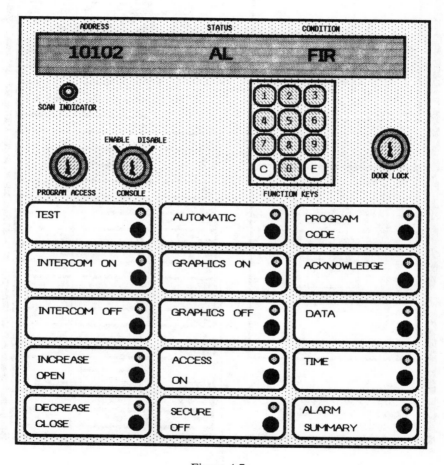

Figure 4.7c

Building Fire Command Center
Graphic Annunciator
ZONE 13 WEST SHOWN IN ALARM

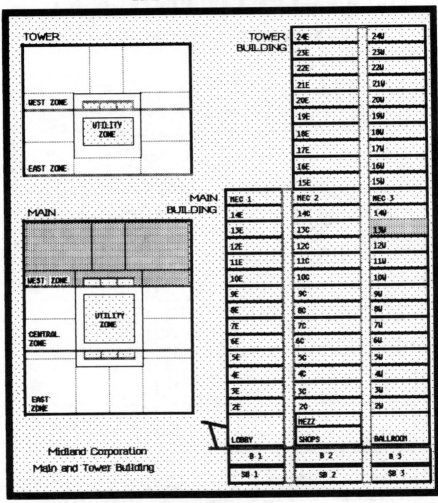

Figure 4.7d

INDUSTRIAL FIRE MANAGEMENT

Industrial fire management must work horizontally as well as vertically. Many if not all the techniques used in high-rise management should be considered in the design and development of an industrial fire management concept.

Zoning and **compartmentalization** of an industrial complex are just as important, if not more so, as in a high-rise situation. The sheer fact that industrial complexes operate in a more volatile environment makes them more susceptible to fire. Fire zoning at the time of initial construction coupled with the compartmentalization of potentially hazardous areas are equally important in the fire protection of the plant.

Retrofitting of existing industrial complexes to provide increased fire protection can also be accomplished. Again, the same fire considerations must be given to the problems of providing adequate fire protection measures. By using care and expert advice, existing facilities may be made considerably safer.

Roof Venting

An important item often overlooked during the design of building fire protection is roof venting. In large industrial, one-storied buildings, automatic roof venting is essential for firefighter safety and building protection. Without automatic roof venting, a fire scenario in an industrial plant might go something like this:

8:00   Fire starts.
8:05   Fire spreads horizontally, smoke spreads to draft curtains, sprinklers open.
8:10   Fire already under the draft curtains, more sprinklers open, unburned gases accumulate.
8:15   The building is effectively smoke logged. All sprinklers have been activated, including many not over the flames. Water pressure drops over the flames. Heat is beginning to melt the steel structural members.
8:20   Firefighters arrive, break windows. Sudden inrush of air causes a backdraft explosion of unburned gases.
8:30   Firefighters attempt to enter; hose stream will not reach the fire. Smoke blocks the view. Firefighters dare not attempt to cut holes in the roof for fear of a collapse.
9:00   Firefighters continue to wet down debris. Building destroyed. Production lost. Customers lost. Employees lost. Business fails.

On the brighter side, with automatic venting, the scenario for the same building might go like this (Figure 4.8, pp. 70–71):

8:00   Fire starts.
8:05   Vents open, sprinklers open, smoke and heat vents.

Fire Management Roof Venting

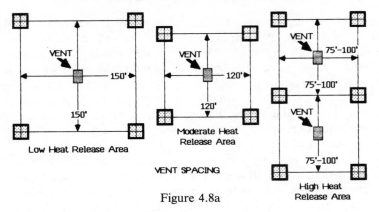

Figure 4.8a

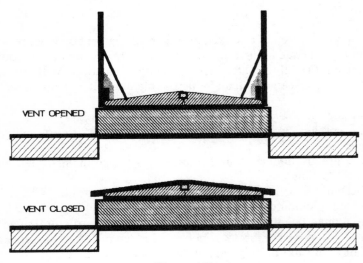

Figure 4.8b

8:10   Fire contained, smoke continues to vent.
8:15   Condition remains essentially the same.
8:20   Firefighters arrive, enter building, and fight the blaze from the floor.
8:30   Fire out.
9:00   Cleanup follows. Production reinstated. Customers sympathetic. Employees become more cohesive. Business survives a potentially fatal fire.

Fire Management

Roof Venting and Curtain Walls

Figure 4.8c

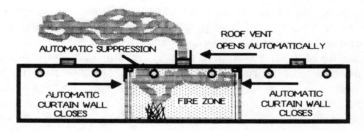

Figure 4.8d

Figure 4.8e

TOTAL FACILITY CONTROL AND FIRE MANAGEMENT

Facility control is very much a part of fire management. The fire protection aspect of fire management will take into consideration such things as heat and smoke propagation through the building. The actual fuel loading of the building and the daily function of internal housekeeping are both important, but they fall under the general heading of fire prevention. Fire detection and alarm are essential to fire protection, but this is also the foundation for building fire management.

High-rise building and industrial complex fire management have a lot in common. Each facility has its own personality, and management must determine the best fire safety approach for each location. Fire management in both situations requires a strong look at the fire prevention aspects of each structure. Where possible, steps should be taken to ensure containment of smoke and flames if a fire should get started. Containment may be anything from physical barriers that inhibit fire propagation to the closing of fire doors either manually or automatically. Fire management activates fire doors and assures that they have in fact closed while doing a whole host of other things at the same time.

Extinguishment is essential to fire management, and care must be taken in the selection, design, installation, checkout, and maintenance of whatever system or systems are used. Incorporation of as many life safety features as practical enhances the total fire management effort.

The ability of the fire system to capture building operating systems is the major thrust of a facility fire management system. By capturing the HVAC it may be possible to contain a fire by air pressure around the zone in alarm and by shutting off air to the zone in alarm. The ability to pressurize stairwells, capture elevators and take them to the ground level, release and verify the closure of smoke doors and dampers, call the fire department, and record all system activity is what fire management is all about.

Emergency communications that will automatically notify occupants at the first hint of trouble are important. Following an occupant alert, management's ability to inform specific floors or areas of what is going on will considerably reduce panic and stress. The ability of firefighters to clearly send and receive information over a dedicated and supervised emergency communications system in private and without the threat of steel masking from protected areas is extremely important to successfully fight fires in high-rise buildings or industrial plants.

System reporting of alarms and subsequent actions is an important asset during the aftermath of a fire. Logs of various points or systems are also valuable. The ability to review all automatic activity through system-generated reporting aids in bettering future system response. When this is coupled with a log by time and function of manual system override commands, true realization of the value of fire management comes into focus.

Fire management is the integration of fire detection and alarm systems with sprinkler system water flow monitoring, supervised audio communications, security systems, building HVAC systems, building equipment, elevator control system, and stand-alone fire and explosion suppression systems. When these and other building functions are incorporated with established physical constructions such as roof venting, lives can be protected and disasters avoided.

Fire management is one of the gems in the total facility control crown.

By averting a single disaster or saving one life this technique will have easily paid for itself. If it can prevent the shutdown of the manufacturing process for even one day it will probably pay for itself. Like total facility control, facility fire management is well worth the effort and expense of installation, because it improves safety and morale and pays for itself.

5

Suppression Systems

There is a wide variety of suppression systems. These systems are broadly designed to provide spot protection of points that are highly vulnerable to spontaneous fire, explosion, or outbreak of flames during industrial processes. They are intended to provide immediate, manual or automatic, suppression at the point of ignition to snuff out the combustion as quickly as possible. They are specifically designed to provide spot, point, or area fire extinguishment. Special application systems can suppress explosions before they reach a critical, over-pressure point.

Many computer rooms are equipped with special suppression systems that have been developed specifically to combat combustion within a tightly controlled area. Other systems are designed for installation in and around equipment or process operations with a high potential for dangerous combustion. Some of these installations are inside buildings, while others protect outdoor locations such as tank farms or bulk fuel loading docks. Still others can be used to combat fire at off-shore oil platforms.

SPRINKLER SYSTEM APPLICATIONS

Automatic sprinklers are the most common type of suppression system for protecting buildings. **Factory Mutual (FM)**, speaking on behalf of a number of structural insurance companies, has for many years been the guiding force behind the installation of sprinkler systems in public and private buildings. More recently, sprinkler systems have become commercially available for installation in private dwellings.

Firefighters strongly support the use of sprinkler systems and would prefer that all buildings be completely covered by automatic sprinklers. A properly installed and maintained sprinkler system certainly makes their job easier. This accounts for the vast number of building codes that require some buildings to have sprinkler systems. Sprinklers do aid in protecting the building, but unfortunately in some instances they do little in the way of protecting lives.

Automatic sprinkler systems are really plumbing systems designed to shower the fire area with water. A general requirement for a sprinkler system

75

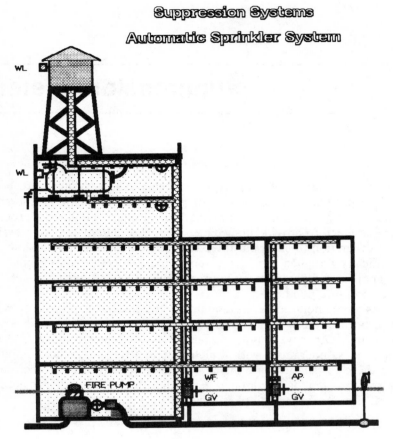

Figure 5.1

is capacity for 15,000 gallons of water or a minimum of a twenty-minute supply of water (Figure 5.1).

To ensure that the system is in a constant condition of readiness, sprinklers must be regularly tested. These tests must be recorded to receive insurance credits. Many jurisdictions require a representative of the fire or building department to be present during these tests.

Because arsonists prefer to shut off sprinkler systems prior to setting a fire, the system should be equipped with tamper switches. These switches indicate whether a valve has been tampered with in some way. The water supply may have been inhibited or valves placed in a mode that would reduce the flow of water in an emergency.

The lowest temperature at which a **sprinkler head** will normally activate or start its spray of water is 135 degrees Fahrenheit. In most cases, sprinkler heads will not activate until temperatures of 190 to 210 degrees are reached. A life-threatening blaze can occur in that temperature range. This is a serious constraint to efficient fire control. The key to holding losses to a minimum is early warning followed by a quick response. Waiting for sprinkler systems to activate at 190 degrees may not be fast enough.

Use of sprinklers must be confined to those areas where water can be tolerated. Agents such as potassium, sodium, and sulfuric acid have a particularly violent way of reacting when doused with water and may actually explode. Sprinklers must not be used in such areas. Water will cause the spread of a petroleum-based fire, so this also must be considered. Judicious use must be made of sprinklers in and around areas of specialized electrical equipment and high voltage transformers, as water and live electricity make a deadly combination. Sprinklers should not be used in areas that contain important records, valuable soft goods, paintings, or expensive hard goods with fine finishes. Water flow in these cases might cause as much damage as the fire.

Many localities require that sprinkler systems be installed for certain applications, but they should always be used in conjunction with modern **fire alarm monitoring** and reporting systems. Such systems must include automatic fire and smoke detectors. These will give early warning before sprinkler heads are activated and thus provide an opportunity to extinguish the blaze without danger of water damage. It is possible for an automatic sprinkler to spray water all night if there is no signal to indicate water flow in the system. Sprinkler activation without an alarm could create large quantities of smoke from a smoldering fire. This can be more dangerous and life-threatening than flames. If the fire alarm system is not brought into action very quickly and proper notifications made, even a single sprinkler head running all night can cause extensive damage.

The typical sprinkler system usually consists of one or more pressurized or gravity flow water sources. It has water flow controlling valves or devices and a piping network, not unlike a manifold system, to supply water to the protected areas. Attached to this basic network are sprinkler heads at the water discharge points, an alarm that indicates water flowing in the system and supervisory devices to protect the system's integrity.

Water flow switches are an integral part of these systems and automatically signal a flow of water within the sprinkler system. This results in a **water gong** sounding without requiring any outside stimulation or power. A water gong may also be capable of actuating electrical alarms and controlling electrical equipment.

Sprinkler heads are located throughout each facility according to codes and engineering requirements. There are generally two basic types of sprinkler head activation. The solder type has a metal device that melts when exposed to various temperatures. Standard melting points for these metal **fusible links** are at temperatures of 165, 212, 286, and 350 degrees Fahrenheit. A second type of sprinkler head uses a water flow triggering device called a **frangible bulb.** At temperatures of 135, 155, 175, 250, 325, 400, 500, and 650 degrees

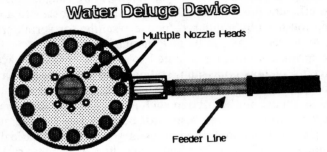

Figure 5.2

Fahrenheit, the bulb will melt and allow the water to flow from the sprinkler head. The working environment will determine the temperature at which the sprinkler heads will activate.

A **gate valve** is used to control the water within the sprinkler system piping (Figure 5.2). **Post indicator valves (PIVs)** may be located inside or outside the facility and are used as a control to operate underground gate valves. **Alarm valves** can be used in combination with gate valves or **retarding chambers** to actuate electric or water motor alarms in **wet pipe sprinkler systems**.

A water control valve is located in the main **riser** of each piping system.

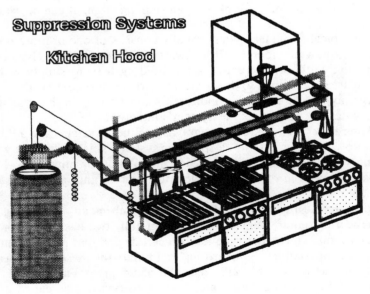

Figure 5.3

This control valve may be any type of valve such as a gate valve, **globe valve**, or a special **alarm check valve** (Figure 5.3). Water is contained in the entire manifold of the sprinkler system right up to the sprinkler head in a wet pipe system. Conversely, the **dry pipe system** is used where there is danger that the piping might freeze. Dry pipe valves are used as water supply control valves in dry pipe sprinkler systems. They are specifically designed for installation where piping and sprinklers, but not valves, are exposed to freezing temperatures—warehouses, parking garages, attic spaces, loading docks, and so forth. Deluge valves respond rapidly and are designed to control water volume supplied to the discharge outlets of deluge and preaction suppression systems. They are actuated by manual, electrical, pneumatic, and hydraulic devices that will signal their activation. They offer a greater flexibility in design and engineering for sprinkler systems (Figure 5.4). Automatic sprinkler systems generally fall into six major classifications:

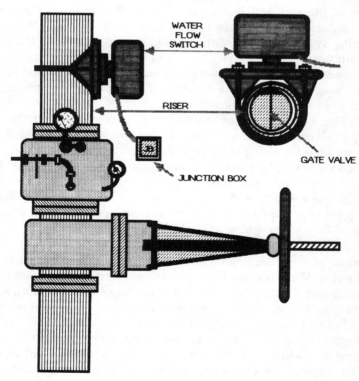

Figure 5.4

1. A wet pipe system uses closed automatic sprinkler heads attached to the piping system. This piping system contains water under pressure at all times. The system is activated at the sprinkler head when heat or flame actuates the sprinkler head opening.
2. A dry pipe system also uses automatic sprinkler heads that are closed and attached to the piping system. The dry pipe system contains air under pressure. This system is activated at the sprinkler head by fire. Heat from the fire melts the **ustulate metal**, or frangible bulb, or otherwise causes the sprinkler head to open, allowing the air to escape. The loss of air pressure allows a clapper valve to release water within the system and discharge it at the opened sprinkler head. A dry pipe system is primarily used where there is a possibility of freezing temperatures that would block a wet pipe system.
3. A **preaction system** is a dry pipe system containing air that may or may not be under pressure. A supplementary fire detection system (pneumatic, electric, electronic, etc.) in the protected area detects the presence of fire and initiates the flow of water.
4. A deluge system is similar to the preaction system, except that all or a portion of the sprinkler heads are open at all times. The fire detection system senses the fire and opens the deluge valve and water flows through the piping system and out of the sprinkler heads, deluging the protected area with water.
5. A combined dry pipe and preaction system uses the actuating features of the dry pipe and the preaction systems. The loss of air pressure or the activation of a supplementary fire will activate the flow of water in the piping. The main purpose of this system is to provide water through two dry pipe valves, connected in parallel, to a sprinkler system of larger size than permitted for a single dry pipe valve.
6. A **limited water supply system** is an automatic sprinkler system where water is supplied by a pressure tank of limited water capacity. This system is generally used where public water, gravity tank, or other conventional water sources are not available, or where local codes require a secondary source of fire system water.

Sprinkler systems are a valuable tool in firefighting and must be considered in all cases. Various other fire detection and alarm options are discussed in this chapter and should also be properly investigated. An in-depth study and comparison must be made prior to any final decision. It may well be that finite zoning and fire-wall compartmentalization would be more cost-effective, while providing increased protection. Management must be assured that whatever system is installed will provide the required early warning, control **air handling units** (AHU), capture the elevators, and so on, for proper protection of the facility and its occupants. Additionally, the cost-effectiveness of any integrated system must be considered.

STAND-ALONE FIRE SUPPRESSION SYSTEMS

Usually there are any number of **stand-alone** fire suppression systems within industrial complexes. These subsystems may include kitchen hoods, Halon systems, carbon dioxide systems, and other specialty deluge systems (Figure 5.5).

The majority of these suppression systems are designed to function as a single operating system and are completely self-contained. However, when the system is activated, an indication signal should be transmitted to a central location for alerting building management. A grease fire on one of the kitchen ranges would trigger the suppression system, but if the fire spreads beyond the

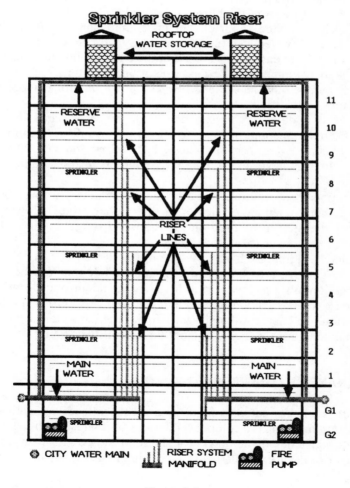

Figure 5.5

capability of that automatic stand-alone system, it could spread throughout the building. This example emphasizes the importance of tying individual stand-alone systems to the facility control center. Each individual subsystem should be properly zoned and linked to the facility control system fire detection and alarm system. Activation of a single signal from a stand-alone system can create a cascade of events generated by the CPU to assist in containing a fire.

AUTOMATIC CARBON DIOXIDE SYSTEMS

Carbon dioxide extinguishing systems are noted for their swift reaction. Within seconds they will smother the fire and hold damage to a bare minimum. Carbon dioxide penetrates the entire hazard area and quickly snuffs out the flame by removing the oxygen from the burning material.

The carbon dioxide vapor chokes off combustion and at the same time carbon dioxide snow reduces the temperature to prevent reignition. In most instances, there is no damage as a result of the extinguishment. Carbon dioxide is harmless to equipment, materials, and property. It leaves nothing to be cleaned up, mopped up, or scraped off. The downtime for equipment is held to a minimum.

Carbon dioxide is effective over a wide range of flammable materials involving both surface and deep-seated fires. Carbon dioxide can be used almost everywhere, even on high-voltage electrical equipment, without danger or damage. It is capable of handling large and small fires, both indoors and out.

Protection from multiple hazards can be achieved through a common supply by using a pneumatic selector or directional valves. However, this is an economy measure to be used only if there is strong assurance that only a single hazard will occur at any one time.

An electrical impulse from any type of fire detection system is all that is necessary to activate a carbon dioxide system. While this may be an efficient fire suppression system, there are others. Independent outside professionals should check the application and recommend the best type of protection for each situation. To ensure an unbiased opinion, the consultant should not represent a manufacturer of the equipment under consideration.

HALOGENATED EXTINGUISHING SYSTEMS

Halon 1301 is a halogenated extinguishing agent that breaks the chain of combustion reaction. Halon is a colorless, odorless gas that is five times more dense than air. It squelches flame quickly without causing extinguishment damage. A potential fire hazard can be held to a minimum as the Halon gas penetrates the entire area.

Halon systems are generally used to protect high-value areas where a clean, electrically nonconductive, nontoxic, safe-for-people agent is needed. Areas that must remain operational, where people work with valuables and sensitive documents, are ideal for the clean, vaporizing nature of Halon 1301.

Halon is not effective on chemicals containing their own oxygen supply, such as cellulose nitrate or reactive metals such as sodium, potassium, magnesium, titanium, zirconium, uranium, and plutonium. Another forbidden area for Halon is where metal hydrides are present.

Halon cylinders can be at floor level or wall mounted for ease of servicing. Smaller systems may have pressurized bottles of Halon mounted in the false ceiling or plenum area over the protected room.

Design of Halon suppression systems must be left to the experts. Actuation control and supervisory circuitry are available in nearly all voltages, so this suppression technique is adaptable for almost any interior enclosed space. An electrical impulse from the detection devices will energize the solenoid

Closed Area

Halogenated Suppression System

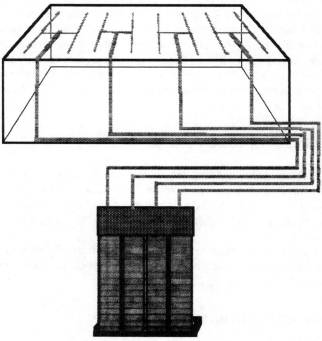

Each Cylinder Protects 1000 Cubic Feet
Used for Class C and Class B Hazards

Figure 5.6

actuator valve, causing the system to discharge automatically. However, this approach is entirely unacceptable when this device must be depended upon for release of the primary fire extinguishing system. Any Halon suppression system must be capable of the performance required to meet the necessary protection requirements for life and property. Generally speaking, Halon systems must meet a design criteria to totally fill the protected space in less than ten seconds (Figure 5.6, p. 83).

A halogenated system may also be manually activated. There is always the possibility that an alert employee may spot the fire before an automatic device activates the system. Remember that Halon is expensive enough to make accidental discharge unacceptable.

Any fire suppression system must have a high degree of reliability. This relates to the ability of the system and each of its components to be in proper working condition at all times. Manufacturers of fire detection and suppression systems should have definitive and reliable information on their detectors available for review.

A system's maintainability varies directly with the complexity of design. In designing a detection system for halogenated agents, it is best to use a cross-zoned series of **products of combustion** smoke detectors. Halon installations are precise and expensive. Design of Halon systems is for experts only and should never be attempted by corporate in-house engineering.

Consultation is recommended with a disinterested professional concerning the high-value area protection requirements. A performance specification should be prepared for bidding. Before deciding on a manufacturer, an insurance underwriter should be contacted to determine whether a reduction in insurance premiums would become effective on the date of the halon system's installation acceptance test.

AQUEOUS FILM-FORMING FOAMS

AFFF is a broad generic term referring to a number of suppression agents appropriate for chemical and petroleum fires. These foams are generally suitable for use with both fresh and salt water as well as nominal low temperature operations. Specific requirements should be checked prior to the selection of any light water system.

Foam systems are primarily designed for firefighting and the mitigation of spills of hazardous liquids. There are a number of **foam concentrates** and **high expansion foams** (Figure 5.7).

FOAM TYPE CONCENTRATES

- **Protein.** This cost-effective agent has proved effective on many extinguishments. It is burnback resistant and water bearing and seals against hot metal. It also provides long-term vapor suppression and is noncorrosive. Normal

Suppression Agents

Aqueous Film-Forming Foam (AFFF)

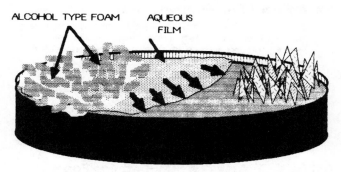

HYDROCARBON FLAMMABLE LIQUID (WATER SOLUBLE)

Figure 5.7a

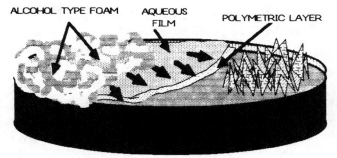

POLAR SOLVENT FLAMMABLE LIQUID (WATER SOLUBLE)

Figure 5.7b

applications include fuel storage tanks, boiler fronts, dikes, offshore platforms, pumping stations, dip tanks, oil-cooled transformers, truck loading
racks, processing areas, dock facilities, and gasohol tanks. This concentrate
is also available in versions that meet military specifications and U. S. Coast
Guard approval.

- **Floroprotine.** Advantages are that it is oil resistant, water-bearing, burnback
  resistant, sealable, self-sealing, noncorrosive, and dry-chemical compatible.
  Floroprotine also resists **plunging** and provides long-term vapor suppression. In addition to the applications of the protein foam, floroprotine foams
  can also be used for subsurface injection.
- **Aqueous Film-Forming Foam (AFFF).** This foam was designed to be a quick

Suppression Agents

Aqueous Film-Forming Foam (AFFF)

Concentrates

1% Aqueous Film-Forming Foam

THIS IS A COMPLETELY SYNTHETIC AQUEOUS FILM-FORMING FOAM USED PRIMARILY ON CLASS "B" HYDROCARBON AND WATER MISCIBLE FUEL (POLAR SOLVENT) FIRES. ITS EXCELLENT WETTING CHARACTERISTICS MAKE IT USEFUL IN COMBATING CLASS "A" FIRES.

3% (AFC-3) Aqueous Film-Forming Foam

THIS IS A COMPLETELY SYNTHETIC AQUEOUS FILM-FORMING FOAM USED PRIMARILY ON CLASS "B" HYDROCARBON AND WATER MISCIBLE FUEL (POLAR SOLVENT) FIRES. ITS EXCELLENT WETTING CHARACTERISTICS MAKE IT USEFUL IN COMBATING CLASS "A" FIRES.

6% (AFC-3) Aqueous Film-Forming Foam

THIS IS A COMPLETELY SYNTHETIC AQUEOUS FILM-FORMING FOAM USED PRIMARILY ON CLASS "B" HYDROCARBON AND WATER MISCIBLE FUEL (POLAR SOLVENT) FIRES. ITS EXCELLENT WETTING CHARACTERISTICS MAKE IT USEFUL IN COMBATING CLASS "A" FIRES.

Alcohol Resistant Concentrate (ARC) 3% and 6% AFFF Concentrate

ARC IS A COMPLETELY SYNTHETIC AQUEOUS FILM-FORMING FOAM USED PRIMARILY ON CLASS "B" HYDROCARBON AND WATER MISCIBLE FUEL (POLAR SOLVENT) FIRES. ITS EXCELLENT WETTING CHARACTERISTICS MAKE IT USEFUL IN COMBATING CLASS "A" FIRES.

Premium 3% (AFC-5A) Aqueous Film-Forming Concentrate

THIS IS A COMPLETELY SYNTHETIC AQUEOUS FILM-FORMING FOAM USED PRIMARILY ON CLASS "B" HYDROCARBON FIRES. ITS EXCELLENT WETTING CHARACTERISTICS MAKE IT USEFUL IN COMBATING CLASS "A" FIRES AS WELL.

Premium 6% (AFC-5) Aqueous Film-Forming Concentrate

THIS IS A COMPLETELY SYNTHETIC AQUEOUS FILM-FORMING FOAM USED PRIMARILY ON CLASS "B" HYDROCARBON FIRES. ITS EXCELLENT WETTING CHARACTERISTICS MAKE IT USEFUL IN COMBATING CLASS "A" FIRES AS WELL.

AFFF 3% Freeze Protected Concentrate -20%

THIS 3% FREEZE PROTECTED (FP) AGENT IS A COMPLETELY SYNTHETIC AQUEOUS FILM-FORMING FOAM USED PRIMARILY ON CLASS "B" HYDROCARBON FIRES IN AREAS WHERE THE TEMPERATURE CAN BE EXPECTED TO GO BELOW FREEZING AND I T WILL REMAIN EFFECTIVE TO -20 Deg F (-29C). ITS EXCELLENT WETTING CHARACTERISTICS MAKE IT USEFUL IN COMBATING CLASS "A" FIRES.

Figure 5.8 (See Figure 5.7)

fire knock-down, self-sealing aqueous film. It is also compatible with dry-chemical and nonaspirating equipment that meets Military Specification F-24385. Common applications include aircraft crash and rescue, aircraft hangars, fuel processing facilities, fuel storage tanks, subsurface injection, dikes, offshore oil platforms, truck racks, and conversion of existing sprinkler systems.

• **Alcohol-based foam.** This foam is a cost-effective, burnback resistant approach to alcohol fires. It also offers sealability, is **polar-solvent**-resistant, and is effective on hydrocarbons. UL (Underwriters Laboratories) listing should be checked before acceptance of a specific product. Normal applications for alcohol-based foams include petrochemical refineries, polar-solvent tanks and processing areas, highway accidents, and truck loading areas.

• **High-expansion foam.** These foams have a low water requirement and are effective on hydrocarbons and many of the polar solvents. In addition to being cost-effective, high-expansion foams provide for vapor suppression and total flooding with a minimum of water damage. There is generally no hazard to life when dealing with high-expansion foams. They are most effective in suppressing fires connected with LNG (liquid natural gas) tanks or spills. Additional applications include fire suppression in class A and class B warehouses, aircraft hangars, railroad accidents, ship engine rooms, three-dimensional fires, turbine peaking units, drum storage, and where multilayer flows are involved.

This information is little more than a primer and has been provided strictly as a guide to understanding the various types of foam systems and their applications (Figure 5.8). When dealing with specialized suppression applications, the user should always seek the services of a professional.

Table 5.1 (p. 88) is supplied as a reference for possible suppression system applications.

HOODS AND DUCTING

Kitchen hoods, hood ducts, rangetops, and appliances connected with food-service operations are generally protected by an automatic fire suppression system (Figure 5.9, p. 89). The short form of an architectural specification generally reads something like this:

All cooking grease exhaust hoods, ducts, deep fat fryers, complete range tops, upright broilers, griddles, and charbroilers shall be protected against fire by the installation of an automatic dry chemical fire extinguishing system. Each system shall be installed by a qualified supplier in accordance with Underwriters Laboratories listing and conform to all local authorities having jurisdiction.

Table 5.1   Suppression System Applications

Hazard	CO_2	Halon	Dry Chemicals
Aircraft hangars	*	*	*
Alcohol storage	*	*	*
Bank vaults		*	
Battery rooms	*		
Carburetor overhaul shops	*		*
Cleaning plant equipment	*	*	*
Computer rooms	*	*	
Dip tanks	*		
Drying ovens	*		*
Engine test cells	*	*	*
Flammable liquid storage		*	*
Flammable solids storage		*	*
Fractioning towers	*		
Fuel oil storage		*	*
Heat treating	*		*
Hydraulic oil	*		*
Infrared drying ovens			*
Jet engine test cells	*	*	
Museums	*	*	
Oil quenching bath	*		
Paint manufacturing	*		*
Paint spray booths	*		*
Paint storage	*		*
Petrochemical storage	*	*	*
Petroleum testing labs	*	*	*
Printing presses	*	*	
Range hoods	*		*
Reactor towers	*		
Rack storage	*		
Record vaults	*	*	*
Service station, inside	*		*
Shipboard storage	*	*	*
Solvent cleaning tanks	*	*	*
Storage vaults, furs	*	*	
Switchgear rooms	*	*	
Telephone exchanges		*	
Textile machinery		*	
Wire manufacturing equipment	*		*

Stand-Alone System Integration

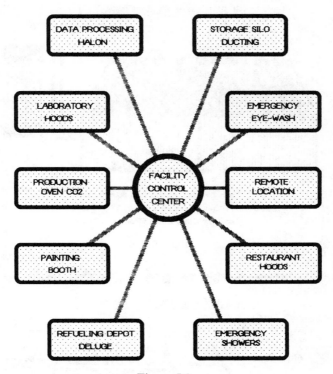

Figure 5.9

This is fine as far as it goes, but the building could end up with multiple stand-alone fire suppression systems having no connection with a total facility protection system. It is relatively simple to devote a single zone to each of the stand-alone systems, thus including them in the overall scheme of building control.

INDUSTRIAL SUPPRESSION SYSTEMS

Industrial fire suppression systems must meet a wide range of applications. While many of these are designed to function in a stand-alone capacity, the majority are also connected electrically to provide trouble or alarm initiation to a central location.

Industrial suppression applications include:

Industrial Suppression Applications
Tankside Suppression

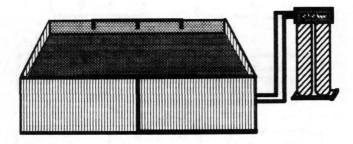

Each Cylinder Protects 40 Square Feet
Illustration Shows an 80 Square Foot Tank Surface Hazard
Used for Class B and Class C Hazards

Figure 5.10

Industrial Suppression Applications
Overhead Suppression

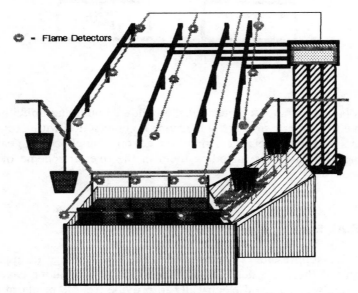

- Flame Detectors

Each Cylinder protects 30 Square Feet
Used for Class B and Class C Hazards

Figure 5.11

- **Tankside.** The suppression agent piping surrounds the edge of a tank containing a cleaning, painting, bathing, or otherwise volatile liquid. At the first indication of a fire, the suppression agent is released to cover the surface of the tank's liquid, snuffing out the fire (Figure 5.10).
- **Overhead.** Overhead systems supply a suppression agent to the area below through a series of nozzles at the end of a manifold system. A typical industrial application uses a carbon dioxide agent to protect a conveyor dipping action or sensitive production line operation (Figure 5.11).
- **Total flooding.** This suppression system is designed to protect an enclosed and uninhabited area. Sensors within the area trigger the suppression system, flooding the area with the suppression agent, usually carbon dioxide or a similar agent (Figure 5.12).

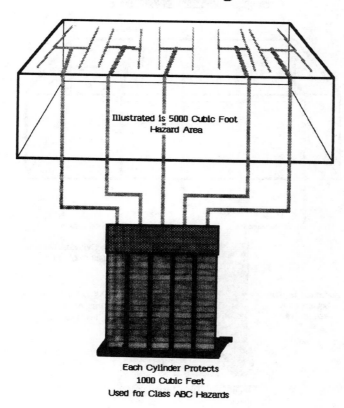

Closed Area Suppression

Total Flooding

Illustrated is 5000 Cubic Foot Hazard Area

Each Cylinder Protects
1000 Cubic Feet
Used for Class ABC Hazards

Figure 5.12

- **Combined hazards (ABC).** Here again is a total flooding technique, but due to the combined or multiple fire sources—oil, solvent, paper, cloth, or electrical equipment—a dry-chemical agent is the suppression agent (Figure 5.13).

A typical architectural specification might read something like this:

> The (location to be protected described in full) shall be protected by a pressurized automatic (dry chemical, carbon dioxide, or special suppression agent) fire suppression system. The system shall be approved by the local authority having jurisdiction and be listed by Underwriters Laboratories.

These systems are usually self-contained systems using dry chemical, aqueous film-forming foam (AFFF), or twin agent (foam and dry powder) sys-

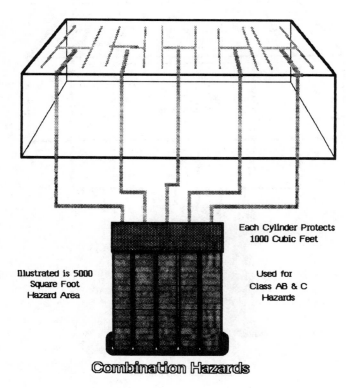

Figure 5.13

tems for a broad spectrum of special hazards. These systems consist of a chemical tank or tanks, a cylinder of nitrogen and a propellant for the chemical, a pneumatic or manual actuation system, and a single or twin hose line with an appropriate nozzle.

The dry-chemical, AFFF, and twin-agent systems can be standard or custom designed to meet specific applications. They may be permanently installed to protect a particular site or area, as well as skid or trailer mounted for transport to the hazard area.

WATER DELUGE

Where extremely high-speed water deluge is required, such as in propellant processes, an explosively actuated deluge valve can provide essentially the same high-speed response from a water line that the high-rate discharge extinguishers can provide with their stored agent. Typical applications of the deluge valve operation include the following:

- Where materials such as nitrocellulose, black powder, or other propellants are involved and high-speed cooling is the only effective means of control, high-speed water deluge is an extremely effective suppression technique.
- In closed vessels such as mixers or reactors and in situations where an imminent runaway reaction can be detected before it actually develops, rapid dilution and cooling can be an effective preventive measure.

These deluge valves can be used in combination with suppressors or high-rate discharge extinguishers for providing optimum fire control (Figure 5.14, p. 94).

EXPLOSION SUPPRESSION

Explosion suppression was developed by the British Royal Air Force shortly after World War II, while seeking a means for controlling aircraft fuel tank explosions resulting from small arms fire. This basic research resulted in the principle that is still used today to protect commercial aircraft from lightning strikes. The logical outgrowth of the aircraft system was the development of a system to provide protection in explosion-prone industrial processes.

Explosions can, in fact, be stopped before they become critical. An explosion is really nothing more than a very rapidly burning fire which, when confined, develops destructive pressures. Like the slower fire, however, it can be extinguished. The secret to suppression of an explosion is speed—speed in detection and speed in actual extinguishment. The system can sense an incipient explosion and discharge a highly efficient extinguishing agent in under 60 milliseconds, faster than the blink of an eye.

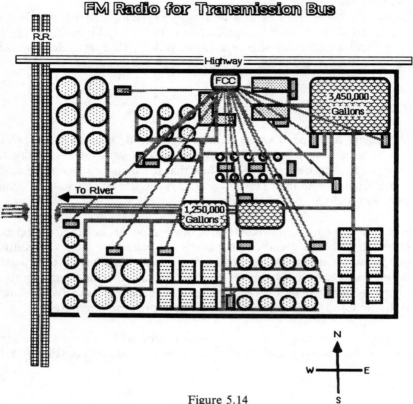

Water Deluge System

Petro-Chemical Special Problem

FM Radio for Transmission Bus

Figure 5.14

Figure 5.15 illustrates an explosion curve. The black line indicates the normal extrapolation of an unchecked explosion. The gray line illustrates the curve of an interrupted explosion with the suppression system providing a reaction that shuts off the overpressure at about 60 milliseconds and returns pressure to normal.

The best defense against potential explosions is to build the defensive system right into the plant. Good housekeeping and safe operating procedures must be developed and enforced. Manufacturing processes with a known potential for explosions can be designed for maximum safety:

- They can be flooded with inert gas.
- They can be structurally designed to alleviate explosive overpressures.

Explosion and Explosion Suppression Curves

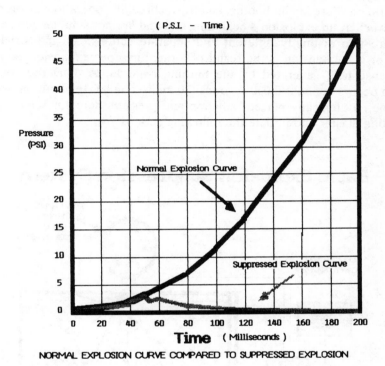

NORMAL EXPLOSION CURVE COMPARED TO SUPPRESSED EXPLOSION

Figure 5.15

- The roofing can be vented to minimize the damage.
- Storage tanks can be vented to reduce explosive damage.

Because no two industrial operations are the same, design of suppression systems must be done independently by suppression system experts. This does not mean that it will be excessively costly or that a particular plant will require special equipment developed for a single application. This individual design approach merely consists of a careful evaluation of materials and methods.

Design experts will locate the detection devices, both radiation and pressure, and the agent containers for maximum effectiveness. They will make recommendations concerning venting and equipment shutdown. In many cases, the explosion detection and suppression system can be combined with existing fire protection systems for additional safety and economy.

EXPLOSION SUPPRESSION SYSTEM
APPLICATIONS

Typical applications for individualized explosion suppression systems are grain elevators, powdered paint booths, and trash-shredding operations. Contrary to popular belief, an explosion's beginning and end are not simultaneous events. They are two distinctly different and separate actions. An industrial dust, vapor, or gas explosion is the result of a rapid gaseous expansion caused by the intense heat generated by the burning material. A dangerous pressure buildup occurs in about 0.030 seconds (30 milliseconds). In about one-sixth of this time, strategically placed radiation and pressure detectors can sense an impending diaster and initiate the following actions:

Basic Explosion Suppression System

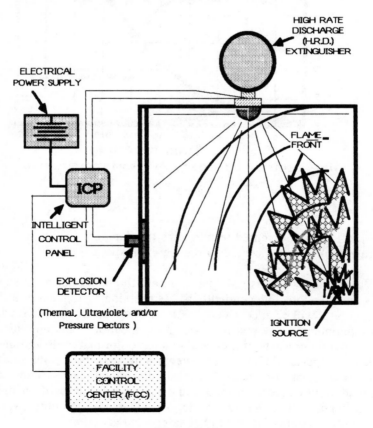

Figure 5.16

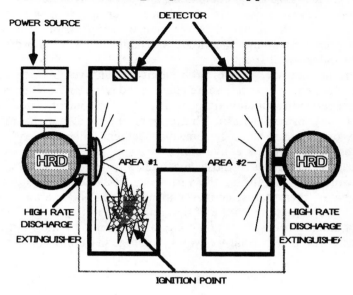

Figure 5.17

1. Discharge suppressant agent.
2. Open vents.
3. Discharge suppressant agents into adjacent areas.
4. Shut down affected machinery.
5. Sound alarms and give visual signal and audible indication of the system's activation.
6. Call in additional fire protection devices according to the design criteria.

By the time 60 milliseconds have elapsed, all these actions will have taken place and the explosive pressures will be on the decline, as illustrated in Figure 5.15. The basic arrangement for a typical suppression system is illustrated in Figure 5.16.

In more sophisticated arrangements the technique of advance inerting is installed. This will guard against an explosion in a routinely hazardous area by activating **high rate discharge (HRD) extinguishers** in adjacent areas (Figure 5.17).

TOTAL FACILITY CONTROL AND SUPPRESSION SYSTEMS

Suppression systems have their place in the protection of facilities, but designing such systems must be left to the experts. There are many highly specialized techniques, sensors, equipment, and devices available. Only a professional would have the depth of experience to ensure proper protection. To ensure proper application of these specialized suppression systems and resultant insurance premium reductions, the money invested in professional assistance is indeed well spent.

There are several types of both monitored and stand-alone suppression systems, and they all have a definite place in today's world. When relating this type of independently functioning system to a facility control system the general reaction is not to mess with it. That may be the case, but regardless of the efficiency of the stand-alone system, management still needs to know when, how, where, and why it is activated.

The best way to have those questions answered is through the facility control center. By monitoring the various stand-alone systems at the facility control center, their status, active or inactive, can become an appendage of the total system. With that type of tie into the overall system, a single event, such as a stand-alone system going into alarm, can activate the full force of the system. And that is what we want—total facility control.

6

Security Protection

SECURITY REQUIREMENTS

Security consists of those measures taken by a company to provide for the protection of property, personnel, material, and facilities against unauthorized entry, trespass, theft, damage, sabotage, espionage, or any other dishonest, illegal, or criminal act that might be taken against the firm.

To the board of directors, security means providing adequate protection with the most efficient expenditure of funds in order to protect corporate assets. To customers, security means keeping the cost of this overhead item to a minimum in order to maintain a competitive edge. Reducing the cost of operational expenses allows savings to go into the profit column, which pleases stockholders.

To the employees, security is probably one of the major factors affecting their morale. If employees have the feeling that management is providing for their safety and that they are working in a well-protected facility, morale goes up and pilferage decreases. Thus, the company benefits by retaining expensively trained personnel.

To the architect, engineer, and consultant, security is all the above, plus attention to new developments and applications of security devices. They must be aware of innovations in order to develop cost-effective techniques that provide enhanced protection.

In developing a sound corporate security philosophy, all these considerations are important. In today's world one cannot be complacent about security. Adequate protection is simply good business.

BASIC SECURITY RESPONSIBILITIES

Security departments are faced with a variety of responsibilities, depending upon the nature of the facility. Basic duties involve protection of the building and its occupants. Protection officers are expected to be first on the scene of any incident or accident, taking charge and resolving whatever problem confronts them. Individual officer tasks range from providing information to de-

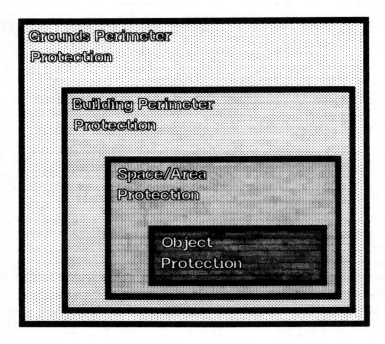

Figure 6.1

tention of troublemakers. They also patrol the building and grounds for increased protection and to reduce insurance rates.

A single line of protection is never adequate. Security protection must be developed in depth. Physical security lines of demarcation are essential for the protection of property and occupants. These rings of security usually start at the property line and are referred to as **perimeter protection**. In some cases the building walls and property line are one and the same. In this case, the protection ring is called **building perimeter protection**. Certain spaces within the facility such as vaults, research laboratories, or hazardous areas will also require security protection and this is referred to as **area security** or **space security**. The innermost point of protection is called **object protection**. In this case an individual safe, art object, or piece of equipment will have a high enough value to require specific security attention devoted to its protection (Figure 6.1).

Some of the routine security problems encountered might include typewriter theft, office breakin, or an employee's need to enter the office after hours. Twenty-four-hour operations require constant monitoring, while deserted loading docks and open storage yards present further problems. For years building managers have been coping with these situations as they arise. Now, however, there is the capability to preclude, or at least minimize, the majority of these security problems.

SPECIAL PROTECTION PROBLEMS

Once we have an appreciation for the number and magnitude of basic security responsibilities, it is time to look at special problems relating to certain operations.

Hospitals have an estimated 3,000 items on their shelves that can be used in the home. The pilferage problem associated with most hospital food-service operations is enormous. The volume of visitors and ambulatory patients combined with free access creates many problems for administrators. The availability of drugs, small items of costly equipment, and expendable supplies provide targets for theft. Health care facilities have additional problems associated with unusual fire hazards, evacuation procedures, dangerous gas monitoring, remote parking lots, nurse residential buildings, distraught people, and the routine handling of emergency situations. All these factors combine to create specialized problems.

Research facilities also have unusual security needs. Some of these are compartmentalization of special access areas, buddy system requirements, tracking of individuals within the facility, and controlled access by time and place. Special requirements for additional security might include explosive area monitoring and sensitive material protection. All call for special security solutions.

Administrators of educational institutions have the responsibilities of a small city with their multiple buildings, traffic problems, residence dorms, eating establishments, athletic events, transient populations, medical and research functions, laboratories, and agricultural activities. These facts place educational institutions in a class by themselves in dealing with security.

Key problems at industrial plants revolve around shift changes, twenty-four-hour operations, shipping and receiving activity, assembly line and key equipment monitoring, proprietary information, and tool theft. These all eat away at the profit margin in one way or another.

PROTECTION MONITORING, CONTROL, AND RESPONSE

The most cost-effective resolution to this wide variety of problems and responsibilities is a total **systems approach** to facility control. Only a survey of the factors affecting a given installation can actually illustrate where these security savings can be achieved. With a well-designed system, operational expenses can be significantly reduced. An economy of force can be realized. This may be achieved by either a reduction in personnel or their more effective use. For every seven-day, twenty-four-hour security post eliminated, the annual savings may exceed $100,000. Regardless of the approach, a well-planned security system can readily pay for itself. Additionally, management will have the satisfaction of knowing that it has provided the most cost-effective personnel and property protection possible for the facility.

A careful study and evaluation of all security systems available should be made before any implementation decision is reached. Present systems offer a wide variety of applications. Personnel involved in developing a security system for their facility, or expanding an existing one, need to think about the economics of various systems.

There are several important factors to consider in system design. A **central control console** is required to assist the protection staff in coordinating their work. The proper selection of electronic sensors is important to provide definitive information that will reduce reaction time. With this type of electronic support, existing personnel will be free to perform more critical protection functions. This continuous electronic surveillance and status reporting will ensure that there are no gaps in the protection of critical areas. The system design must provide for the automatic preparation of written records for all security transactions.

There are many security systems on the market; however, there is no one system that is best for all situations. The application of security to a building complex depends on the industry involved. Building security requirements are only one side of the equation. The other side is the proper application of security sensors and devices.

One of the primary functions of the **design team** is to develop the security requirements for the facility. This must be done in concert with safety, fire, maintenance, and operational considerations. In this way, all will have their specific problems addressed by the ultimate system arrangement selected. When these requisites are presented at the first meeting of the design team, they will have a better idea as to how to approach the task.

PERFORMANCE SPECIFICATION

When the broad facility control requirements have been identified, a professionally prepared **performance specification** can be written. This specification must be prepared in conjunction with those individuals who will be involved with the eventual management and operation of the facility.

The breadth of security responsibility, at all levels of facility operations, is important and must be fully understood. When security is in question, it is usually a case of the weakest link being the point of vulnerability. Resolution of these problem areas should be the task of the individual charged with facility security responsibility and a professional security consultant who specializes in system development. Each shares in the process of developing the security system. The consultant is responsible for maintaining knowledge in the state of the art, but does not know all the security requirements for a particular facility, even though he or she probably has broad general knowledge concerning security operations. The security director, on the other hand, understands the facility's security problems, but due to daily pressures on the job cannot hope to maintain currency in security system innovations and new devices. The salesperson of security products is there to sell security products.

The first two individuals will complement one another and serve to guarantee an effective security program that is integrated to mutually support the other facets of the total facility control system.

TOTAL FACILITY CONTROL AND SECURITY PROTECTION

The security provided by the **protection rings** can be greatly enhanced when coupled with other building management systems. Just as every facility has its own personality, the effective functioning of the security system is a factor of the innovativeness of those who design, install, and operate the system.

Security control, when integrated, will provide increased protection to both building and occupants. When a single control center can manage the security throughout the facility, an economy of personnel will have been achieved. If this same centralized control can also monitor the fire detection and alarm system, an additional safety factor will have been added. Forethought and design are essential for a security protection system to function as the nerve endings for the building. Intelligently designed, an integrated security system will sense those areas or points that require immediate attention.

Normally, closed circuit television (CCTV) systems are purchased and installed as a completely separate control element. They are totally devoid of interface with any other system without some type of intervention by the control center operator. Today's CCTV systems may quite readily be linked functionally with security systems. They may be initially installed as an integral part of the primary security control of the facility. Coupled with the security system, CCTV becomes the unsleeping eyes that aid in protecting the facility.

An audio system may be installed to serve as the voice and ears of the security personnel. Activated by security devices, the audio system will automatically tune in, listen, and record activity at the point in alarm, and do it all without human intervention. The audio system can provide a link for the rapid flow of timely information without the delay and confusion of attempting to use the telephone system without knowing where to call. When coupled with other systems in an integrated fashion, the audio control network will provide an invaluable life-saving service in support of the security system.

Security control over locked doors and the movement of personnel during a fire or similar emergency can be the difference between success and failure of the building's protection system. In such an instance, integration is imperative.

Monitoring the protection of the physical envelope of the building and working inward, controlling access to space, and even specific objects within the space, is a primary function of the security staff. Once all other major building control systems are integrated, monitored, and where appropriate, controlled, the overall security protection of the facility and its occupants will be greatly improved, even though fewer personnel may be required.

7

Physical Security

Physical security is concerned with the physical measures designed to safeguard personnel; prevent unauthorized access to the grounds, equipment, buildings, materials, and proprietary information; and protect against espionage, sabotage, damage, and theft. Physical security is the first line of defense for any facility.

It is imperative for the design team to thoroughly understand physical security, sensors and their applications, and monitoring and response requirements in order to develop a satisfactory facility security system. Monitoring, control, and response are the key words in understanding how security relates to other aspects of facility control.

The protection afforded by physical security is generally classified into broad categories. These categories include **grounds perimeter protection, building perimeter protection, space protection,** and **object protection** (Figure 7.1, p. 106).

GROUNDS PERIMETER PROTECTION

The outermost ring of physical security is referred to as **perimeter protection**. In some cases this might also be called **outdoor protection** or **grounds perimeter protection**. A pedestrian gate or vehicle entrance is often classified as a *point of entry* and falls under the perimeter protection category. Also in this category is **building perimeter protection,** which includes the exterior walls, roof, and underground areas. If a fence line is the outer boundary of the property, the building perimeter security measures serve as a second ring of protection for the facility.

Perimeter protection can provide deterrence, delay, detection, and, in the more sophisticated systems, discrimination and identification. It is at this outer point that the facility is generally first attacked or penetrated. In an *attack* the attackers do not care if they are killed or captured in the act. They make no effort to conceal their thrust. A *penetration* is overt if the penetrators use stealth to make their entry, but fail to cover their tracks, and covert if the penetration is made with the intent of entering and exiting undetected.

Security in Depth

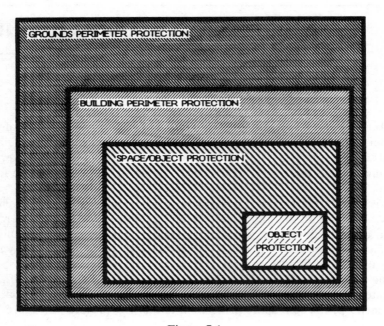

Figure 7.1

Physical protection of the perimeter may also be overt or covert. For some facilities, overt perimeter protection is not only essential as a deterrent, but expected. It is perfectly acceptable for an industrial plant or a military reservation to be surrounded by chain-link fence and protected by visible security devices. However, this approach to perimeter protection might not be esthetically acceptable or permitted by zoning at a downtown office building or hospital complex.

Detection and Protection Techniques

There are many outdoor perimeter protection techniques. They range from protective shrubbery and bare fencing to sophisticated electronic sensors and reporting systems. A listing of electronic sensors that may be used for various perimeter protection applications follows.

- **Taut-wire detectors.** A series of wires under tension are attached to switches at various points along the fence. An intruder attempting to climb over,

Grounds Perimeter Protection
Low Risk Facilities

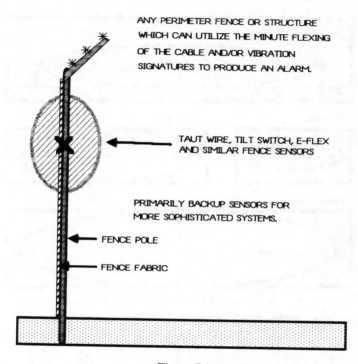

ANY PERIMETER FENCE OR STRUCTURE
WHICH CAN UTILIZE THE MINUTE FLEXING
OF THE CABLE AND/OR VIBRATION
SIGNATURES TO PRODUCE AN ALARM.

TAUT WIRE, TILT SWITCH, E-FLEX
AND SIMILAR FENCE SENSORS

PRIMARILY BACKUP SENSORS FOR
MORE SOPHISTICATED SYSTEMS.

FENCE POLE

FENCE FABRIC

Figure 7.2

under, or through or to cut the fabric of the fence will cause taut-wire detectors to sound an alarm (Figure 7.2).

- **Tilt switch detectors.** A tilt switch detector may also be referred to as a fence disturbance sensor (FDS). This device has several sensing switches, usually of the mercury switch type, connected either in series or parallel to a central processing unit or control panel designed to provide an alarm when fence movement causes the sensor to activate (see Figure 7.2).
- **Microwave sensors.** Microwave energy is beamed from a transmitter to a receiver. An alarm is sounded when an intruder breaks or deflects a sufficient amount of the microwave energy being beamed (Figure 7.3, p. 108).
- **Electric field fence sensors.** This form of perimeter protection is referred to as an E-Field system. This is a two- or three-wire fence through which an

Grounds Perimeter Protection

Outdoor microwave intrusion detection systems must be installed in an area that is free of moving objects, to include trees and bushes. This systems works well over flat open areas, but will not follow rolling terrain and the microwave pattern will spread as a function of distance and transmitter / receiver settings.

1. Typical Outdoor Microwave Transmitter / Receiver Single Zone.

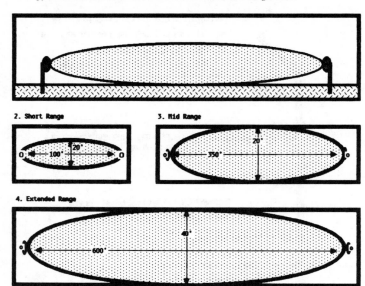

5. Typical Microwave Layout Illustrating Corner Crossover.

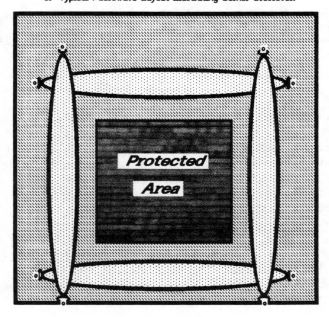

Figure 7.3

108

alternating current excites a field wire which is one element of the fence. There is also a more sophisticated technique called an H-Field system. The other wires are sensing wires and will couple with energy from the field wire resulting in an electric field or aura about the fence. The monitoring system generates an alarm when the electrical field is disturbed by an intruder (Figure 7.4).

- **Electrical capacitance fence sensors.** This system is unaffected by wind, rain, or passersby. They are generally used to detect attempted penetrations over walls, fences, building tops, or other barriers. The system detects the presence of an intruder by measuring changes in electrical capacitance between sensing wires and a ground wire as the intruder approaches or touches a sense wire (Figure 7.5, p. 110). Figure 7.6 (p. 111) illustrates multiple fence sensor applications for very high-risk facilities.
- **Seismic buried-line sensor.** There are two general types of seismic buried-line sensors. These geophone sensors, normally buried in sequence along

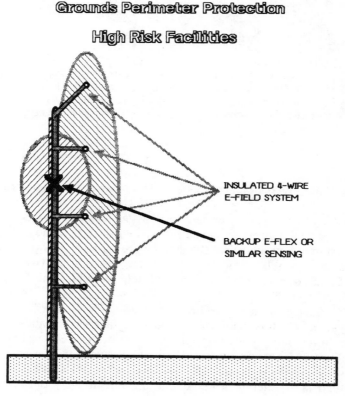

Figure 7.4

Electric Capacitance Fence

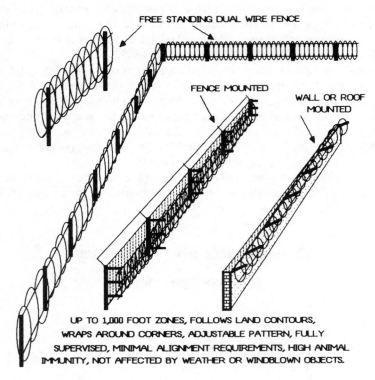

FREE STANDING DUAL WIRE FENCE

FENCE MOUNTED

WALL OR ROOF MOUNTED

UP TO 1,000 FOOT ZONES, FOLLOWS LAND CONTOURS, WRAPS AROUND CORNERS, ADJUSTABLE PATTERN, FULLY SUPERVISED, MINIMAL ALIGNMENT REQUIREMENTS, HIGH ANIMAL IMMUNITY, NOT AFFECTED BY WEATHER OR WINDBLOWN OBJECTS.

Figure 7.5

an outer perimeter, pick up seismic vibrations and cause an alarm to sound.

- **Pressure sensitive buried-line sensor.** This system employs two or more oil filled hoses with pressure sensitive switches at tl ends of the tubing. Human movement over the area creates pressure on the hose and activates the pressure switches. This type of system usually has two or three lines of hose buried in parallel and this will help to reduce the false alarm rate (Figure 7.7a, p. 112).
- **Magnetic buried-line sensor.** This system consists of a buried wire loop passive system which is sensitive to magnetic field disturbances. Since it responds to ferromagnetic material, this type of device is primarily used by the military to sense an individual carrying a weapon. It has some seismic sensitivity and the pressure effect of a footfall might affect the earth's magnetic field and generate a detectable current in the loop, resulting in an

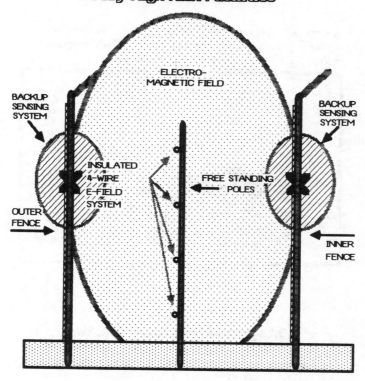

Figure 7.6

alarm (see Figure 7.7a). Grounds perimeter protection is best accomplished with a minimum of false alarms and a maximum of coverage where integrated sensor systems are utilized. Figure 7.7b (p. 112) and c (p. 113) illustrate the progress of an intruder through a buried sensor line and a microwave beam with the subsequent audio, lighting, and closed circuit television (CCTV) automatic response to the intrusion.

- **Infrared beam sensors.** These are active exterior infrared sensors which consist of a modulated light source transmitter and a photocell receiver. Any disruption of the beam will result in the system generating an alarm. This type of sensor is subject to reduced effectiveness during bad weather such as fog, rain, or snow, but it is unaffected by wind unless debris is blown through the beam (Figure 7.8, pp. 114–115).

Of these sensor systems, the microwave beam and the electric field fence sensor

Grounds Perimeter Protection
Buried Line Sensor

BURIED LINE SENSOR DETECTS ACTIVITY (SEISMIC, PRESSURE OR MAGNETIC) AND INITIATES WARNING SIGNAL TO FACILITY CONTROL. CENTER.

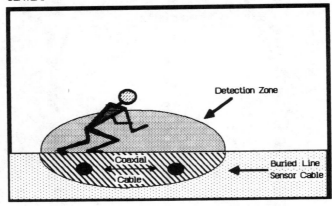

Figure 7.7a

Integrated Sensors - Alerting

MICROWAVE IS USED AS A BACKUP TO BURIED LINE SENSORS. A PRE-RECORDED, AUDIO MESSAGE IS ACTIVATED AND BROADCAST WHEN BOTH THE BURIED LINE AND MICROWAVE SENSORS ARE IN ALARM. CENTRAL CONSOLE MAY ALSO BROADCAST TRESPASS WARNINGS, TURN ON AREA LIGHTS AND CCTV IF REQUIRED.

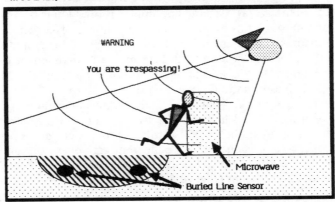

Figure 7.7b

Grounds Perimeter Protection

Integrated Sensors - Alarm

AS THE INTRUDER PROCEEDS, THE CCTV SWITCHES TO A MASTER
MONITOR, ACTIVATES A VIDEO RECORDER WITH A DATE-TIME-
GENERATOR, AND RECORDS ALL VIDEO VIEWED ACTION. THE
FACILITY CONTROL CENTER WILL AUTOMATICALLY RECORD ALL
VERBAL AND SENSOR ACTIONS UNTIL THE INCIDENT IS TERMINATED.

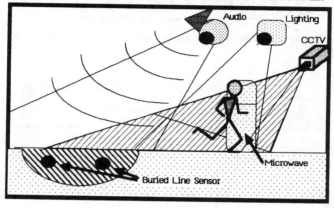

Figure 7.7c

(E-Field) are far superior in the areas of sensitivity and stability when properly installed outdoors. The buried systems are most effective where esthetics or concealment are prime considerations.

Video motion detectors do not really fall into the area of perimeter protection in the sense that fences do, but video cameras outfitted with motion detection units can truly enhance the security department's response to intrusions. With this CCTV enhancement, an alarm is sounded when the electrons on the face of the CCTV camera tube are excited by an object moving into the field of view or a designated portion of the field of view of the camera. CCTV cameras with motion detection capability can also provide an unobtrusive means of detection with covert installations (see Chapter 9).

Nighttime video applications may use either low light level camera tubes or an infrared illumination arrangement for this type of camera system. The biggest single advantage of this type of perimeter surveillance is the support it provides to the security force. One operator in the security control center can easily monitor numerous locations and provide guidance to the responding force.

Numerous turnstiles and gates are available for pedestrian access to the property. Where appropriate, these can be remotely controlled by television

Grounds Perimeter Protection
Infrared Beam Sensors

Outdoor infrared (IR) intrusion detection systems must be installed
in an area that is free of moving objects, to include trees and
shrubs. Infrared beams will only be effective over flat open areas.
IR does not follow rolling terrain and the beam pattern must focus
on individual receivers.

1. Typical Outdoor Infrared Beam Single Zone.

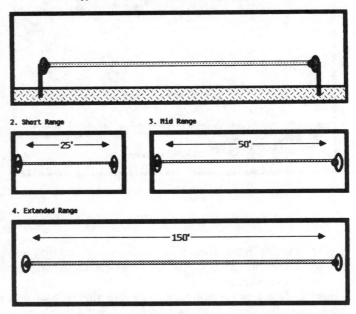

Figure 7.8a

viewing, audio, cypher lock, or an access control card system. Regardless of
the method selected, care must be taken to ensure the required degree of protection and monitoring of the portal.

Depending upon the facility, vehicle entry and exit control can be simple
or complex. Both flexible and rigid roadway pressure sensitive switches are
designed to initiate a signal with the passing of a vehicle. Magnetic sensors
buried either under the roadway or parallel with it perform the same signaling,
but covertly. Vehicle entry points are often neglected in perimeter security
design, yet they can be the most vulnerable to penetrations. Companies that
permit shipping and receiving from the same loading docks without controlling

Outdoor Infrared Beam Application

While outdoor applications are effective, it must be remembered that any one security system, by itself, is insufficient for adequate protection.

5. Typical Infrared Beam Layout Illustrating Corner Crossover.

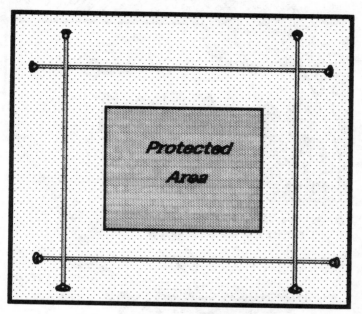

Figure 7.8b

the movement of the drivers often experience considerable losses from failing to monitor and control this area.

Vehicle Control

Vehicle control should be precise and conform to the protection requirements of the facility. Failure to control vehicular movement in and around the facility can be not only dangerous, but also fatal, as it was in the attacks on the marine barracks and U.S. embassy in Lebanon in the early 1980s. There are standard pieces of equipment which can be automatically activated in a **fail-safe** or **fail-secure** mode as a preventive measure against terrorist attack. It may not be possible to prevent the attack, but its effect can be minimized.

Vehicle Entrance Monitoring

BURIED MAGNETIC SENSORS DETECT VARIATIONS IN THE EARTH'S MAGNETIC FIELD WHICH RESULTS FROM THE MOTION OF FERROUS METAL OBJECTS. EFFECTIVE AGAINST CARS, TRUCKS, BICYCLES AND MOTORCYCLES.

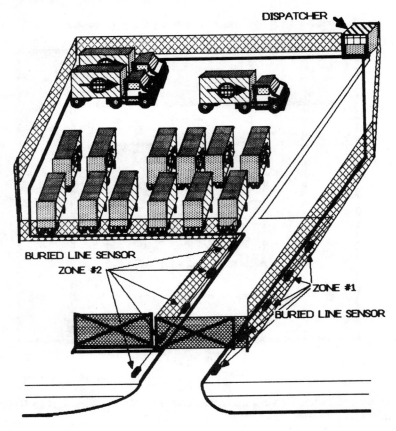

Figure 7.9

Vehicle movement monitoring, as illustrated in Figure 7.9, is primarily designed to alert a dispatcher in shipping and receiving of the arrival or departure of a vehicle. The same sensor system may be used as an automatic gate control device when security requirements are minimal. They may also be used to activate more stringent control devices.

For lesser vehicle problems there are fixed sabre-tooth traffic controllers such as those seen in some parking lots. Motorized traffic controllers similar to those shown in Figure 7.10 (pp. 117–118) are also available. Motorized bar-

Motorized Traffic Controller

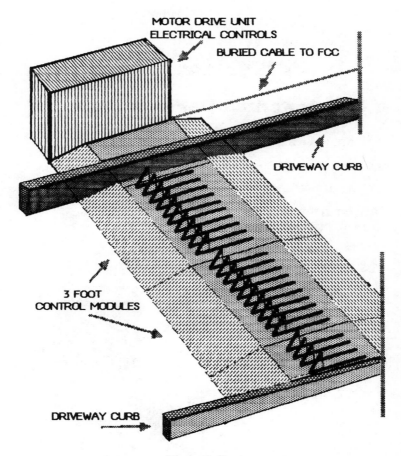

MOTOR DRIVE UNIT
ELECTRICAL CONTROLS

BURIED CABLE TO FCC

DRIVEWAY CURB

3 FOOT
CONTROL MODULES

DRIVEWAY CURB

Figure 7.10a

ricades have been designed for high-security locations where ramming or forced entry is a possibility. They are applicable where conventional gates or barriers are impractical. Such a barrier is designed to elevate from 13 to 30 inches in 1.6 to 2.5 seconds and designed to stop a 16,000-pound vehicle moving at 80 feet per second (55 mph) (Figure 7.11, pp. 119–120).

BUILDING PERIMETER CONTROL

It should be remembered that the total perimeter of the building includes all openings, walls, ceilings, roofs, floors, and basements. Other factors for con-

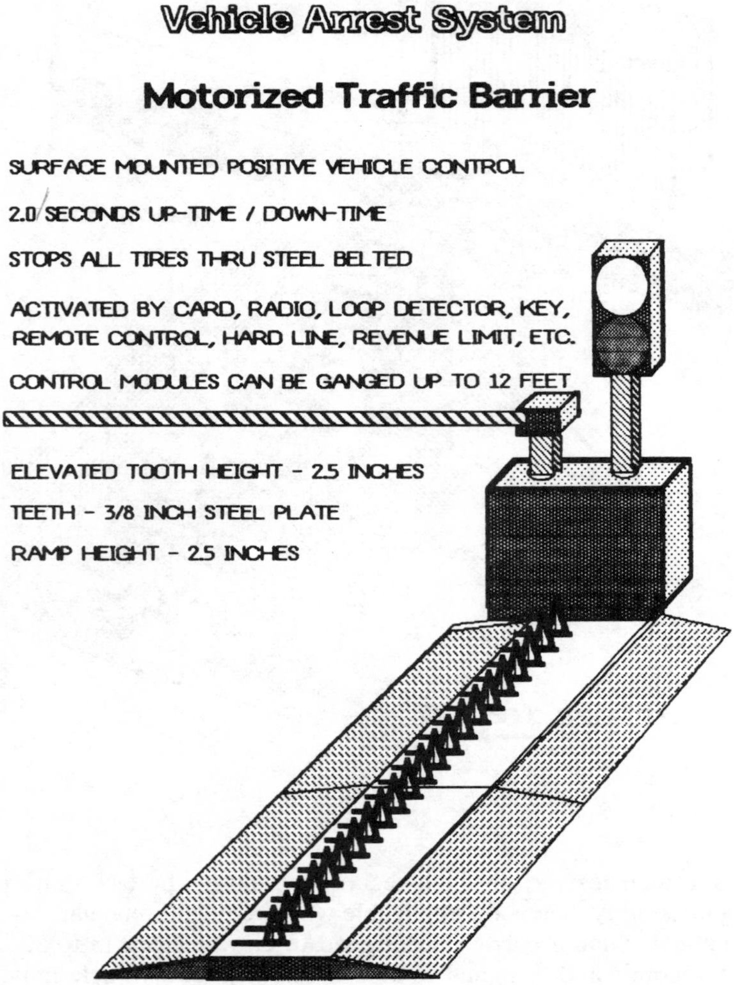

Vehicle Arrest System

Motorized Traffic Barrier

SURFACE MOUNTED POSITIVE VEHICLE CONTROL

2.0 SECONDS UP-TIME / DOWN-TIME

STOPS ALL TIRES THRU STEEL BELTED

ACTIVATED BY CARD, RADIO, LOOP DETECTOR, KEY, REMOTE CONTROL, HARD LINE, REVENUE LIMIT, ETC.

CONTROL MODULES CAN BE GANGED UP TO 12 FEET

ELEVATED TOOTH HEIGHT - 2.5 INCHES

TEETH - 3/8 INCH STEEL PLATE

RAMP HEIGHT - 2.5 INCHES

Figure 7.10b

Motorized Barricade

BARRIER WILL SUPPORT 22,000 POUNDS WITHOUT DAMAGE WHEN UP AND LOCKED.

ACTIVATED BY CARD, RADIO, LOOP DETECTOR, KEY, REMOTE CONTROL, HARD LINE, REVENUE UNIT.

2.0 SECOND ACTIVATION TIME, UP AND DOWN

BARRIER HEIGHT = 13.0 INCHES

BARRIER WIDTH = 72.0 INCHES

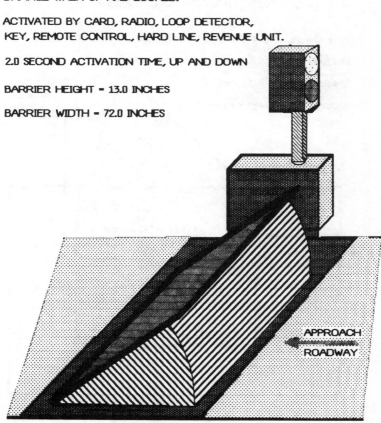

Figure 7.11a

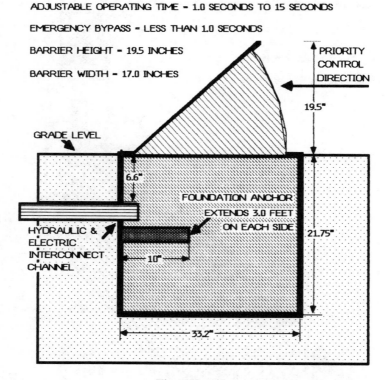

Vehicle Arrest Systems

Single Lane Barricade

ADJUSTABLE OPERATING TIME - 1.0 SECONDS TO 15 SECONDS

EMERGENCY BYPASS - LESS THAN 1.0 SECONDS

BARRIER HEIGHT - 19.5 INCHES

BARRIER WIDTH - 17.0 INCHES

PRIORITY
CONTROL
DIRECTION

19.5"

GRADE LEVEL

6.6"

FOUNDATION ANCHOR
EXTENDS 3.0 FEET
ON EACH SIDE

HYDRAULIC &
ELECTRIC
INTERCONNECT
CHANNEL

10"

21.75"

33.2"

Figure 7.11b

Magnetic Door Lock

ELECTROMAGNETIC LOCK MOUNTS ON DOOR FRAME AND A STEEL PLATE IS FASTENED TO THE DOOR. LOCK KEEPS DOOR CLOSED WITH A HOLDING FORCE OF FROM 1,200 TO 3,000 POUNDS OF MAGNETIC FORCE.

THERE ARE NO MOVING PARTS TO WEAR OUT OR JAM AND THERE IS NOTHING TO BE TAMPERED WITH. A MAGNETIC CONTACT SWITCH IS INHERENT WITHIN THE LOCK.

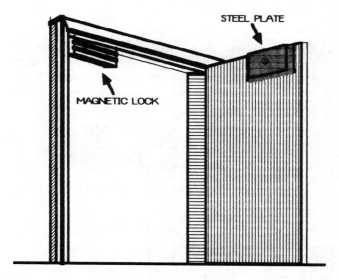

STEEL PLATE

MAGNETIC LOCK

DOORS MAY BE CONTROLLED INDIVIDUALLY OR IN GROUPS. A FIRE ALARM REQUIRING A DOOR TO BE UNLOCKED WILL AUTOMATICALLY RELEASE THE MAGNETIC HOLD AND PERMIT EVEN A SMALL CHILD TO EXIT SAFELY.

Figure 7.12

Magnetic Contact Devices

1/4 INCH DRILL MINIATURE MAGNETIC CONTACT SWITCH

PRESS—TO—FIT MAGNETIC CONTACT SWITCH

SUPERVISED WIDE GAP MAGNETIC CONTACT SWITCH

STEEL DOOR MAGNETIC CONTACT SWITCH

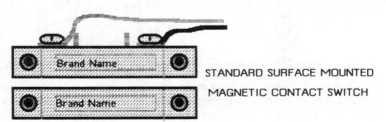

STANDARD SURFACE MOUNTED
MAGNETIC CONTACT SWITCH

Figure 7.13

sideration are the outside configuration of the building as well as the layout of the walls and partitions within. In most cases the cost of total building perimeter protection is impractical. Thus the most typical approach is to protect the normal points of access such as doors and windows (Figure 7.12, p. 121). The second approach, **area protection**, is addressed later in this chapter.

Contact devices are widely used to protect doors and windows. When the door or window is opened, the magnetic field is broken, activating an electrical impulse that signals an alarm. The devices are available in both surface and flush type mountings. Doors can be purchased with built-in **magnetic contact devices**. There are also high-quality hinges with built-in, unobtrusive switches (Figure 7.13).

Pressure sensitive mats can be used in connection with flooring and can be installed under carpet and padding or used under plywood or masonite. Some mats are even suitable for use under linoleum or tile. Good mats are quite thin, ranging from $^{40}/_{1000}$ of an inch to $^3/_{32}$ of an inch in thickness. The better mats are hermetically sealed to provide moisture protection (Figure 7.14 below and p. 123).

Protective window screens have the outward appearance of normal window screens, but are nevertheless security sensors that, if cut or penetrated, will activate an alarm.

Pressure Sensitive Mats

ENTRANCE WAY PRESSURE MAT

STAIR TREAD PRESSURE MAT

HALLWAY PRESSURE MAT

25 FEET X 30 INCHES
CUT TO DESIRED LENGTH

Figure 7.14a

Pressure Sensitive Mats

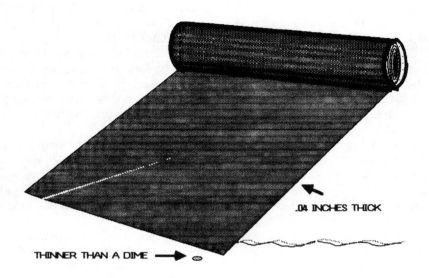

.04 INCHES THICK

THINNER THAN A DIME ➤ ⊗

ULTRA THIN UNDER CARPET SENSOR * EASY TO INSTALL
HERMATICALLY SEALED * COMPLETELY MOISTURE AND WATERPROOF
NO METAL STRIPS * AVAILABLE IN 100 FOOT ROLLS * NON-MAGNETIC
WIRING CRIMPED ON * SIX INCHES MINIMUM WIDTH
INSTALL OVER OR UNDER PADDING * RESILIENT TO HEAVY LOADS

Figure 7.14b

Wooden screens are actually grills made of wooden dowels or slats arranged in a grill-like fashion with no more than a 4-inch opening. A fine but brittle wire runs through the wooden frame. Any attempt at entry would break the wire and cause an alarm (Figure 7.15).

Lace paneling is a term used where the surfaces of walls, door panels, and safes are protected by lacing or weaving a metallic foil or fine brittle wire over the surface. A panel of wood is usually placed over the lacing to prevent it from being accidently broken and activating the alarm (Figure 7.16, p. 126).

Metallic foil is widely used to monitor glass surfaces. Strips of foil are affixed to the glass in such a fashion that if the glass is broken, the flow of current through the foil is lost, activating an alarm (Figure 7.17, p. 127).

Vibration detectors, often referred to as **window bugs**, are used for the protection of glazed areas. Window bugs are small specialty microphones tuned to the sound frequency of breaking glass. They are an obvious sign of a security system and in that respect alone are a deterrent (Figure 7.18, p. 128).

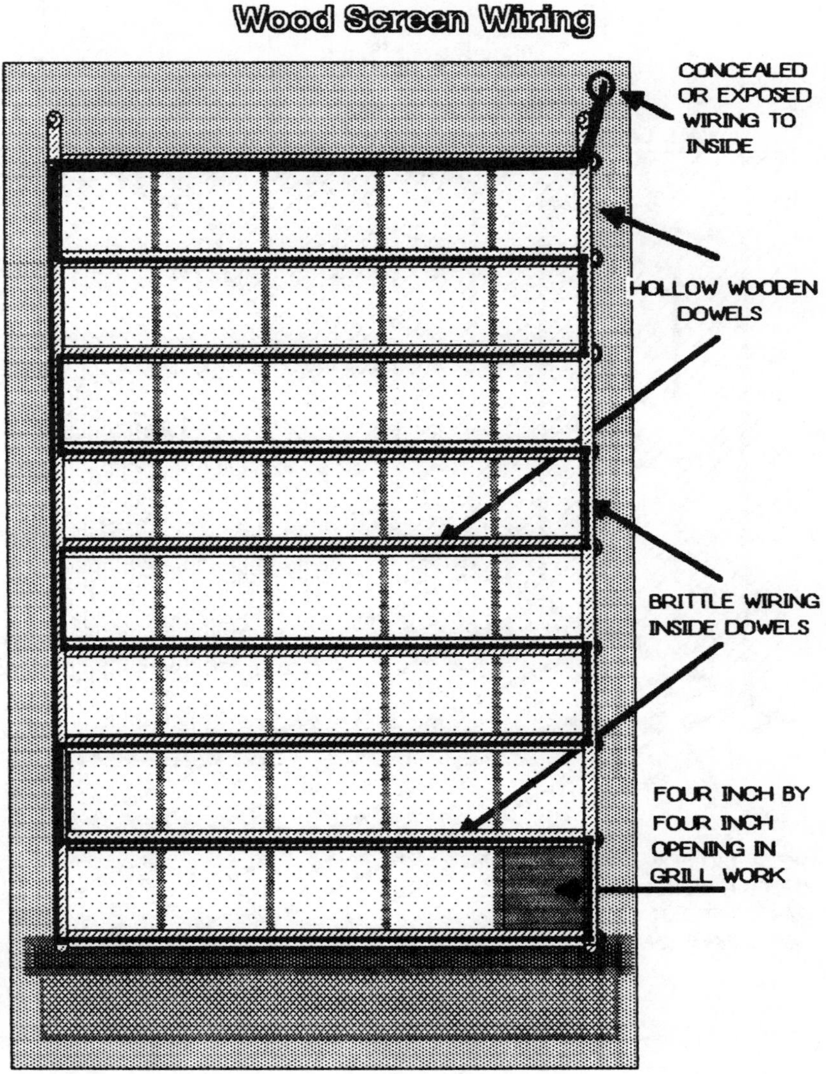
Wood Screen Wiring
CONCEALED OR EXPOSED WIRING TO INSIDE
HOLLOW WOODEN DOWELS
BRITTLE WIRING INSIDE DOWELS
FOUR INCH BY FOUR INCH OPENING IN GRILL WORK

Figure 7.15

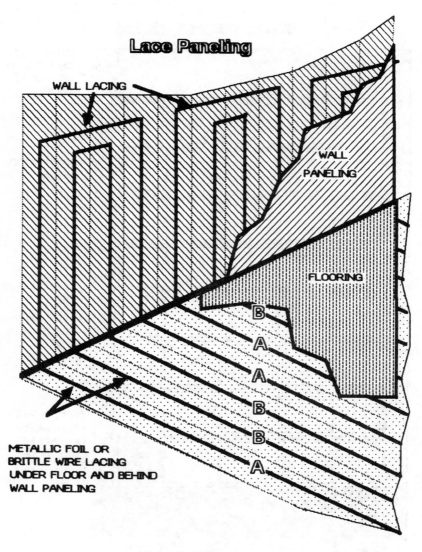

Figure 7.16

Metallic Foil Window Tape

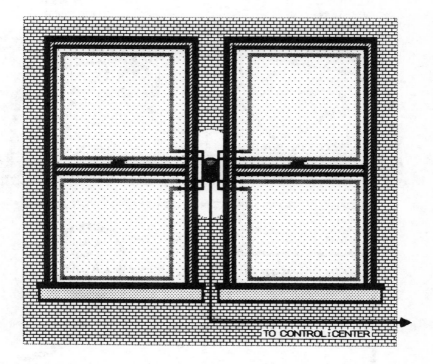

TO CONTROL CENTER

STRIPS OF THIN LEAD-TIN FOIL ARE AFFIXED TO THE SURFACE OF THE
WINDOW OR OTHER GLASS SURFACE. SHOULD THE GLASS BE BROKEN,
THE FOIL WILL BREAK CAUSING AN ALARM. THIS TECHNIQUE REQUIRES
FREQUENT MAINTENANCE, ESPECIALLY ON GLASS DOORS.

Figure 7.17

Electronic Vibration Detection (EVD)
Windows and Walls

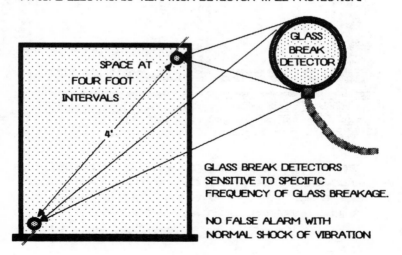

ELECTRONIC
VIBRATION
DETECTORS

ALARM
RECEIVER

30'

15'

15'

CRACK
IN WALL

NOMINAL SPACING

TYPICAL ELECTRONIC VIBRATION DETECTOR WALL PROTECTION.

GLASS
BREAK
DETECTOR

SPACE AT
FOUR FOOT
INTERVALS

4'

GLASS BREAK DETECTORS
SENSITIVE TO SPECIFIC
FREQUENCY OF GLASS BREAKAGE.

NO FALSE ALARM WITH
NORMAL SHOCK OF VIBRATION

Figure 7.18

Photoelectric devices work on the principle of a beam of light striking a receiving photocell. As long as the light continues to land on the photocell, an electrical current flows to the cell. When the photoelectric beam of visible or invisible light is interrupted, an alarm sounds. Photoelectric devices operate on visible light as well as invisible light. **Infrared** and **ultraviolet** light from both ends of the visible spectrum used in conjunction with a photoelectric device make the system exceptionally difficult for all but the most sophisticated intruder to identify or defeat. Mirrors can also be used with photoelectric devices to crisscross beams over a wide area or an entrance point or even to surround an object (Figure 7.19).

SPACE PROTECTION

Space or **area protection** systems are designed to protect interior spaces of a facility. Devices used in space protection are particularly effective against

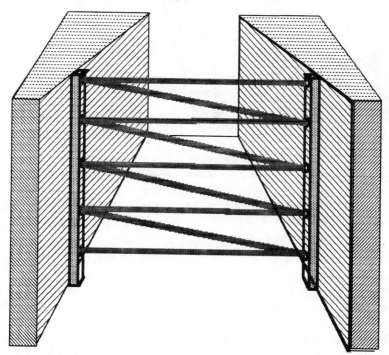

Photoelectric Beam Devices

INVISIBLE BEAMS MONITOR CORRIDOR, BUT DO NOT IMPEDE TRAFFIC.

Figure 7.19

Area Protection – Audio Detection

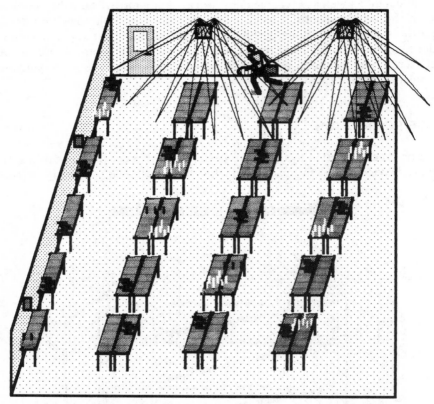

AUDIO DETECTION IS A QUICK AND VALUABLE AID IN VERIFYING
INTRUSION ALARM, ESPECIALLY IN LARGE FACILITIES WHERE TIME
OF RESPONSE COULD BE LENGTHY.

Figure 7.20

"stay behind" intruders. The four general categories of detection sensors normally used in space protection are audio, pressure, electronic vibration, and motion detection.

Audio detection systems use basically a microphone-speaker arrangement installed within an area to listen for intrusion sounds. Abnormal sounds such as those a vandal or burglar might make are immediately picked up and reported to an alarm receiver. These systems are extremely flexible. With advances in solid-state electronic technology, a wide selection of audio detection devices have been developed (Figure 7.20).

Pressure detection devices can have specialized applications in area protection. **Pressure-sensitive mats** can be cut to match stair treads or used in 100-foot hallways. There are also **stress-sensitive devices** that provide greater reliability and longer service than the mats and should be considered wherever mats might also be used (Figure 7.21 below and p. 132).

Electronic vibration detectors fastened to the walls, floors, and ceilings are designed to sense any attempt to penetrate the protected surface. These sensors are wired back to a detector control unit and from there to the facility control center (FCC). This type of system is applicable for rooms of ordinary construction to make them as secure as bank vaults through the use of elec-

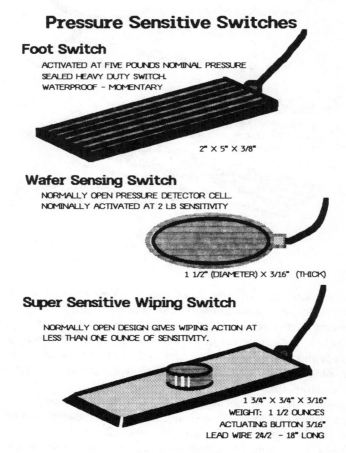

Pressure Sensitive Switches

Foot Switch

ACTIVATED AT FIVE POUNDS NOMINAL PRESSURE
SEALED HEAVY DUTY SWITCH.
WATERPROOF – MOMENTARY

2" X 5" X 3/8"

Wafer Sensing Switch

NORMALLY OPEN PRESSURE DETECTOR CELL.
NOMINALLY ACTIVATED AT 2 LB SENSITIVITY

1 1/2" (DIAMETER) X 3/16" (THICK)

Super Sensitive Wiping Switch

NORMALLY OPEN DESIGN GIVES WIPING ACTION AT
LESS THAN ONE OUNCE OF SENSITIVITY.

1 3/4" X 3/4" X 3/16"
WEIGHT: 1 1/2 OUNCES
ACTUATING BUTTON 3/16"
LEAD WIRE 24/2 – 18" LONG

Figure 7.21a

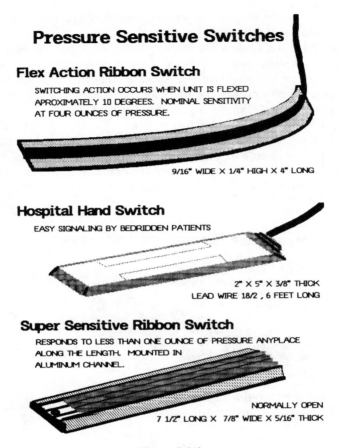

Pressure Sensitive Switches

Flex Action Ribbon Switch

SWITCHING ACTION OCCURS WHEN UNIT IS FLEXED
APROXIMATELY 10 DEGREES. NOMINAL SENSITIVITY
AT FOUR OUNCES OF PRESSURE.

9/16" WIDE X 1/4" HIGH X 4" LONG

Hospital Hand Switch

EASY SIGNALING BY BEDRIDDEN PATIENTS

2" X 5" X 3/8" THICK
LEAD WIRE 18/2 , 6 FEET LONG

Super Sensitive Ribbon Switch

RESPONDS TO LESS THAN ONE OUNCE OF PRESSURE ANYPLACE
ALONG THE LENGTH. MOUNTED IN
ALUMINUM CHANNEL.

NORMALLY OPEN
7 1/2" LONG X 7/8" WIDE X 5/16" THICK

Figure 7.21b

tronics. These rooms are, of course, subject to physical overt penetration, but are relatively safe from covert penetration (Figure 7.22).

Microwave (MW) detectors have a greater range than ultrasonic sensors. Since microwave motion detectors do not use sound as ultrasonic sensors do, they are less prone to false alarms caused by air currents. They do have limited application since **radio frequency interference (RFI)** cannot be contained without expensive shielding.

Ultrasonic systems do not require shielding but if not properly tuned and serviced are subject to false alarms, and the sonic frequency sometimes dips into the upper levels of female hearing (Figure 7.23, p. 134).

Infrared (IR) systems have proved to be most versatile for space protection. The IR sensors can focus across wide areas or beam down long hallways.

Interior Vibration Devices

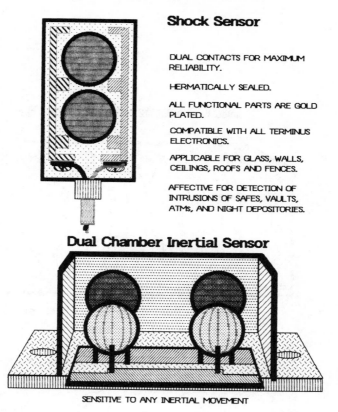

Shock Sensor

DUAL CONTACTS FOR MAXIMUM
RELIABILITY.

HERMATICALLY SEALED.

ALL FUNCTIONAL PARTS ARE GOLD
PLATED.

COMPATIBLE WITH ALL TERMINUS
ELECTRONICS.

APPLICABLE FOR GLASS, WALLS,
CEILINGS, ROOFS AND FENCES.

AFFECTIVE FOR DETECTION OF
INTRUSIONS OF SAFES, VAULTS,
ATMs, AND NIGHT DEPOSITORIES.

Dual Chamber Inertial Sensor

SENSITIVE TO ANY INERTIAL MOVEMENT

Figure 7.22

These IR beams can be **cross-zoned** to eliminate false alarms and intrusion alarms by pets, rodents, bats, and the like (Figure 7.24, p. 135).

Dual IR/ultrasonic devices are also available. While a bit more expensive than single devices, the dual arrangement is less prone to false alarms when properly installed and calibrated than independent single devices of either type. Using both the infrared and ultrasonic technologies, the dual sensors are designed to give an alarm only if both devices go into alarm. There are many applications where these devices are superior to any single unit (Figure 7.25, p. 136).

Capacitance proximity detection systems can be used to protect false ceiling areas, the tops of partitions, hallways, and stairwells. Capacitance systems work well when applied correctly, but they must be properly installed and maintained to preclude nuisance alarms. Capacitance techniques are also used

Indoor Ultrasonic Motion Detection

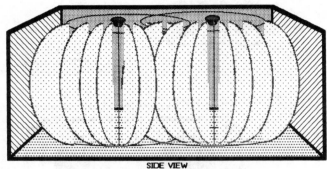

SIDE VIEW
CEILING MOUNTED ULTRASONIC MOTION DETECTORS

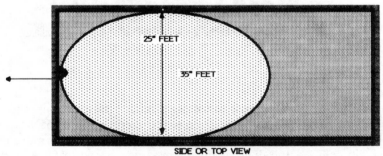

25" FEET

35" FEET

SIDE OR TOP VIEW
WALL MOUNTED ULTRASONIC MOTION DETECTOR

Figure 7.23

Indoor Infrared (IR) Motion Detection

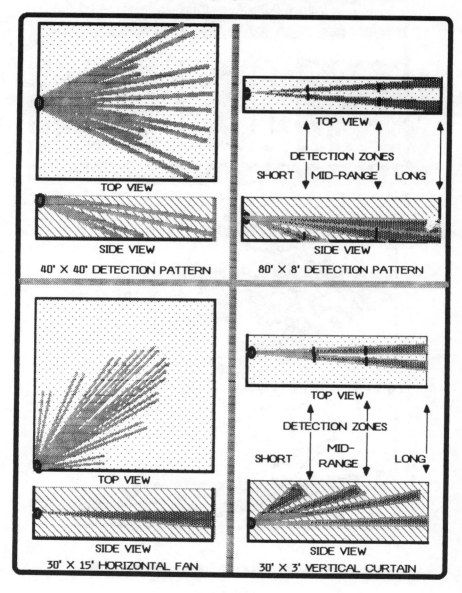

TOP VIEW

DETECTION ZONES

SHORT   MID-RANGE   LONG

SIDE VIEW

TOP VIEW

SIDE VIEW

40' X 40' DETECTION PATTERN

80' X 8' DETECTION PATTERN

TOP VIEW

DETECTION ZONES

SHORT   MID-RANGE   LONG

SIDE VIEW

TOP VIEW

SIDE VIEW

30' X 15' HORIZONTAL FAN

30' X 3' VERTICAL CURTAIN

Figure 7.24

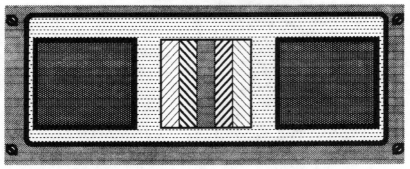

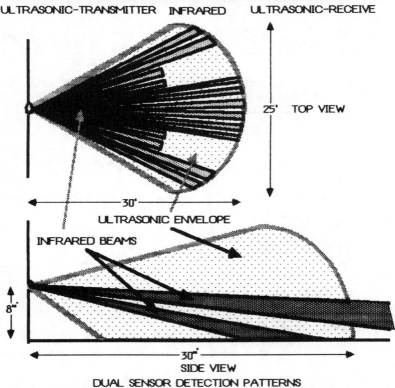

Figure 7.25

Capacitance Proximity Detection

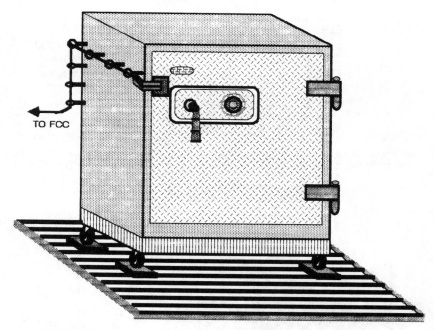

TO FCC

PROTECTION OF SAFES, FILE CABINETS OR OTHER LARGE METALLIC OBJECTS.

NORMALLY REQUIRES A MINIMUM SPACING OF 12" FROM WALLS AND, WITH PLASTIC OR GLASS ISOLATION BLOCKS, THREE TO FOUR INCHES FROM THE FLOOR.

EACH INSTALLATION WILL REQUIRE EXPERT ASSISTANCE.

Figure 7.26

to protect free-standing safes, file cabinets, and similar metal containers. In this case the protected object or its container actually becomes the sensor. A light electrical current passed through the object being protected causes an electrical field to develop through and/or around the object. Any disruption of the electrical field will result in an alarm (Figure 7.26).

Application of these various space protection sensors and systems requires more than a passing degree of knowledge and installation experience. They are exceptionally effective when properly integrated into the overall scheme of security protection.

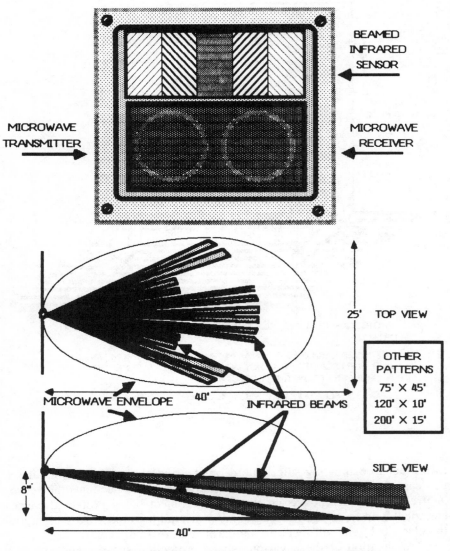

DUAL SENSOR (MICROWAVE - IR) DETECTION PATTERNS

Figure 7.27

More sophisticated space protection sensors are currently on the market. They are less prone to false alarms because they are **dual sensored devices**. These are single devices using the dual technologies of infrared and microwave (IR-MW) (Figure 7.27), infrared and infrared (IR-IR) (Figure 7.28), and infrared and ultrasonic (Figure 7.25). Within these devices are combined technologies that will cross-check each other to avoid random false alarms.

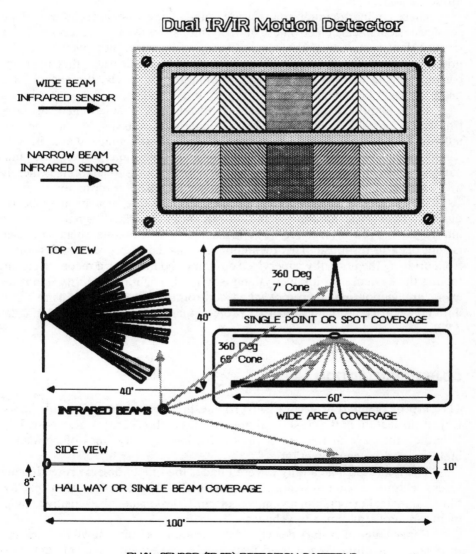

DUAL SENSOR (IR/IR) DETECTION PATTERNS

Figure 7.28

Compartmentalized Areas

Compartmentalized areas differ from space or area protection in that the compartmentalized area must be protected at all times. In some cases the compartmentalized areas are active twenty-four hours a day, while in others, they might normally be closed most of the time and only opened to a select few on rare occasions.

These compartmentalized areas are found in government facilities and the aerospace, chemical, electronics, and toy industries where management has learned that the future of the company may well rest on how well their proprietary secrets are protected. These industries have learned that by compartmentalizing their proprietary information and materials, the chance of a major loss can be minimized, if not rendered useless.

To be totally effective, compartmentalized areas must automatically control who is permitted entry and when. It is important to the corporation that individuals having business associated with a compartmentalized area be subjected to extensive background investigations and periodic polygraph examinations. This is not to imply that these individuals are dishonest; this is merely a solid approach to the protection of compartmentalized information.

Where high-quality security is essential, **high-line security** may be required. This is a technique whereby a randomly generated signal is used to interrogate the sensor(s) concerned and a unique, to the original signal, message is sent back in response. This technique is designed to prevent professionals from bridging the normally supervised circuitry and inserting a recorded signal, fooling the system to think everything is normal. High-line security is not for every application and therefore when confronted with such a sensitive and difficult security problem, unbiased professional assistance is needed (Figure 7.29).

OBJECT PROTECTION

The purpose of **object protection** is to provide direct protection to specific items. Object protection is the final focal point of in-depth security (see Figure 7.1). It is the bull's eye at the center of the multiple security rings of perimeter, building, and space protection.

The items most generally covered under the title of object protection are safes, sculpture, paintings, drug cabinets, high-value items on open display, filing cabinets, key personnel vehicles, aircraft, desks, models, sensitive equipment, and construction site vehicles.

Capacitance proximity detection systems are generally known for their use in object protection. When used in this role, capacitance systems are most effective when dealing with relatively small ferrometallic items. With this system the object or the materials surrounding the object actually become an

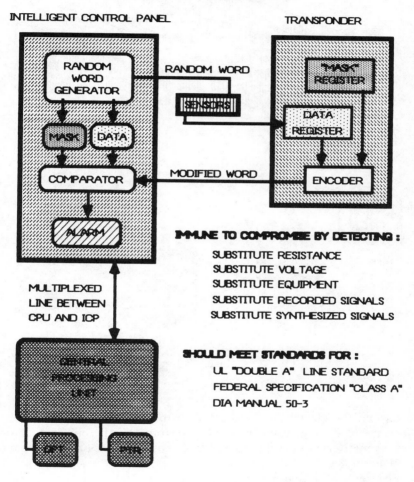

Figure 7.29

Object Capacitance Protection

Sample Applications

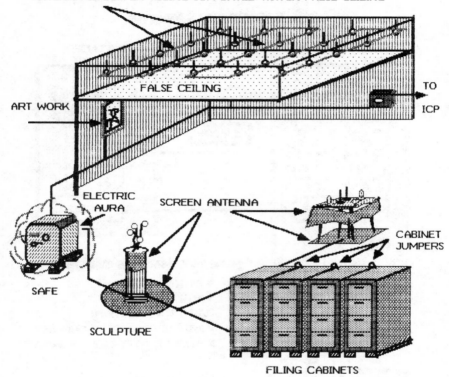

ANTENNA IS COPPER TUBING SUPPORTED WITHIN FALSE CEILING

FALSE CEILING

ART WORK

TO
ICP

ELECTRIC
AURA

SCREEN ANTENNA

CABINET
JUMPERS

SAFE

SCULPTURE

FILING CABINETS

Figure 7.30

antenna and are electrically connected to the Facility Control Center. Any disturbance of the electromagnetic aura surrounding the object, touching the object, or interfering with the capacitance sensor, cable, or control panel creates an alarm (see Figure 7.30).

Electronic vibration detectors (EVD) use a highly sensitive and specially designed microphone referred to as an EVD. The EVD is attached directly to the object to be protected. When an intruder causes a vibration within the EVD's monitoring or sensing range, an alarm is sounded. These devices are adjustable in range from a sledge hammer to the tinkling of breaking glass.

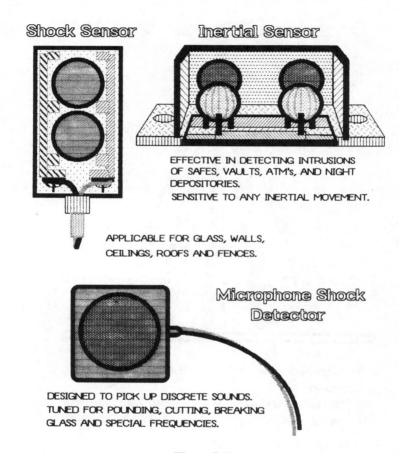

Electronic Vibration Devices

Shock Sensor

Inertial Sensor

EFFECTIVE IN DETECTING INTRUSIONS
OF SAFES, VAULTS, ATM's, AND NIGHT
DEPOSITORIES.
SENSITIVE TO ANY INERTIAL MOVEMENT.

APPLICABLE FOR GLASS, WALLS,
CEILINGS, ROOFS AND FENCES.

Microphone Shock Detector

DESIGNED TO PICK UP DISCRETE SOUNDS.
TUNED FOR POUNDING, CUTTING, BREAKING
GLASS AND SPECIAL FREQUENCIES.

Figure 7.31

EVDs differ from capacitance detectors in that they can protect even non-metallic objects (Figure 7.31).

Infrared motion detectors can be used effectively to protect large objects indoors. This requires the services of an expert for proper application, but an object as large as the MX missile in a checkout bay can be protected in this manner without any hindrance to the activity surrounding the vehicle (Figure 7.32, p. 144).

Electromagnetic locks are capable of protecting large movable objects such as vehicles on a construction site or sensitive high-value items in transit. Ve-

Infrared Object Protection

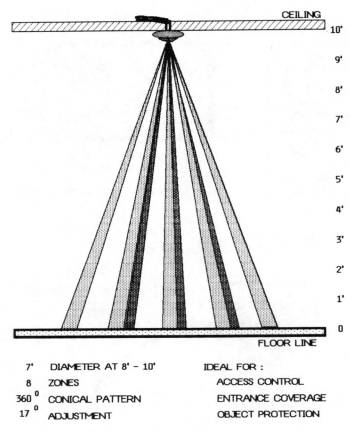

7'	DIAMETER AT 8' - 10'	IDEAL FOR :
8	ZONES	ACCESS CONTROL
360^0	CONICAL PATTERN	ENTRANCE COVERAGE
17^0	ADJUSTMENT	OBJECT PROTECTION

Figure 7.32

hicles at a construction site can be interconnected with an electrical harness of electromagnetic locks tied into an alarm control system. These expensive vehicles can be protected for as little as 1 percent of their value (Figure 7.33).

Nuclear weapons can be hermetically sealed in protective canisters and be under constant electromagnetic lock protection and internal controls. The canister is powered by internal or transport vehicle power sources while in transit and will generate an alarm if access procedures or power elements are tampered with (Figure 7.34, p. 146).

Photoelectric beams in the visible or invisible light spectrum can be an effective object protection technique. Beams of light designed to surround the

Electro-Magnetic Locking Devices

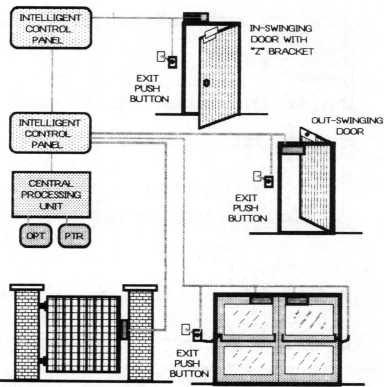

INTELLIGENT CONTROL PANEL

IN-SWINGING DOOR WITH "Z" BRACKET

EXIT PUSH BUTTON

INTELLIGENT CONTROL PANEL

OUT-SWINGING DOOR

CENTRAL PROCESSING UNIT

DPT   PTR

EXIT PUSH BUTTON

EXIT PUSH BUTTON

A COMPLETE ELECTRO-MAGNETIC LOCK INCLUDES MAGNET, STRIKE PLATE, AND BUILT-IN MAGNETIC CONTACT SWITCH. IT MUST BE INSTALLED IN A FAIL-SAFE MODE ON EXTERIOR DOORS AND TIED INTO THE FIRE ALARM SYSTEM TO OPEN AUTOMATICALLY IN THE EVENT OF A FIRE. INTERIOR SECURE AREAS MAY BE INSTALLED IN A FAIL-SECURE MODE SO ESCAPE IS ASSURED. CHECK WITH THE "AUTHORITY HAVING JURISDICTION" BEFORE INSTALLATION TO ASSURE CODE COMPLIANCE.

Figure 7.33

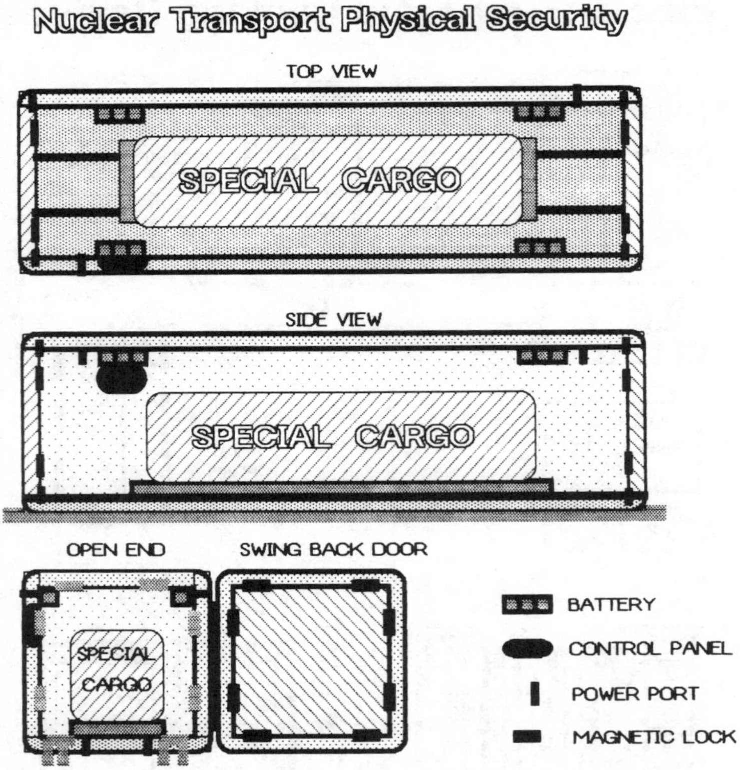

Nuclear Transport Physical Security

TOP VIEW

SPECIAL CARGO

SIDE VIEW

SPECIAL CARGO

OPEN END   SWING BACK DOOR

SPECIAL CARGO

BATTERY

CONTROL PANEL

POWER PORT

MAGNETIC LOCK

SPECIAL CARGO CONTAINER DESIGNED FOR TRANSPORT VIA TRUCK AND
AIRCRAFT. POWER PORT PROVIDES EXTERNAL POWER WHEN CONTAINER IS
IN TRANSIT OR DURING STORAGE. CONTAINER IS HERMETICALLY SEALED
BY EIGHT MAGNETIC LOCKS ON DOORS AT EACH END OF CONTAINER.
INTERNAL NOXIOUS GAS REPELS PENETRATORS WHILE SIREN, AUTOMATIC
RADIO AND BEACONS ALERT SECURITY PERSONNEL TO INTRUSION ATTEMPT.
CONTAINER IS SECURED BY INTERNAL POWER AND BIOMETRIC ACCESS
CONTROL WHILE IN TRANSIT AWAY FROM MAIN POWER AND NORMAL
SECURITY FORCE.

Figure 7.34

Photoelectric Beam Object Protection

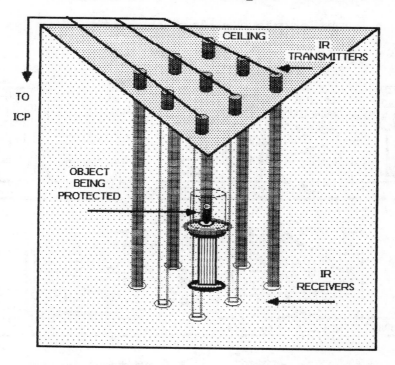

PHOTOELECTRIC BEAMS OF LIGHT ARE TRANSMITTED FROM THE CEILING
TO RECEIVERS FLUSH IN THE FLOOR TO PROTECT A SINGLE HIGH VALUE
OBJECT. LIGHT BEAMS MAY BE MADE INVISIBLE BY USING INFRARED
FILTERS. ANY DISRUPTION OF THE PHOTOELECTRIC BEAMS WILL INITIATE
AN ALARM, VIA THE INTELLIGENT CONTROL PANEL, TO THE FACILITY
CONTROL CENTER.

Figure 7.35

object, either on a direct beam basis or through the use of mirrors, will sound
an alarm if any of the beams are broken or obscured (Figure 7.35).

PHYSICAL PROTECTION

Physical security techniques are essential for the protection of personnel, property, and proprietary information. The physical protection methods employed
must be cost-effective and complete, if the facility is to be properly secured.

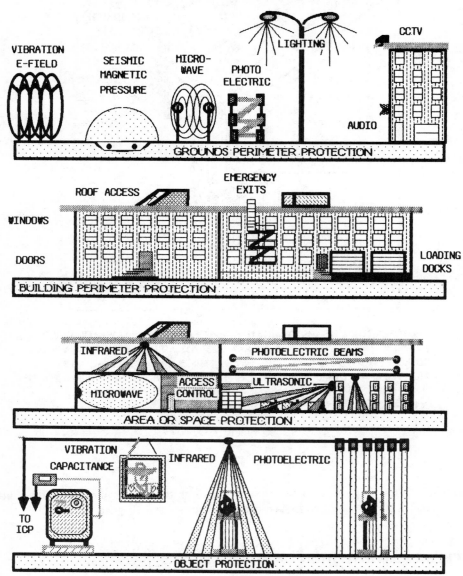

Figure 7.36

The first step toward achieving an efficient protection system involves preplanning and developing a list of security priorities. Additional steps require proper sensor application and effective alarm controls that can be integrated into the overall protection plan for the facility.

To be effective, a minimum of two rings of security should be developed. For instance, perimeter and space protection systems present two lines of defense. The use of dual sensors prevents blind spots and reduces false alarms. Linking two or more separate systems can be extremely effective. A security sensing system developed on a prioritized basis and linked with audio detection, access control, and CCTV is extremely difficult to defeat (Figure 7.36).

Various staff and department heads should coordinate their respective security requirements with the director of security. These requirements can then be balanced to ensure full coverage through effective application of security sensors and their integration into the total facility control system.

WATERFRONT PROTECTION

Many security people would view a water frontage on their property as part of their perimeter protection and stop at that. Failure to add electronic surveillance along the water frontage could leave a facility open to all sorts of vandalism, thievery, and even sabotage.

Underwater intrusion detection is not an occult science, but standard equipment that is readily available. Underwater detection devices, such as those illustrated in Figure 7.37 (p. 150), are available for emergency deployment or permanent installation underwater.

The sonar scope is designed to provide a color rendition of underwater objects, stationary and mobile. Where appropriate, stationary objects such as reefs, pilings, and sunken wrecks may be erased from the screen. This way, only moving objects will be visible on the scope. Color variations of submersibles will provide the trained and experienced operator with immediate identification. The density of the underwater mobile objects are reflected in the color shading from light yellow, orange, red, green, blue, and indigo. This color shading, coupled with the erratic movement of fish, aids in the identification.

Waterside intrusion detection uses a combination of underwater sonar-type devices and overwater radar-type surveillance working in conjunction with each other to provide water frontage physical security protection. The surface skimming radar, usually installed on a tower to increase the detection range, coupled with the underwater intrusion sonar sensors, provides protection on the waterfront side of the property (Figure 7.38, p. 151).

Underwater Intrusion Detection

Rapid Deployment and Stationary Devices

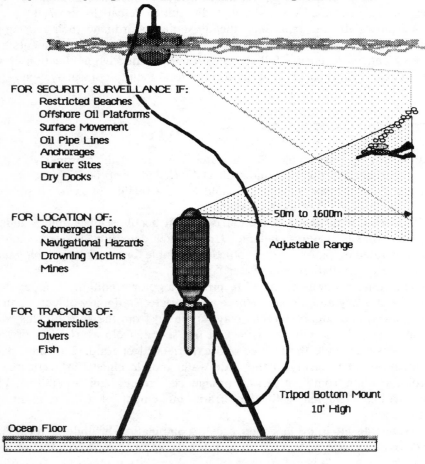

FOR SECURITY SURVEILLANCE IF:
Restricted Beaches
Offshore Oil Platforms
Surface Movement
Oil Pipe Lines
Anchorages
Bunker Sites
Dry Docks

FOR LOCATION OF:
Submerged Boats
Navigational Hazards
Drowning Victims
Mines

FOR TRACKING OF:
Submersibles
Divers
Fish

50m to 1600m

Adjustable Range

Tripod Bottom Mount
10' High

Ocean Floor

Figure 7.37

Waterside Intrusion Detection

Combined Surface and Underwater Sensors

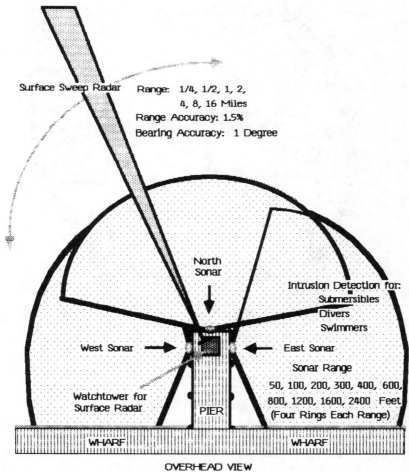

Surface Sweep Radar

Range: 1/4, 1/2, 1, 2,
4, 8, 16 Miles
Range Accuracy: 1.5%
Bearing Accuracy: 1 Degree

North
Sonar

Intrusion Detection for:
Submersibles
Divers
Swimmers

West Sonar →

← East Sonar

Sonar Range
50, 100, 200, 300, 400, 600,
800, 1200, 1600, 2400 Feet
(Four Rings Each Range)

Watchtower for
Surface Radar

PIER

WHARF

WHARF

OVERHEAD VIEW

Figure 7.38

Perimeter Intrusion Protection

E—FIELD SENSOR SYSTEM USES PARALLEL WIRES, TWO OR MORE OF WHICH ARE EXCITED BY A FIELD GENERATOR TO DEVELOP AN EXTREMELY SENSITIVE ELECTROMAGNETIC FIELD. THE SYSTEM EXHIBITS HIGH IMMUNITY TO FALSE ALARMS AND CAN DISTINGUISH SLOW HUMAN MONEMENT FROM SMALL ANIMAL AND BLOWN OBJECTS.

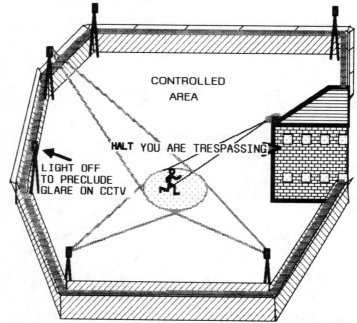

CONTROLLED
AREA

HALT YOU ARE TRESPASSING

LIGHT OFF
TO PRECLUDE
GLARE ON CCTV

E—Field makes undetected intrusion or escape virtually impossible. Automated systems would incorporate lighting, video and audio to provide in—depth protection and control.

Figure 7.39

TOTAL FACILITY CONTROL AND PHYSICAL SECURITY

Efficient and effective protection of personnel, property, and proprietary materials are paramount in an integrated facility security system. Building protection systems will automatically interact to provide maximum security protection with minimal personnel.

Should there be a penetration of the facility at the property line, the perimeter sensors will audibly alert the Facility Control Center of the intrusion,

Perimeter Intrusion Protection

Buried line sensors are either of an audio, magnetic or a seismic type.

The principle of detection involves discriminator (D) sensors at the fence line to filter out ambient disturbances from traffic and yet have detection (F & 6) and capture (a) sensors to readily detect intruders.

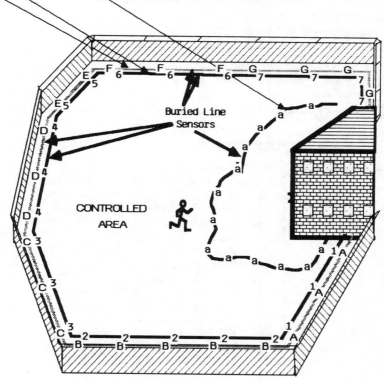

Figure 7.40

identify the location, and create a hard-copy record of the event by date, time, location, and time of FCC operator acknowledgment (Figure 7.39).

The facility control system will seize the appropriate CCTV camera and point it at the area in alarm. At the same time, the CCTV system will activate a **video cassette recorder (VCR)** and a **date-time generator (DTG)** and begin recording the scene (Figure 7.40).

Where applicable, the nearest audio sensor will automatically be switched to permit immediate listening and two-way communication with the zone in alarm. All the FCC operator needs to do is look at the CCTV monitor and

Intrusion Alarm Sequence

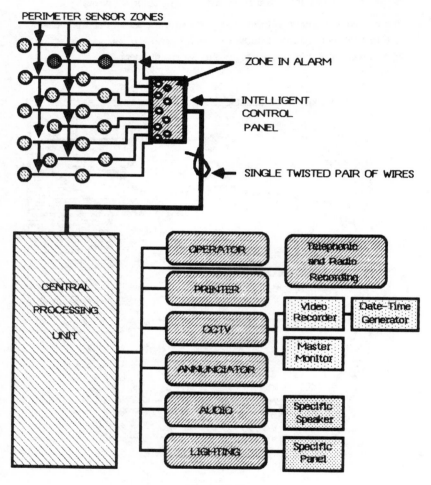

Figure 7.41

listen for sounds of intrusion. With this added visual and oral information, appropriate decisions can be made (Figure 7.41).

This is where the **Facility Control Center** (**FCC**) enhances its interface capability. Based on the intrusion-initiated alarm, and in addition to these actions, the FCC will automatically commence recording all telephonic and proprietary radio activity. This permits management to accurately review all actions causing the alarm, as well as actions taken to resolve the problem. This information will be contained on the videotape from the CCTV system, the recordings of radio and telephone conversations, and the hard-copy recording of events reported on the facility control system.

Management can then respond effectively to change or update procedures to preclude any shortcomings that might have occurred. By having complete and accurate information available, every step of the incident can be reconstructed. Integrated security is protecting people, property, and proprietary information.

8

Movement Control

It is essential that the importance of controlling the movement of personnel and vehicles in and around a facility be thoroughly understood. This chapter concentrates on access control requirements, techniques, and devices. Their integration with a facility control system is also described.

ACCESS CONTROL

Just as every building has its own personality, each building also has its own unique movement control requirements. Failure to recognize this element of facility control can be not only expensive, but also disastrous.

As facility managers review the loss potential of their buildings, consideration must be given to the movement and control of people within its confines. An access and movement control system designed to complement the management procedures will go a long way toward reducing losses and making the other protective systems efficient and cost-effective. Management directives and policies are designed to meet a variety of conditions. The access control system must show this same flexibility in order to provide predictable regulation and monitoring of the movement of people and vehicles.

In many cases, access control must go beyond simple entry to the building. Employees need ready access to the building and their work locations; however, they do not necessarily need access to the entire facility. Movement of visitors should be monitored and controlled to ensure their safety and the protection of proprietary material. This can be handled quite discreetly with appropriate access control techniques. Access to high-value items, research and development laboratories, and data processing centers should also be regulated.

LOCKS AND KEYS

The normal approach to building security has been locks and keys. Generally speaking, locks will keep out the honest people, but leave much to be desired in the realm of movement control and protection of corporate secrets. Con-

Master Key System

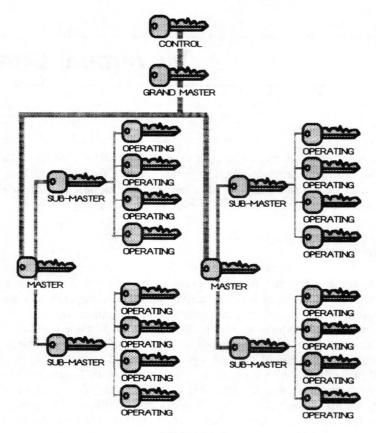

Figure 8.1

ventional lock-and-key arrangements may be satisfactory for some applications, but there are also some distinct disadvantages. Locks are easily picked and keys can be readily duplicated. Keys are cumbersome to carry and subject to loss. Where time is of the essence, keys can be uncomfortably slow. It must be recognized that even the finest key control system will not be adequate without proper support from management. Along with the responsibility of managing the key control system must go the authority to control keys in the very best interests of the company.

Master keying has long been thought to be the ultimate way to protect property and prevent loss, but operating a **master key system** can be difficult and costly. Master keying must be specifically accomplished for each facility. There is a grand master key that will open every lock in the system, and a series of submaster keys that open various groups of locks. On the lowest rung of the master key ladder is the operational key that has been specifically cut to open a particular lock. For the locking system to be effective, the lock cores should be periodically changed. Figure 8.1 illustrates the typical master key arrangement.

Whenever locks are master-keyed, they are keyed to a specific chart. This chart lists all available codes for future use. The person responsible for facility security should request a copy of the master key charting for the lock system that is used in his or her buildings. With this master key chart it is then possible to have additional keys reproduced from the codes on the chart.

It must be recognized that these codes are also available to others. This makes control of the master key charts critical, and steps must be taken to ensure adequate protection. The real question still remains, do locks and keys provide the level of protection required? An integrated access control system can definitely provide more positive protection than a master key arrangement.

GUARD SERVICE

Use of a uniformed guard service might be a solution to the movement control of people throughout a facility, but the use of guards to control exits and entrances may prove to be excessively expensive. Federal government figures indicate that it takes 5.2 individuals to staff a single twenty-four hour guard post, and the cost may run as high as $100,000 a year.

While there is a definite role for the human element in the protection of corporate assets, standing guard over a door may not necessarily be the most cost-effective way to use security personnel. Proper use of protection personnel lies in their ability to apply intelligence and resources at the point or points requiring specific attention during an emergency situation or at known peak traffic times.

CARD ACCESS CONTROL SYSTEMS

Time and technology have increased the sophistication of access control systems. Today's popular systems are microprocessor based, and the majority use an access control card of one type or another. These cards are about the size of a standard credit card and come in a wide variety of encoding techniques.

All systems do not take the same size card. There is little interchangeability where the different encoding methods are concerned. This is also true of card readers. While one card may be used in several variations of card reader, there is little commonality among readers.

In a normal card access system, the individual presents his unique card to a card reader at a controlled location. The sensor extracts information from the card and the reader translates that information into a code number and

Magnetic Stripe Card

ILLUSTRATING POSSIBLE MAGNETIC RECORDED PATTERN

Figure 8.2

sends it to the system's central processing unit (CPU). The number is compared with the user's programmed access criteria and either grants or denies entry. In the latter case, an alarm may or may not be sounded, depending upon the system. There may also be a printed record of each alarm or, if desired, a recording of each access granted by the system for a permanent historical record of individual card activity.

Magnetic Stripe Cards

Of the variety of **magnetic cards** available, probably the most popular are the magnetic stripe cards that are similar to typical credit cards (Figure 8.2). They can be used in a card reader that is relatively inexpensive and has few or no moving parts. With this type of card a pattern of digital data is encoded on the magnetic stripe. When the card is withdrawn from the reader, it moves across a magnetic head, similar to a tape recorder head, that "reads" the data, sends the information to the system CPU for verification, and if valid for entry at that point and that time, the CPU sends a signal to release the door.

Magnetic Dot Card

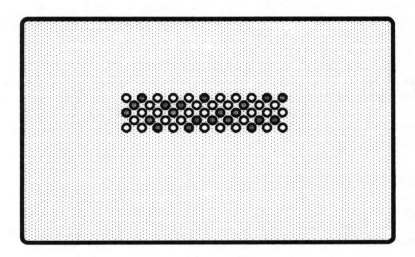

ILLUSTRATING POSSIBLE MAGNETIC DOT PATTERN

Figure 8.3

These cards are relatively low in cost, and an exceptionally large amount of data can be stored on the magnetic stripe as compared to other types of cards. The cards can be supplied in standard vinyl plastic; however, they tend to chip and break with prolonged use. The magnetic stripe on this card will usually be supplied in a single layer, three-track, low coercivity of 400 **oersteds**.

A superior medium for the magnetic stripe card is a mylar/polyester core material that will maintain its properties and flexibility over a temperature range from minus 50 degrees to over 350 degrees Fahrenheit without cracking or breaking. This mylar type card is also available with a single layer **high-coercivity** stripe of 4,000 oersteds and a Teflon coating to protect the magnetic stripe from flaking or wear induced by friction. An insert is also available which is pre-die-cut with a recessed aperture in the top layer of the dual mylar center core. This allows for consistent registration of miscellaneous bits of information on each card. This mylar type card is only slightly more expensive, but has an active life more than ten times greater than the standard 400 oersteds plastic card. It also causes fewer malfunctions. For long-term applications this type of card is highly recommended.

Magnetic Dot Cards

In magnetic dot cards, very small dots or pieces of magnetic materials, often barium ferrite, are laminated between plastic layers. These dots are magnetically charged either positively or negatively in a variety of configurations (Figure 8.3, p. 161). When this magnetic card is inserted into the reader, internal sensors are actuated by the magnetically encoded areas on the card.

Disadvantages of this type of card include its vulnerability to being deciphered, card vandalism, and the problems associated with handling and wear. A major factor in the selection of the magnetic dot card might be lower cost, but it is still more expensive than the standard magnetic stripe card. This type of card and reader are less durable than other types and may require more frequent replacement.

Weigand Cards

Weigand effect access control cards, also known as **embedded wire** cards, use a coded pattern on the magnetized wire within the card to generate a code number (Figure 8.4). When the card is passed through a slot containing a sensing device, the wire pattern is retrieved and forwarded to the reader for decoding.

The technology of this reader makes it less vulnerable to weather and vandalism than readers with more conventional slots. The cards are moderately priced and can contain a modest amount of information. A major drawback is the wear and tear on the card as it is passed through the tracklike slot. The card must also be properly oriented when it is passed through the slot to achieve a correct reading. This type of card will effectively handle a large volume of traffic during opening and closing surges of card reader activity.

Proximity Cards

Proximity card readers work on the basis of a number of passively tuned circuits that have been embedded in a high-grade fiberglass-epoxy card (Figure 8.5). To gain access, the bearer of the card holds the card within 2 to 4 inches of a concealed device that senses the pattern of the resonant frequencies contained in the card. This pattern is then transmitted to a remote card reader which digests the pattern and unlocks the door.

A major asset of the proximity system is the durability of the sensing element. It is encased in a weatherproof, vandal-proof, dust-proof, and shock-resistant enclosure. The sensing element can be concealed within walls, mounted behind glass, or simply attached to a surface. This provides considerable flexibility in installation and higher sensor security.

Since the cards can be read through most materials, they do not generally need to be removed from a pocket or purse for the cardholder to gain entry. A primary disadvantage of the proximity card system is higher cost.

Weigand Card

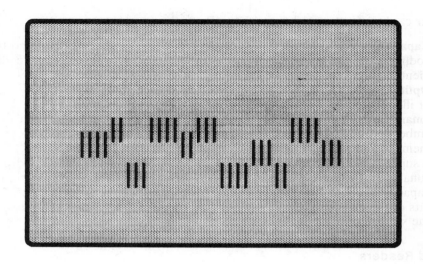

CUT-AWAY SHOWING POSSIBLE EMBEDDED WIRE PATTERN

Figure 8.4

Proximity Card

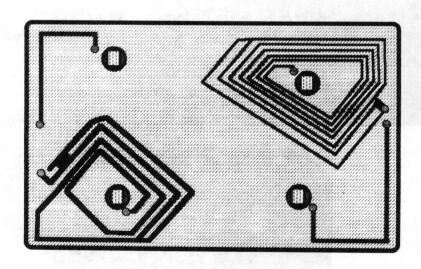

(CUT-AWAY SHOWING CIRCUITS INSIDE CARD)

Figure 8.5

Other Types of Card Access Systems

Other card systems include:

- **Capacitance cards.** Capacitor material is enclosed within the card and the coding is effected by connecting selected plates to provide a specific coded identification.
- **Optical cards.** These cards have a pattern of light spots which can be read or illuminated by a specific light source, frequently infrared.
- **Smart cards.** The card itself actually contains an integrated circuit chip embedded in the plastic of the card. This type of card has both a coded memory and a microprocessor with inherent intelligence. The card acts as a super-miniature computer as it records and stores information and personal identification codes in its memory. Smart cards have a nominal storage capacity of about 4,000 bits of data. This compares favorably with the 1,700 bits of the magnetic stripe card. All other cards fall far below these two in the storage of data.

Card Readers

Before selecting an access control system, the user should be familiar with access control readers and their operation. This will help avoid buying a system incapable of providing the necessary mix of access control functions.

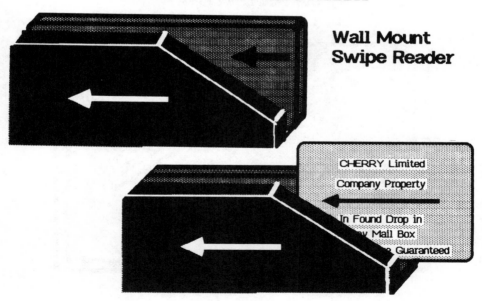

Figure 8.6

The wall-mount swipe card reader mounts on the wall and the user simply "swipes" the card through the slot to obtain access to the controlled point (Figure 8.6).

The turnstile card reader is similar to the swipe card reader in that the card is run through the reader from front to rear and releases a turnstile after reading the information. These are commonly used at high-volume and shift-change check points (Figure 8.7).

The insertion card reader is common, and various models are available. They are not normally interchangeable with each other, so a thorough understanding of the total access control system's capability is required (Figure 8.8, p. 166).

There are also insertion card readers with keypads for more sophisticated applications. This control device requires insertion of a valid card at the proper place and time and the entering of a unique, to the card holder, four-digit number on the keypad, followed by the card's withdrawal. If all information

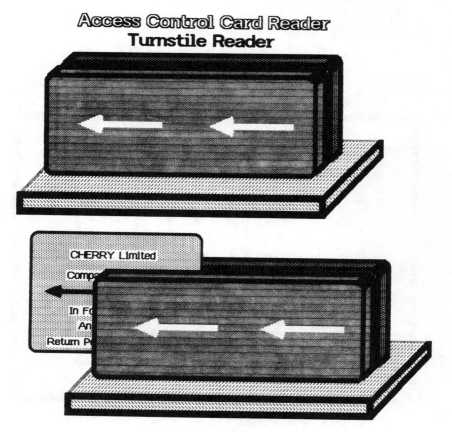

Figure 8.7

Access Control Card Reader
Insertion Reader

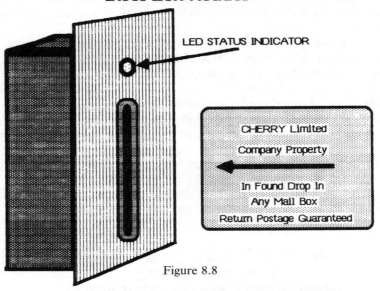

LED STATUS INDICATOR

CHERRY Limited
Company Property

In Found Drop In
Any Mail Box
Return Postage Guaranteed

Figure 8.8

Access Control Card Reader
Insertion Reader with Keypad

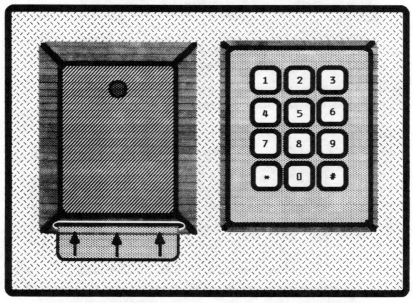

INSERTION CARD READER   KEYPAD WITH DURESS

Figure 8.9

and requirements have been met, the door will open. A duress feature should be part of any keypad card reader installation. Vendors and manufacturers will supply specific information on the functioning of their keypad card reader (Figure 8.9).

The key type reader is almost in a class of its own. In this access control function, a rigid plastic key is issued to the user instead of a card. This special key is inserted into the reader slot and withdrawn for access (Figure 8.10).

BIOMETRIC ACCESS CONTROL

Going beyond the card reader systems, there is a new generation of personal identification and verification that may or may not be used in conjunction with

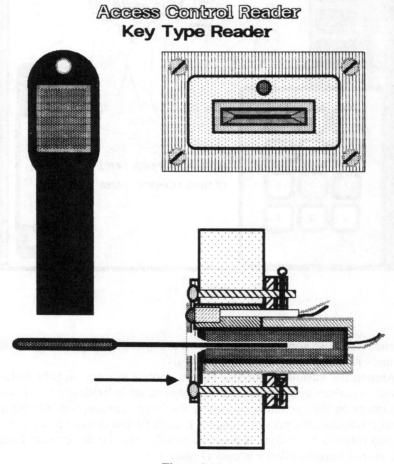

Figure 8.10

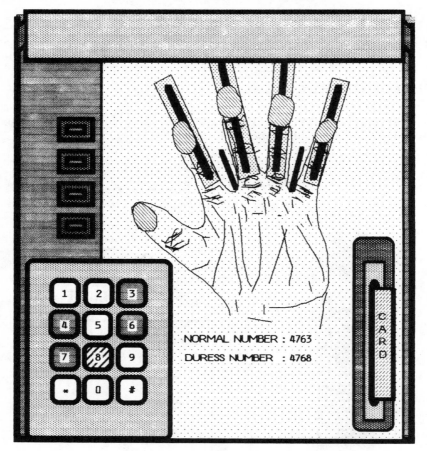

Figure 8.11

card readers. These sophisticated systems are specifically personalized and are sometimes referred to as biometric systems.

Among the various biometric access control systems are the following:

- *Hand geometry* systems electronically scan an individual's hand and store the image in the system's repository for future comparison. On future system activations, the present image is measured and compared with the initial stored reference version. A positive match between the current image and the stored version allows access (Figure 8.11).
- *Fingerprints* are unique to an individual. Initially a person's fingerprint from

one finger is collected and stored by the system. The reference file may also be done manually, but this calls for a trained operator to compare the prints on a card. A computerized system uses an electro-optical recognition technique to establish a positive comparison from stored data before permitting access.

- *Palm prints* are as individual as fingerprints. A biometric system based on palm prints works much the same as the fingerprint technique. Palm print measurements are taken, digitized, processed, and stored. The large amount of memory required prevents broad use of this approach.
- *Retinal patterns* are captured by a device that recognizes the retinal vessel pattern of an individual's eye. A scanned picture of the back of the eye is converted to analog signals that are then converted into digital data for storage. This digital data is stored in the system's computer as a standard for later comparison and matching.
- *Signature verification* requires that the individual make a minimum of three copies of his or her signature. The average of these signatures is retained and stored in memory. The system's signature verification system is based on the dynamics of the individual's pen motion and is related to time. These measurements are taken by using a specially wired pen or, in some cases, a sensitized pad. Future signatures made to gain access are compared with the original averaged signatures and when a match is made, access is granted. Early versions of this system went through a series of pen malfunctions and breakdowns, but later versions seem to have solved this problem.
- *Voiceprints* are taken by the system and recorded in an analog signal that, like the retinal pattern technique, is converted to digital data. Measurements are derived and stored in the host computer. Future references are based on an individual voice pattern of a few single words. The system may require the individual to speak three or four words from a reference file of seven or so words. A match of the voice patterns from the reference file permits access.

VEHICLE ACCESS CONTROL

Vehicular movement control begins in the parking area. No system designed to control the movement of personnel within a facility can be effective unless combined with proper management of vehicle access. The need for regulation of vehicle access naturally varies from one facility to another. Management of vehicle movement in and about a theme park differs considerably from that of an embassy.

There are many factors to consider in controlling access to any normal industrial manufacturing complex: a fenced perimeter; shipping and receiving docks; employee, visitor, and executive parking; service, vendor, and construction vehicles; emergency vehicle access lanes. Shift changes, parking structures, and odd-hour operations serve to magnify the vehicle control problem.

An integrated card access control system, which is automatically responsive to fire, security, and closed circuit television (CCTV) systems can easily manage employee, executive, and vendor traffic. In this way management determines who parks where, giving them a controlled flow of traffic during shift changes for ease of employee vehicle movement. Parking areas should not be located where employee theft might be fostered by easy access.

Key personnel can be tracked throughout the facility from the moment they arrive on the premises. An access control system can readily monitor their progress as they move from one access control point to another. This is an

Vehicle Access Control Gate

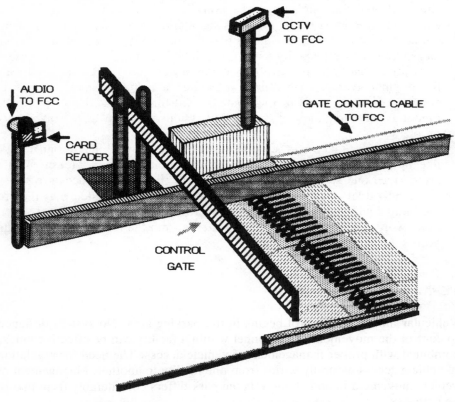

MANAGED BY CARD ACCESS OR REMOTE CONTROL
FROM FACILITY CONTROL CENTER.

Figure 8.12

important capability for locating doctors in a large hospital complex. Proper application of vehicle access control allows effective management of available parking space. Data processing collusion can occur when programmers and operators get together. Subtle measures, such as assigning separate parking areas to the programmers and operators, can be an effective first step in reducing the opportunity for collusion.

Loading docks for shipping and receiving are particularly vulnerable to theft and require close control. Where feasible, shipping docks should be isolated from receiving areas. The movement of drivers can be regulated by providing them a warm and comfortable place to rest while their trucks are being loaded or unloaded. CCTV and audio may be subtly used to monitor driver activity. Uniformed or management personnel can unobtrusively intercept any undesirable movement discovered by the integrated control system.

Control of hourly, salaried, and external vehicles by a variety of control point devices may be achieved by integrating these access control devices with security and CCTV systems. A relatively simple wooden drop-gate can be paired with a sabre-tooth vehicle control device for normal card access entry or exit. Both devices may be tied to the integrated control system for automatic opening in the event of an emergency (Figure 8.12).

More massive and heavy-duty vehicle barriers can be unobtrusively embedded into the driveways. These are antiterrorist devices designed to stop even the largest trucks. When these devices are integrated into the protection of a sensitive facility they can be activated in less than two seconds in response to a manual or electronic signal. An entire cascade of security precautions can be coupled with this signal (Figure 8.13, p. 172).

ACCESS CONTROL SYSTEM APPLICATIONS

A fully integrated access control system permits the card holder access to authorized building, laboratory, office, and parking areas. Building access is permitted at the times management decides the individual should have access, yet the system can still be flexible enough to permit variations in access time. For example, management can decide when and where vending machine service personnel may have access to the building. They do not need twenty-four-hour access to the entire facility if 9 to 11 on a Tuesday morning is adequate. For food service delivery, set hours can be established and monitored by the access control system. These set hours will permit tighter control of delivery personnel and more efficient scheduling of food service employees. Protection personnel may be programmed to be in the food service area during the designated delivery times, and this alone should result in a considerable reduction in losses.

There are numerous other ways in which access can be controlled within a building. Elevators can be controlled to permit card holders access to certain floors only. Entry to offices can be limited to those individuals having man-

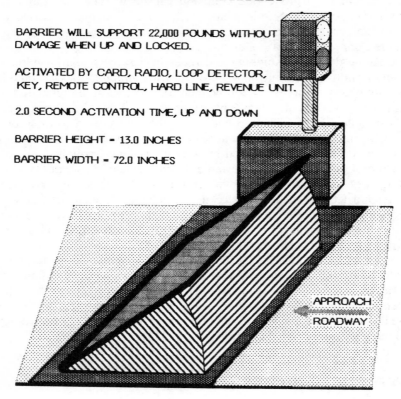

Vehicle Access Control Systems
Motorized Barricade

BARRIER WILL SUPPORT 22,000 POUNDS WITHOUT
DAMAGE WHEN UP AND LOCKED.

ACTIVATED BY CARD, RADIO, LOOP DETECTOR,
KEY, REMOTE CONTROL, HARD LINE, REVENUE UNIT.

2.0 SECOND ACTIVATION TIME, UP AND DOWN

BARRIER HEIGHT = 13.0 INCHES

BARRIER WIDTH = 72.0 INCHES

APPROACH
ROADWAY

Figure 8.13

agement approval and for the time of day for which this access has been granted. Access to computer terminals can be prevented unless the proper access control card opens the terminal and both the access-controlled work station and the date and time are correct. Only then will a sign-on procedure be accepted by the computer terminal. The same card access can be used to control copying machines. They will not operate without the proper access card and entry code. Entry to mechanical equipment rooms can be limited to maintenance personnel and then only if they are authorized to work during that time. Even the amount dispensed by fuel pumps can be controlled through an integrated access control system.

The access control system must be interlocked with the fire detection and alarm systems to ensure a **fail safe**, ready exit from the fire zone in case of an alarm. Computer tape libraries, biohazard areas, and other sensitive areas can be designed **fail secure** to prevent firefighters and others from inadvertent exposure to dangers more deadly than fire. The fail-secure technique can also be used to preclude corporate records from being damaged during an emergency. Such an arrangement will permit people within the fail-secure areas to exit, but will automatically relock doors to prevent reentry or damage from excessive smoke or water. Any such fail-secure system must have prior approval from the *authority having jurisdiction* for the facility in question.

The access control system can easily interface with the fire, security, audio, and CCTV systems. The effectiveness of any building's access control system is limited only by knowledge of the access system and the imagination of the staff.

In planning for initial installation and future facility growth, management would be well advised to require the architect and consultant to specify the following standard access control features in the central processing unit.

- At least an 8,000-card capacity.
- Backup power supply, to include batteries.
- Automatic time programs to secure access readers.
- **Anti-passback.**
- Capability to add a large number of additional card readers without having to increase the CPU's memory.
- Printers that will provide data segregation and suppression of valid entry transactions.
- Assurance that the system will not be subjected to trunk-line noise from unintentional electrical interference.
- Provision for a service maintenance contract as part of the access control system.
- Built-in redundancy with backup power, backup keys, and whatever else may be necessary.

The access control system must meet the Underwriters Laboratories (UL) Standard for Safety for Access Control System Units, UL 294. This means that the units of the system have been subjected to and successfully passed a rigid battery of tests such as the following:

- Power interruption and standby power
- Voltage variation
- Temperature variation
- Humidity
- Jarring
- Dust
- Rain
- Radio frequency interference
- Nondestructive attack
- Destructive attack

A UL 294 listing means that representative samples of the access control system have been investigated and found to comply with UL 294. The UL 294 mark on the access control device is also an indication that periodic UL factory follow-up visits have been made as a countercheck on the manufacturer's program for continuing compliance with UL requirements.

A high-quality access control system, complete with the UL listing, when properly installed by a qualified electrician, is a positive step in protecting corporate assets. In addition, the access control system should be integrated with other building control systems for maximum effectiveness.

There are many things that an access control system can do for the owners and managers of large facilities. The access control system manages who has access to what space or place and when that access may be made. **Audit trail** for each point or each card is available upon request. Retention of any or all activity may be collected, stored, and retrieved when required, even years later with the proper advance planning.

Typical Card Reader System

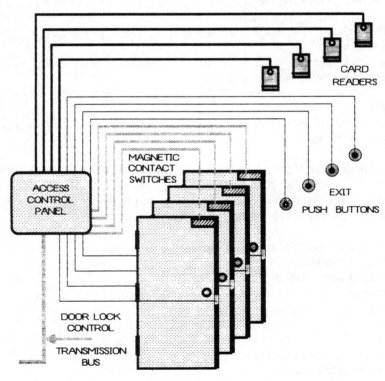

Figure 8.14

With proper application, the access control system will be cost-effective and efficient, while reducing the security personnel requirements and increasing the overall protection of assets and improving safety (Figure 8.14).

SELECTION OF ACCESS CONTROL SYSTEMS

Card access control systems control and record entry and exit of the doors under their protection. It is the responsibility of the owner, therefore, to weigh the myriad factors discussed in reaching the proper access control approach for each situation. This includes the level of security required, the cost of the system when measured against what it is to protect, and the convenience or inconvenience for the personnel who will actually be using it.

Reaching an optimum level of security protection is not easy. The optimum level is that point at which additional expenditures for security controls will exceed in value what the reduction of loss might actually be worth. Professional advice, not associated with a vendor or manufacturer, is the most likely source of assistance to management. Through this type of consultant service, the owner/operator will receive recommendations and suggestions on standard equipment and approaches to resolve personnel and vehicle movement control problems.

Setting a value on the information to be protected may not be an easy task. Estimating the cost of equipment in the area to be protected should not be too difficult. These value judgments will have an effect on the equipment selected to provide the protection, just as a government contract would have an effect on the amount and type of security to be afforded under the contract.

A personnel movement control system should allow workers to have ready access to their work place. Management must determine who can be where at what time. There must be flexibility in the system to allow for coping with changes in requirements on short notice. Controlling the movement of people is not meant to impede the movement of people; it is meant to protect property and personnel.

There are several things to look for in any personnel movement control system, regardless of the manufacturer. Ease of operation can prevent the majority of problems before they happen. This must include the ability to make quick and easy changes in programming. These programming changes should be in plain English rather than computerese. The system itself should be able to provide records of who used what door when by card, by door, or by time.

The system must be capable of coping with weather, should outdoor applications be considered, as well as future expansion to accommodate corporate growth. Along these same lines, all exposed hardware should be relatively strong to reduce the effects of vandalism and should have a minimum of moving parts to reduce maintenance problems. Techniques to preclude **tailgating** and an antipassback feature should be standard.

TOTAL FACILITY CONTROL AND MOVEMENT CONTROL

It is important that portal, gate, and door control be successfully integrated with other building control systems in order to provide automatic operation. Locked entrances must be designated to automatically unlock in the event of a fire emergency. High-security areas need to go to a fail-secure condition to preclude access during an emergency.

Integrated Access Control System

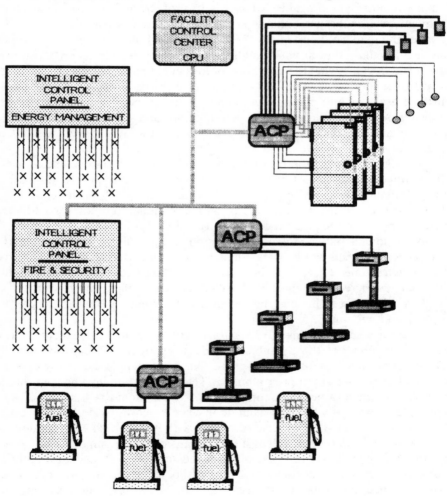

Figure 8.15

Integration of the access control system with CCTV can save time and effort, while increasing security operations. The integrated access control system will also provide hard-copy records of who is, or was, on the property at any given time. This capability can be extremely important in determining if a given area has been successfully vacated in an emergency situation.

Card access is a valuable control tool for building management; when integrated with the elevator system for after-hours work access, enhanced security is provided. It also provides additional protection to the personnel working after hours and reduces the requirement for extra personnel. A research and development center can provide a fail-safe buddy system for sensitive areas by simply requiring dual access and then managing the requirement through the integrated access control system.

Regardless of the type of facility, an access control system, when integrated into the overall building management system, will provide increased protection, better movement control of personnel, and a reduction in personnel requirements (Figure 8.15).

9

Closed Circuit Television

CLOSED CIRCUIT TELEVISION TECHNIQUES

Closed circuit television (CCTV) is one of the most effective and efficient asset protection systems available. Systems vary from the simple camera-cable-monitor to the most complex arrangement of microprocessor-based programmable control/routing switcher with multiple cameras, monitors, master monitors, and video cassette recording devices with date-time generators. CCTV is initially expensive in terms of capital outlay, but the fact that it will work twenty-four hours a day, year in and year out, makes it an excellent investment.

CCTV INSTALLATION

To be truly cost-effective, a CCTV system must be designed, assembled, and installed by professionals. A single reputable dealer might do a good job, but it is better to have a qualified, but disinterested party design the end product to ensure desired performance. This precludes buying old or loss leader equipment.

While CCTV systems initially appear to be expensive, they are actually cost-effective. The key to successful CCTV system integration is an understanding of the facility's total surveillance requirements. Far too often CCTV systems are designed with only a single function in mind. While this may be effective for the purpose intended, it probably does not begin to cover the potential of a CCTV system designed as an integral part of a comprehensive protection system. For total-facility control and the effective use of the available equipment, it is essential that the facility's control systems be not only automatically mutually supportable, but also capable of instantaneous human override.

To achieve the desired end result of CCTV applications, a thorough site survey is mandatory. The development and design of a CCTV system requires close cooperation between the individuals responsible for the operation and protection of the facility and the CCTV system design professionals. These professionals are qualified disinterested parties, not vendors of the equipment.

It is true that many vendors and suppliers can do a good job on a CCTV site survey, but it is unlikely that they would recommend equipment or a system capability that they could not provide.

A design professional has broad knowledge of CCTV system applications and is able to prepare a **performance specification** that will meet the owner/ operator's requirements. This individual must have specific knowledge of all aspects of facility control, whereas equipment vendors are probably familiar only with their own equipment. Vendors may have little or no understanding of CCTV interaction with security systems, process monitoring, access control systems, or other building management systems. By employing a system design professional who works closely with the owner's personnel, the CCTV system can be tailored to meet specific performance requirements.

Once the CCTV performance specification has been prepared, numerous suppliers and installers are invited to bid on the project. Through the performance specification the owner tells the suppliers how the system is to work and what the CCTV system is to do. It is then up to the suppliers to select and install the proper equipment to meet those performance requirements. It is probably prudent for the supplier to be held responsible for the installation.

It is wise to have the preparer of the CCTV performance specification participate in the system checkout prior to final acceptance. A system guarantee of one year should be obtained even though the CCTV camera tube is usually guaranteed for only thirty to ninety days. The owner should additionally insist upon a minimum three-year maintenance contract as part of the initial purchase cost. This will ensure at least four years of relatively trouble-free operation.

CCTV EQUIPMENT

CCTV is not just a simple camera-cable-monitor arrangement. There is additional equipment associated with CCTV.

Pan and tilt units are devices designed for remote control positioning of cameras in both the horizontal (pan) and vertical (tilt) planes. They come in light, medium, heavy-duty, and extra-heavy-duty models and are specifically designed for indoor or outdoor use. Units are available in either fixed- or variable-speed versions (Figure 9.1).

Scanners rotate the camera back and forth in the horizontal plane only, although the camera tilt position is manually adjustable. These units are usually offered in light- and medium-duty versions for indoor applications (Figure 9.2). Outdoor units fall into the heavy-duty and extra-heavy-duty classes. In operation, these units provide an oscillating surveillance sweep back and forth across a preselected area or **field of view (FOV)** (Figure 9.3, p. 182).

Specialized scanners are designed for certain applications where discreet enclosures are required. For these situations mirrored or smoked spherical, flat, or tunneled scanner enclosures are available. Such scanner arrangements

Closed Circuit Television
Pan and Tilt Units

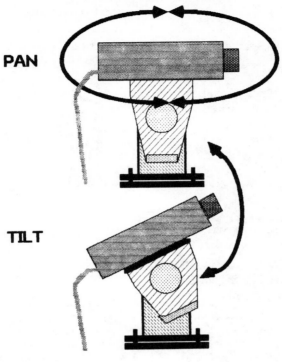

PAN

TILT

Figure 9.1

Closed Circuit Television
Scanner Unit

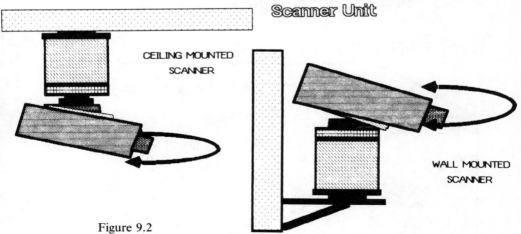

CEILING MOUNTED
SCANNER

WALL MOUNTED
SCANNER

Figure 9.2

Closed Circuit Television
Field of View

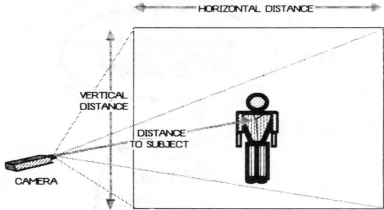

HORIZONTAL DISTANCE

VERTICAL DISTANCE

DISTANCE TO SUBJECT

CAMERA

FIELD-OF-VIEW DESCRIBES THE WIDTH AND HEIGHT OF A
PARTICULAR SCENE BEING VIEWED.

Figure 9.3

Closed Circuit Television
Specialized Scanners

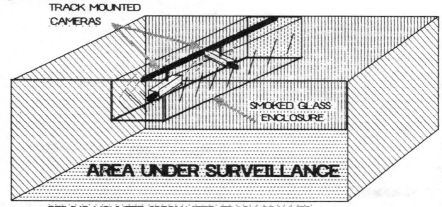

TRACK MOUNTED CAMERAS

SMOKED GLASS ENCLOSURE

AREA UNDER SURVEILLANCE

CEILING MOUNTED SPECIALIZED TRACK SCANNER

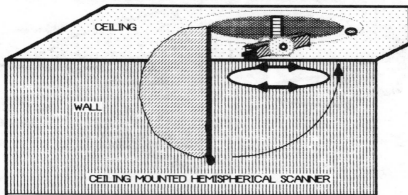

CEILING

WALL

CEILING MOUNTED HEMISPHERICAL SCANNER

Figure 9.4

are generally designed for indoor applications. They are usually pleasing to the eye and offer minimum camera visibility to the uninitiated (Figure 9.4).

Mountings are available in both fixed and adjustable versions for supporting CCTV cameras. Particular applications, such as indoor/outdoor, pan, tilt, zoom, housing, scanner, industrial, and explosion proof, will dictate the basic type of camera support mounting. This will usually be a horizontal or suspended ceiling mount, but there are mountings available for literally every possible application.

Manual video switchers are available in a number of operating configurations. Terminated and looping models manage the switching of from four to sixteen camera inputs. Most switchers are available in desktop and rack-mounted versions.

Automatic video switchers sequence through camera inputs at preselected rates. This type of switcher is available in **homing** (Figure 9.5), **bridging** (Figure 9.6, p. 184), **looping-homing** (Figure 9.7, p. 184), and **looping-bridging** (Figure

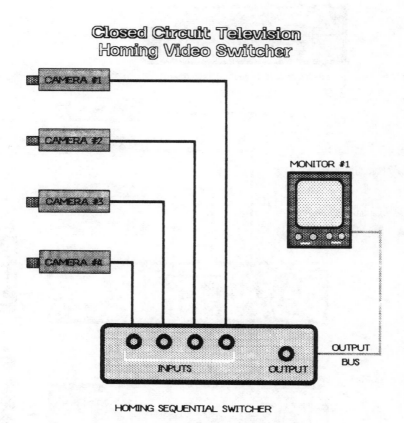

Figure 9.5

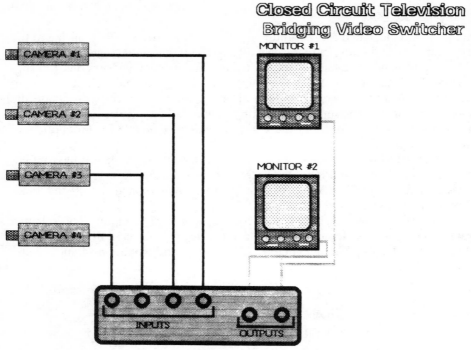

Closed Circuit Television
Bridging Video Switcher

MONITOR #1

MONITOR #2

INPUTS

OUTPUTS

Figure 9.6

BRIDGING SEQUENTIAL SWITCHER

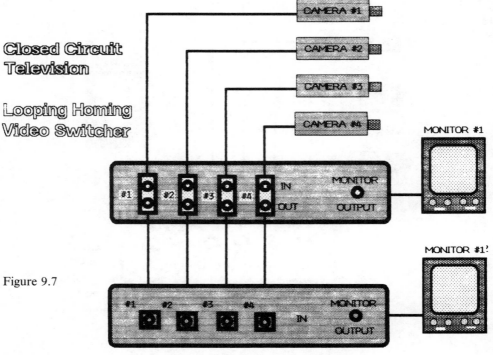

CAMERA #1

CAMERA #2

CAMERA #3

CAMERA #4

MONITOR #1

Closed Circuit
Television

Looping Homing
Video Switcher

#1 #2 #3 #4 IN

OUT

MONITOR

OUTPUT

MONITOR #1!

Figure 9.7

#1 #2 #3 #4 IN

MONITOR

OUTPUT

184

LOOPING HOMING SEQUENTIAL SWITCHER

Closed Circuit Television
Looping–Bridging Video Switcher

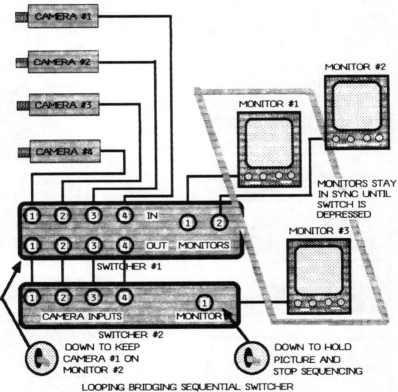

LOOPING BRIDGING SEQUENTIAL SWITCHER

Figure 9.8

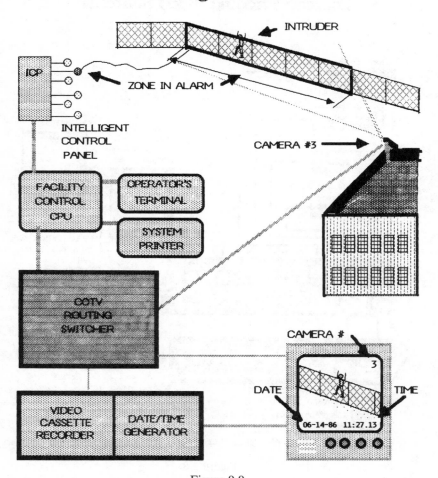

Figure 9.9

Closed Circuit Television
Master Monitor

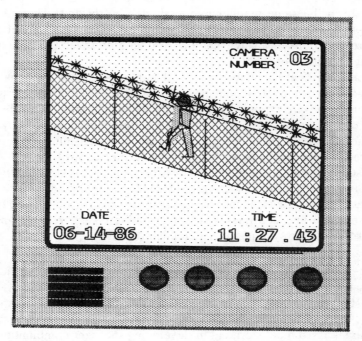

MASTER MONITOR ILLUSTRATING DATE, TIME AND CAMERA NUMBER

Figure 9.10

9.8, p. 185) versions. A new category of automatic switcher, called a "routing switcher" by some suppliers, is available for application in conjunction with integrated facility control systems. The routing switcher will take a signal from the integrated facility control system and automatically turn a particular camera to view a scene as indicated from the signal (Figure 9.9). From here it is simple to activate a video cassette recorder (VCR) and the **date-time generator** (DTG) to automatically record the scene and superimpose the date and time the scene was recorded (Figure 9.10). This application extension should be considered for all CCTV systems at the time of initial design, if not for immediate installation, then at least as a future capability.

CCTV system controls come in a variety of versions:

- Single controls are designed to operate a specific piece of equipment and to form a compatible link with other controls in the complete system, in both the operational and aesthetic sense. Single controls, in desktop or rack mounting, provide for remote operation of pan and tilt units, scanners, lenses, enclosures, and infrared illuminators on a selective basis.

- Multiple controls conserve panel and desktop space. The individual controls operate in the same manner as the single control unit. They also have a dual-station capability, operating a remote piece of equipment from two control locations or a single station, or operating several remote units from a single control location.
- **Digital controls** are available in limited and long-distance versions. They are designed for use over coaxial cable, microwave, or fiber optic transmission systems, and are intended for medium to large system control. They can also use the transmission bus of the multiple facility control system, but require an additional technique for picture transmission.
- **Microprocessor-based controls** generally feature control of CCTV cameras and support units via digital transmission over a dual-shielded twisted pair of wires. There is also an RF (radio frequency) option with modulated control and video signal transmission over single coaxial cables. The full duplex transmission and continuous receiver polling ensure reliable and flexible control of larger systems over extended distances.

There is a wide variety of **video signal equipment** including video amplifiers, distribution amplifiers, motion detectors (Figure 9.11), date-time generators (Figure 9.10), screen splitters (Figure 9.12, p. 190), and camera identifiers (Figure 9.10). These all have their place in various systems, but professional assistance is critical in developing the right combination of video signal equipment.

Video control consoles are essential if a medium-to-large CCTV system is being considered. The console design should permit ease of operator control, ready access to the back of the console, and adequate space for future console expansion (Figure 9.13, p. 191). It is important that access to the rear of the CCTV console has been preplanned; otherwise, a minor adjustment could disrupt the entire control center operation.

Fixed lenses include manual, motorized, motorized with auto-iris, and a variety of specialized types. They are compatible with almost all existing CCTV cameras. A wide range of focal lengths and lens speeds are available for both the one-inch and two-thirds-inch formats. It is important to completely understand lens **depth-of-field** (Figure 9.14, p. 192) and **field-of-view** (see Figure 9.3) and to use this knowledge in determining the proper lens for each location.

Zoom lenses come in a wide range of focal lengths and speeds for both the one-inch and the two-thirds-inch format cameras. They are offered in manual, motorized, motorized with auto-iris and filter, and in various unique configurations. With the zoom lens, the capability of a floating field-of-view and

Closed Circuit Television
Video Motion Detection

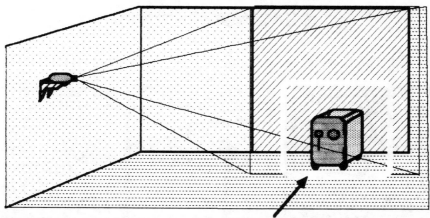

CLOSED CIRCUIT TELEVISION WITH SMALL MOTION DETECTION AREA.

OPERATOR CAN MODIFY
MOTION DETECTION FIELD
OF VIEW TO LIMIT MOTION
DETECTION TO ONLY COVER
SENSITIVE AREAS.

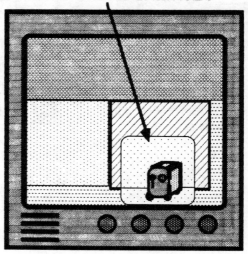

Figure 9.11

Closed Circuit Television
Split Screen Monitors

PRESCRIPTION
DRUG PICK-UP ↑

RECORDS INDIVIDUAL
PICKING UP EACH DRUG
AS WELL AS THE ORIGINAL
PRESCRIPTION.

FOUR-CAMERA SPLIT SCREEN MONITOR

ILLUSTRATES - CASHIER, PARKING LOT,
FENCE LINE, AND LOADING DOCKS.

Figure 9.12

Closed Circuit Television

Standard Video Control Consoles

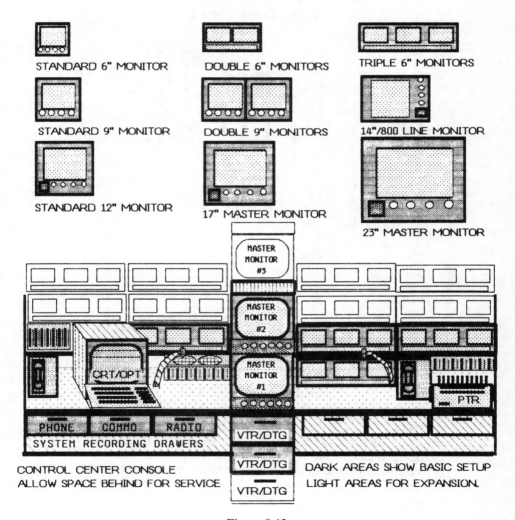

Figure 9.13

Closed Circuit Television

Depth of Field

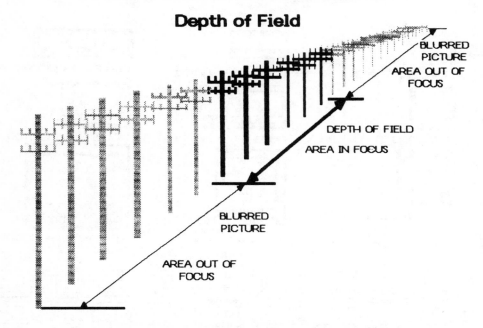

BLURRED
PICTURE
AREA OUT OF
FOCUS

DEPTH OF FIELD

AREA IN FOCUS

BLURRED
PICTURE

AREA OUT OF
FOCUS

WHEN A CCTV CAMERA IS FOCUSED ON AN OBJECT AT A SPECIFIC RANGE,
THERE ARE OTHER OBJECTS BOTH NEARER AND FARTHER AWAY WHICH
ARE IN FOCUS. THE AREA BETWEEN THE NEAREST AND FARTHEST
POINTS FROM THE CAMERA THAT APPEARS TO BE IN FOCUS IS CALLED:

DEPTH OF FIELD

AS THE FOCAL LENGTH OF THE LENS INCREASES, THE DEPTH OF FIELD
DECREASES. A GREATER DEPTH OF FIELD IS ACQUIRED BY MAKING
THE APERTURE (f-STOP) SIZE SMALLER. DEPTH OF FIELD BECOMES
CRITICAL AS LIGHT LEVEL DECREASES. AS THE APERTURE OPENS TO
COMPENSATE FOR THE LOW LIGHT, THE DEPTH OF FIELD SHORTENS.

Figure 9.14

flexible depth-of-field vary widely, so care must be taken in the selection of the individual zoom camera control elements to ensure that they meet application requirements (Figure 9.15).

There is a wide variety of miscellaneous equipment and accessories for all types of CCTV and security applications, such as relay boxes for remote manipulation of pan and tilt units, scanners, enclosures, zoom lenses for extended distances, and **infrared illuminators** (Figure 9.16, p. 194) for nonvisible illumination under low-light conditions.

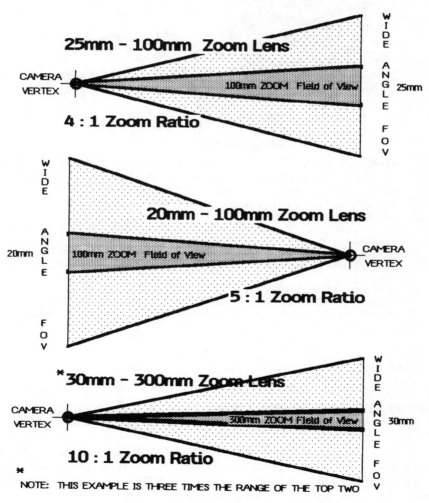

Figure 9.15

Infrared Video Illuminators

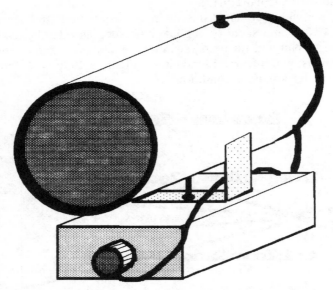

CLOSED CIRCUIT TELEVISION INFRARED CAMERA SYSTEM. THE VIDEO
OUTPUT IS A COMPOSITE SIGNAL AND CAN BE USED WITH ANY STANDARD
CLOSED CIRCUIT TELEVISION SYSTEM OR DEVICES SUCH AS VIDEO TAPE
RECORDERS, TELEVISION MONITORS, VIDEO MOTION DETECTORS, OR
SEQUENTIAL SWITCHERS.
SYSTEM CAN BE OPERATED IN A "NO LIGHT LEVEL" CONDITION, OR BRIGHT
SUNLIGHT. THE ENTIRE SYSTEM IS AUTOMATED FOR HANDS OFF
OPERATION. THESE SYSTEMS ARE DESIGNED FOR OBSERVATION OF AREAS
THAT REQUIRE SURVEILLANCE IN BOTH BRIGHT SUNLIGHT AND TOTAL
DARKNESS.
INFRARED ILLUMINATORS ARE AVAILABLE IN 40 WATT (5-15 FEET);
150 WATT (5-300 FEET); 500 WATT (5 FEET TP800 FEET); AND 1000 WATT
(100-800 FEET) RANGES. CONSULT A SPECIALIST ON SCENE REFLECTANCE
PRIOR TO PURCHASE.

Figure 9.16

Lighting Systems and Lamp Types

Lighting is extremely important to successful CCTV operation. Understanding
the effects of different lamps and lighting will do much to improve the effectiveness of the CCTV system's performance after dark. Incandescent filament
lamps are lamps in which light is produced by a filament heated by an electric
current to incandescence, glowing with intense heat.

Tungsten-halogen lamps are a variation of incandescent filament lamps.

The term halogen is given to a group of negative elements such as bromine, chlorine, fluorine, and iodine. The tungsten-halogen lamp provides a whiter lamp and greater intensity of light, as well as excellent lumen maintenance. This lamp also exhibits relatively more ultraviolet radiation than regular incandescent lamps due to higher filament temperature combined with a transparent quartz envelope.

Fluorescent lamps are electric discharge sources, in which light is produced by fluorescent powders activated by ultraviolet energy generated by a mercury arc.

In low-pressure sodium discharge lamps, the arc is carried through vaporized sodium. The light produced by the low-pressure sodium arc is almost monochromatic, consisting of a double line in the yellow region of the spectrum at 589.0 and 589.6 nanometers.

High-intensity discharge lamps include the groups of lamps known as mercury, metal halide, and high-pressure sodium.

- In a mercury lamp, light is produced by the passage of an electric current through mercury vapor.
- Metal halide lamps are very similar to mercury lamps, although the metal halide arc tube contains various metal halides in addition to mercury. The three typical combinations of halide used in metal halide lamps are (1) sodium, thallium, and indium; (2) sodium and scandium iodides; and (3) dysprosium and thallium iodides.
- In high-pressure sodium lamps, light is produced by electricity passing through sodium vapor. High-pressure sodium lamps radiate energy across the visible spectrum. The light produced by this lamp is golden white (Figure 9.17, p. 196).

CCTV APPLICATIONS

The following is a series of generic situations or application criteria under which a CCTV camera might be used. For clarification, types of lighting for each situation are given as well as some general information and the appropriate camera tube for the situation. This information is intended to be informative and may be used as a guide when dealing with professionals in the CCTV field. It should not be used as a sole criterion for designing a CCTV system.

In the typical indoor situation with illumination by fixed lighting, a relatively simple camera arrangement can be used. The low-contrast background scene preferable in this case is well suited for a two-thirds-inch separate mesh Vidicon tube. Lens selection is subject to field-of-view and depth-of-field requirements. This type of Vidicon tube works in any lighting in which the human eye can see well and functions best under fluorescent lighting. Extreme lighting causes the Vidicon tube to burn.

In indoor/outdoor situations with medium light levels, a two-thirds-inch Newvicon does well. Where there are changing light levels, a two-thirds-inch

Parking Lot Lighting

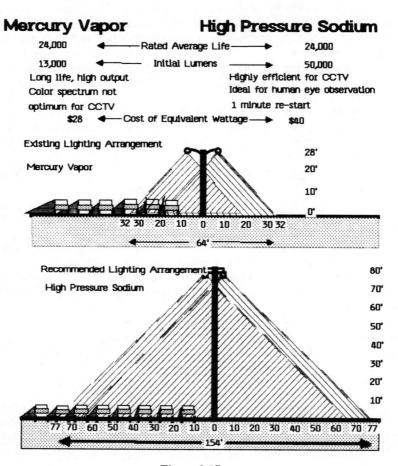

Mercury Vapor		High Pressure Sodium
24,000	◄——Rated Average Life——►	24,000
13,000	◄—— Initial Lumens ——►	50,000
Long life, high output.		Highly efficient for CCTV
Color spectrum not		Ideal for human eye observation
optimum for CCTV		1 minute re-start
$28	◄——Cost of Equivalent Wattage——►	$40

Figure 9.17

Ultracon responds better. Both the Newvicon and Ultracon tubes have low-lag characteristics and are impervious to burn. An auto-iris should be used. The Newvicon and Ultracon tubes give a good rendition under mercury vapor, sodium vapor, fluorescent, or tungsten lighting.

Where indoor high-resolution coverage is required in a low-contrast scene, a standard one-inch Vidicon tube should be used. In the best of conditions under fluorescent lighting, this arrangement will yield about 600 lines of resolution. The Vidicon tube will burn under extreme lighting conditions.

Where high resolution is required outdoors under medium to low light levels, either a one-inch Ultracon or Newvicon tube equipped with an auto-iris should suffice. When used in this application, IR lighting (silicon diode), sodium, or tungsten lighting must be used. The Ultracon provides about 700 lines of resolution and has low lag. The Newvicon produces 800 lines for a good usable picture with similar lighting (Figure 9.18).

The same camera tubes can also be used in medium to low light conditions where high resolution is required, but there are severe environmental considerations. These camera arrangements will also be satisfactory for extremely high noise areas that exceed 150 decibels, underwater up to about 60 feet, up to about two atmospheres of pressure, in 100 percent humidity, in sand, dust,

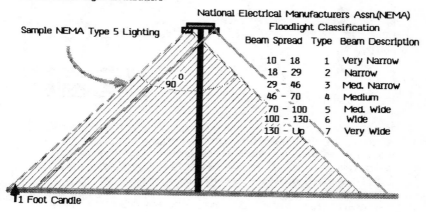

Parking Lot Lighting Considerations

Typical Reflectance Coefficients

Scene/Material	Reflectance (%)
Empty Asphalt Parking Lot	7
Parking Lot With Automobiles	40

Lamp Type	Watts	Rated Life	Lumens	Notes:
High Pressure Sodium	150	24,000	16,000	High output; peaks at
	400	24,000	50,000	550–650 nanometers; Long Life;
	1000	24,000	140,000	highly efficient for CCTV lighting
Mercury Vapor,	250	24,000	13,000	Long life, high output,
Delux White	400	24,000	23,000	color spectrum not optimum for CCTV Lighting

Outdoor lighting for CCTV systems typically requires a uniform light distribution over a wide area. These systems, unlike indoor systems, seldom have nearby reflecting surfaces and therefore must utilize luminaires having high lumen outputs and controlled light distribution.

Sample NEMA Type 5 Lighting

National Electrical Manufacturers Assn.(NEMA) Floodlight Classification

Beam Spread	Type	Beam Description
10 – 18	1	Very Narrow
18 – 29	2	Narrow
29 – 46	3	Med. Narrow
46 – 70	4	Medium
70 – 100	5	Med. Wide
100 – 130	6	Wide
130 – Up	7	Very Wide

1 Foot Candle

Figure 9.18

or salt atmosphere, in explosive environments, at high altitudes and temperature extremes, and even where the mounting is subjected to shock or vibration. However, the camera must be suitably packaged for each environmental problem.

In the outdoors under very low light levels, a one-inch silicon intensified target (SIT) tube equipped with a complete auto-iris lens is required to deliver 600 lines of resolution. In ultra-low-level lighting conditions below starlight, an intensified silicon intensified target (ISIT) tube complete with auto-iris lens produces about 500 lines of resolution.

Special CCTV Applications

There are a number of special application cameras with complete assembly, camera, lens, and housing designed to meet unusual surveillance requirements in confined areas. These cameras come in a wide variety of housings and generally have an exceptionally wide angle lens (4 mm to 9 mm) for installation. These covert camera concealment devices include, but are not limited to, wall clocks, card files, wide three-ring notebooks, stereo speakers, smoke alarms, emergency lighting, radios, paper towel dispensers, decorative furniture, tele-

Basic Closed Circuit Television System

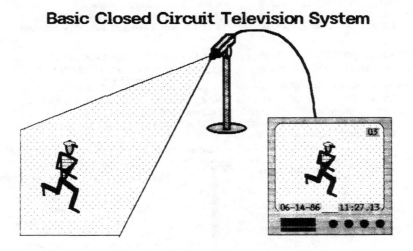

THE BASIC FUNCTION OF A CCTV CAMERA IS TO CONVERT THE PHYSICAL SCENE VIEWED BY THE CAMERA INTO AN OPTICAL PICTURE. BY A FOCUSING PROCESS, THE SCENE IS PLACED UPON A SPECIAL CAMERA IMAGING TUBE WHICH SCANS THE IMAGED SCENE AND BREAKS IT DOWN INTO ITS VARIOUS PICTURE ELEMENTS. THESE SIGNALS ARE THEN CONVERTED INTO VARYING ILLUMINATION LEVELS THAT CORRESPOND TO THE VIDEO SIGNAL WHICH IS ULTIMATELY CONVERTED INTO A VISUAL SCENE ON THE SYSTEMS MONITOR.

Figure 9.19

phones, and even a mannequin where the lens peers out through the mannequin's eye. Actual use dictates the choice of concealment device, and the con-
sequences of being discovered, even by accident, must be well thought out
before installation.

CCTV ILLUSTRATIONS

A series of illustrations is provided in Figures 9.19 to 9.27 (pp. 198–206) to
give some idea as to how the various facets of CCTV perform their functions.
These illustrations are not designed to make one an instant expert on CCTV,
but to provide enough information to speak intelligently with professionals and
to remove some of the mystique from CCTV jargon.

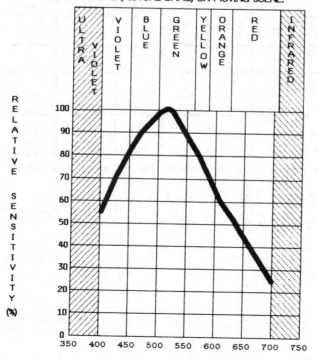

Figure 9.20

Imaging Tube

Spectral Sensitivity Ranges

	Standard Vidicon	Silicon Diode Vidicon	Newvicon	Ultracon	Silicon Intensified Target (SIT)	Intensified Silicon Intensified Target (ISIT)
BRIGHTLY LIT FLOURESCENT	YES	YES	YES	YES	YES	YES
DIMLY LIT INCANDESCENT	NO	YES	NO	YES	YES	YES
DIMLY LIT FLOURESCENT	NO	YES	YES	YES	YES	YES
INCANDESCENT	NO	YES	YES	YES	YES	YES
MERCURY VAPOR	NO	①	①	YES	YES	YES
LOW PRESSURE SODIUM	NO	YES	YES	YES	YES	YES
HIGH PRESSURE SODIUM	NO	YES	YES	YES	YES	YES
NO ARTIFICIAL LIGHTING	NO	NO	NO	NO	②	③

① DEPENDENT ON THE TYPE OF MERCURY VAPOR LAMP UTILIZED (SPECTRAL SENSITIVITY)

② SCENE ILLUMINATION MUST BE AT LEAST 3.3×10^{4} FOOTCANDLES.

③ SCENE ILLUMINATION MUST BE AT LEAST 27×10^{5} FOOTCANDLES.

Figure 9.21

Video Transmission Systems

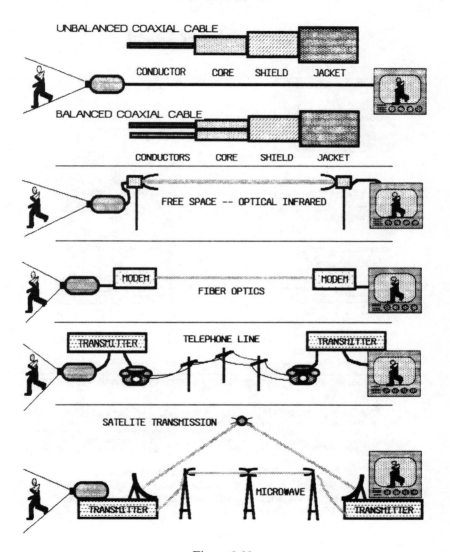

Figure 9.22

CCTV
Video Monitor Sizes

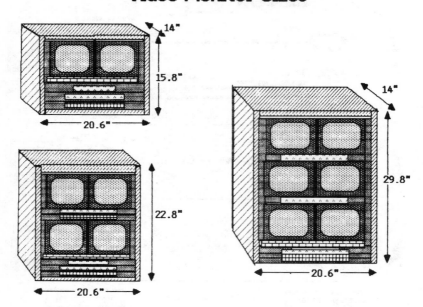

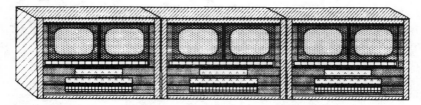

DESK TOP CCTV MONITOR MODULES COME IN A WIDE VARIETY OF
SIZES AND SHAPES. PLAN AHEAD, STICK WITH STANDARD MAKES
AND MODULES THAT WILL PERMIT EXPANSION AND BE READILY
AVAILABLE IN THE FUTURE.

Figure 9.23

Screen Size and Viewing Distance

MONITOR SCREEN SIZE IS A FUNCTION OF THE MAXIMUM VIEWING DISTANCE (VD) OF THE OPERATOR.

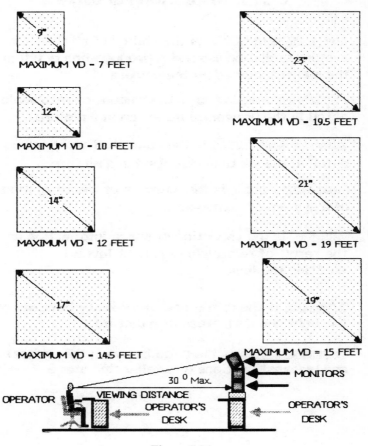

MAXIMUM VD - 7 FEET

MAXIMUM VD - 10 FEET

MAXIMUM VD - 12 FEET

MAXIMUM VD - 14.5 FEET

MAXIMUM VD - 19.5 FEET

MAXIMUM VD - 19 FEET

MAXIMUM VD = 15 FEET

Figure 9.24

CCTV Resolution Factors

Resolution, in CCTV, is the ability of a television system to distinguish and reproduce fine detail in the subject viewed by the camera.

Horizontal Resolution, is the amount of resolvable detail in the horizontal direction in a picture.

Vertical Resolution, is the amount of resolvable detail in the vertical direction in a picture.

Resolving Power, is the measure of the resolution of a system or component.

Blinding, is the reduction of scene information as the result of relatively high light levels entering the lens.

Contrast, is the difference of intensity between the light and dark areas of a picture.

Contrast Range, is the ratio between the whitest and blackest portions of a television image.

Figure 9.25

Closed Circuit Television

Monitor Viewing Angles

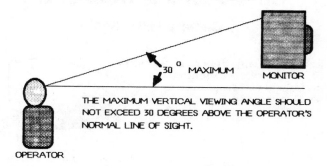

30° MAXIMUM

THE MAXIMUM VERTICAL VIEWING ANGLE SHOULD NOT EXCEED 30 DEGREES ABOVE THE OPERATOR'S NORMAL LINE OF SIGHT.

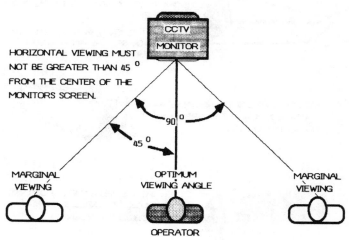

HORIZONTAL VIEWING MUST NOT BE GREATER THAN 45° FROM THE CENTER OF THE MONITORS SCREEN.

Figure 9.26

Closed Circuit Television

Camera Housings

BRACKET MOUNTED INDOOR HOUSINGS COME IN THEFTPROOF, STANDARD, SMALL, SMALL-EXTRA LONG AND MAXIMUM SECURITY VERSIONS.

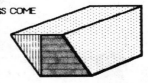

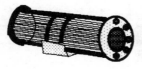

INDOOR CEILING MOUNTED HOUSINGS COME IN STANDARD AND TAMPERPROOF VERSIONS.

SPECIAL HIDDEN CAMERAS COME IN A NUMBER OF SPECIAL APPLICATION COVERT HOUSINGS.

OUTDOOR ENVIRONMENTAL CAMERA HOUSINGS COME IN WEATHERPROOF AND DUSTPROOF STYLES.

OTHER SPECIALIZED CAMERA HOUSINGS ARE AVAILABLE IN EXPLOSION PROOF AND PRESSURIZED VERSIONS.

Figure 9.27

10

Electronic Equipment Monitoring and Control

Equipment monitoring and maintenance response are important facets of facility control that are generally overlooked. Inspections, if performed at all, are probably made on a time based or monthly schedule that may or may not conform to the equipment manufacturer's recommendations.

When integrated with the facility control system, equipment control reaches out to protect manufacturing processes. It is also possible to monitor vehicular use, expendable fuels, flow meters, equipment temperatures, tankage levels, safety devices, and other esoteric areas essential to the operation of the building, as well as manufacturing functions carried out within the facility. As part of the total facility control system, effective monitoring of key equipment is relatively inexpensive.

Figure 10.1 (p. 208) illustrates how the facility control center (FCC) conducts a two-way flow of information between the building systems. In addition to monitoring and controlling the heating, ventilating, and air-conditioning (HVAC) system, lighting, maintenance management, emergency power sources, security, closed circuit television, access control, patrol tours, fire detection and alarm, sprinkler systems, special suppression systems, and specialized building management functions, the FCC can also monitor and control various aspects of the industrial or manufacturing process to preclude costly stoppages.

Practically any kind of equipment, at all types of facilities, can be successfully monitored and, in most cases, also controlled. As a function of energy management, normal HVAC systems are controlled to provide appropriate comfort levels for occupants. When facility management looks beyond typical building management systems, building operators will be able to find unique applications that will increase system efficiency and cut operational costs.

There are pieces of equipment in nearly every building upon which the continued welfare of the business is dependent. Automatic monitoring and control of this equipment can provide early warning of a pending problem or alarm in the event of an unprogrammed shutdown. It also provides the foundation for a preventive maintenance program that will prolong the productive life of each item being monitored.

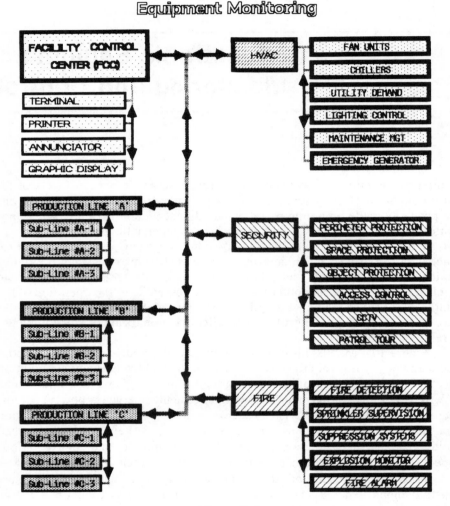

Figure 10.1

For example, if a major bearing burns out for lack of proper attention or maintenance, the entire production line may be shut down. If this causes a lengthy delay, results to the business can be devastating. Employees may be laid off, sales orders cannot be fulfilled on time, and customers may become angry or disenchanted and decide to go elsewhere. That bearing can be very expensive!

Fuel Monitoring

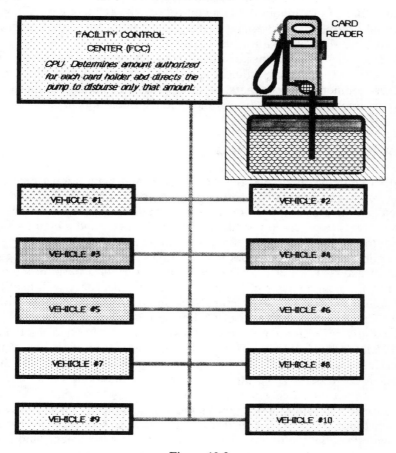

Figure 10.2

By monitoring and remotely controlling rooftop HVAC units, thousands of dollars and many hours of routine inspections can be saved. An additional benefit is increased efficiency of the individual units. Figure 10.2 illustrates FCC control over the disbursement of gasoline. Authorized individuals insert their access control card into the reader at the pumping station. The central processing unit (CPU) at the FCC recognizes that the bearer of this card is authorized to receive X gallons of fuel and will turn on the pump and allow up to that X amount to be pumped, at which time the system shuts off the pump. The CPU will also direct that a record be maintained of this transaction by card number, date, time, and number of gallons actually pumped. This information is stored for printing at a predetermined time or upon operator demand.

Fuel consumption per vehicle may also be tabulated to determine one of the factors in the cost-of-vehicle-maintenance formula. Consumption of gasoline and diesel fuel can be monitored and controlled with relative ease. This technique, while providing cost analysis and consumption rate information, also greatly reduces the potential for fuel theft.

There are many reasons for considering equipment monitoring. It can provide increased operating efficiency, reduced energy consumption, a more secure environment for occupants, lower operating costs, and properly maintained equipment for manufacturing and building operation.

DUST AND VAPOR MONITORING

Firms that deal with toxic and flammable gases and vapors must incorporate the very latest technology to protect employees and plant and surrounding areas from leakage, explosion, and fire. It is imperative to use highly effective detection systems to preclude volatile industrial disasters, and a broad spectrum of standard equipment is available to meet these situations.

Familiarization with sensors is but a first step in learning techniques to prevent disasters. Careful study of the broad nature of a basic problem, followed by technical analysis of possible preventive measures, will lead to potential solutions. The end result must be adaptable to specific applications.

An integrated system will often be the best approach. It should be a modular fail-safe design employing solid-state electronics and **light-emitting diode** (LED) indicators to verify reliable operation. Built-in false alarm prevention, fast response, and electrical and radio interference immunity must be inherent in the design. Accurate sensor readings under the most severe operational temperature and humidity ranges must be guaranteed. The sensors must be explosion proof, and all wiring must be completely encased in sealed, explosion-proof conduits. Figure 10.3a illustrates the sequence of monitoring ducts from detection, actuation, agent injection, extinguishment, and reset.

For such industries as nuclear operations, defense contractors, paint manufacturers, combustible gas manufacturers, or grain elevators, this type of highly sensitive detection is mandatory. Figure 10.3b (p. 212) puts the monitoring functions illustrated in Figure 10.3a into action. In this illustration, dust by-products from the grinding machines exhaust through the ducting and are propelled by a blower. Sensors within the ducting perform the detection function by sensing static electricity (sparks) and initiate release of the extinguishing agent, suppressing the potential of an explosion should sparks reach the collector. This suppression system is generally designed and installed to stand alone. In this stand-alone configuration, a facility control system can monitor the suppression system for activity and, when appropriate, control other equipment to reduce or preclude additional damage.

Manufacturing engineers and petroleum and chemical processing operators understand the requirements for flammable gas detectors, diffusion sen-

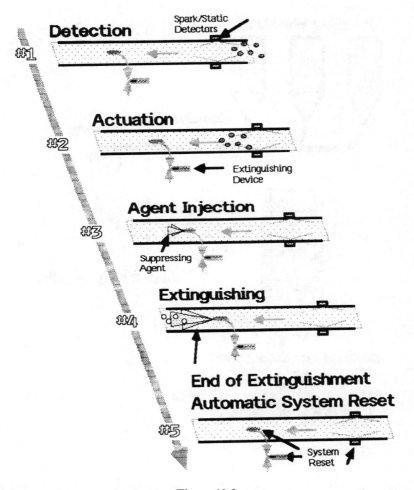

Figure 10.3a

sors, and rapid response explosion-proof devices. However, many of these manufacturing process operators do not always understand that silicones and plasticizers have certain properties that can form coatings on the catalytic elements of the sensors that could render them completely insensitive to flammable gases. Intimate knowledge of sensors that are unaffected by the various contaminants is important. Therefore, professional assistance is recommended.

It is possible to sense and stop explosions, even after they begin. An explosion is really nothing more than a rapidly developing fire, and like a fire,

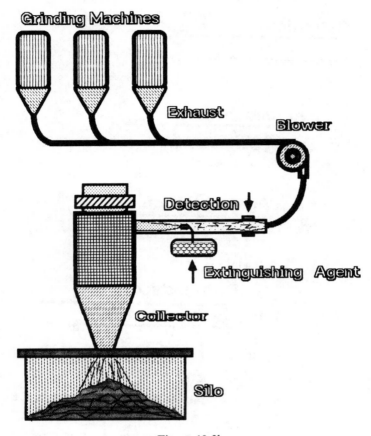

Figure 10.3b

an explosion can be extinguished. The difference between extinguishing a fire and an explosion is time! Two things are required: speed of detection and speed of suppression, or extinguishment.

To meet these two requirements the system must be sufficiently sensitive to detect an incipient explosion and to activate the discharge mechanism on a highly efficient extinguishing agent. Figure 10.4a illustrates an explosion curve pressure in pounds per square inch (psi) and time in milliseconds. In this illustration, the curve indicates the rapid rise in pressure from zero to 50 psi in just 200 milliseconds.

Figure 10.4b illustrates a similar explosion. In this example an explosion suppression system senses the incipient explosion in approximately 50 milliseconds and activates the suppressing agent which quells the explosion. This eliminates the overpressures in considerably less than 200 milliseconds.

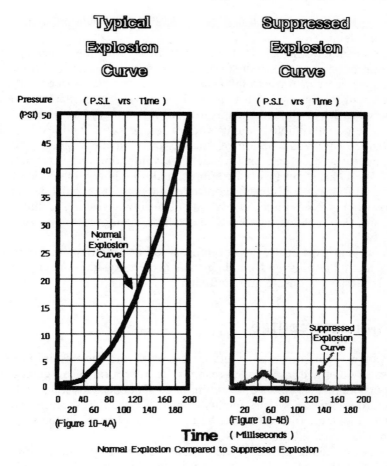

Figure 10.4

When integrated as part of a total facility control scheme, an explosion suppression system can prevent injuries and save lives. Such a system may reduce the possibility of legal claims based on management's neglect to provide a safe working situation. Without this type of protection, insurance coverage is often unobtainable. If initially designed into the structure, explosion suppression systems might even lower construction costs by reducing, or even eliminating, the need for building reinforcement.

MONITORING AND CONTROL OF MANUFACTURING PROCESSES

It is possible to extend the lifetime of manufacturing equipment and to avoid costly breakdowns through monitoring procedures. Preventive maintenance can be scheduled on a more timely basis, and maintenance personnel can be used more effectively.

Routine monitoring of production line flow, equipment usage, and automatic operations provides immediate alerting to work stoppages. Supervision of fuel capacities can provide information for automatic reorder and can indicate leaks in storage tanks. It is possible to sense the temperatures and observe the viscosity in dip tanks to ensure proper coating. Hot and chilled water tankage may be continuously monitored for temperatures and levels. Sensors can recognize the accumulation of volatile gases in fuel loading and spray-painting operations and can ensure adequate ventilation and warning to management when hazardous levels are approached. Fluid flow, manifold switches, and valve status can be closely controlled in petrochemical operations. At hospitals, where the continued availability of various gases is essential, cylinder tank weight, flow volume, and switching can be monitored to ensure constant availability.

To prevent gaps in the flow of information and overlaps in response, the facility's manufacturing and building management systems need to be integrated. To do less is unsafe and inefficient.

EVENT INITIATED CONTROL

A series of cascading events should be designed into the system in order to ensure total coverage and proper response in the event of an emergency or pending problem. This series of event initiated sequences must be well thought out and programmed into the facility control system. Responses vary from incident to incident. In each case, the controlling element in the sequence is the event that initiated the actions.

Figure 10.5 illustrates how the initiating event, in this case a fire alarm, cascades through the fire, HVAC, security, building systems, and FCC. As in Figure 10.5, the fire triggers each of the major cascading areas, and they, in turn, cascade to other areas to accomplish control, monitoring, and recording functions.

Event initiated control functions are managed through the software of the CPU. An event, as viewed by the CPU, will result in facility control system performance of specific actions. An event may be any of the following:

- An alarm
- A return-to-normal following an alarm
- A programmed time
- A programmed number of functions
- A high or low digital signal
- A specific action resulting from an analog reading
- A programmed calculation result
- One of the system's energy management program readings

Event Cascading Actions

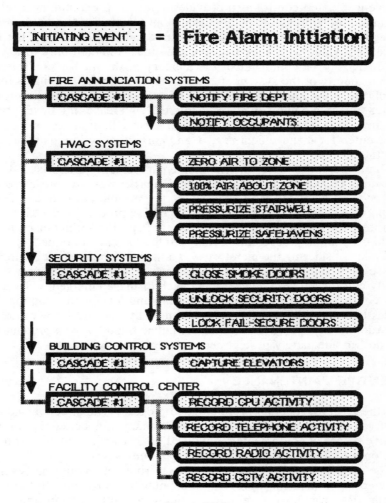

Figure 10.5

- A manual command
- An override command
- Another event initiated control function

Generally speaking, with the application of event initiated programs, the facility control system will permit a single event to command twenty-five to thirty separate actions in a cascading manner. The event initiated control procedure operates in a set/reset mode to produce a variety of on/off, open/close commands that are automatically carried out when the event occurs.

Event initiated control also provides a way of programming a relatively large number of addressable points throughout the facility to react in response to a single event. As one event can also direct additional actions, the facility is literally provided with a control sequence that is limited only to the extent of the devices to be commanded, the memory of the facility control system, and the ingenuity of the system operators. This capability eliminates the need for duplicate programming, provides a wide variety of automatic protective measures to activate upon an alarm, and greatly increases the flexibility of the system in a completely automatic mode. All these actions are recorded, sorted, and presented for management review and corrective action, as required, following the incident.

There are many cases where momentary electrical shorts and ground faults cannot be avoided in certain production processes. An integrated facility control system equipped with solid-state current-limiting units can eliminate this type of power outage. The event initiated approach to electrical current monitoring allows for a switching arrangement to permit automatic replacement of the faulty module in seconds so that production can continue.

While considering the monitoring of a facility's stand-alone systems, it is also wise to monitor any **emergency eye wash** or emergency showers to automatically call for aid. By single zoning each of these emergency devices, the facility control system will provide reporting and logging information. It also indicates to employees that the corporation really does have their interests at heart. Additionally, possible litigation for failing to do "what a prudent person would do" to adequately protect personnel can be avoided.

PREVENTIVE MAINTENANCE

One of the great assets of an event initiated program is an effective and precise preventive maintenance (PM) program. Where large numbers of important and expensive pieces of equipment are involved, this arrangement will probably be second only to demand limiting as a major money saver.

The facility control system is capable of routinely monitoring each piece of selected equipment for a preventive maintenance program. In the simplest form, the PM program can remotely monitor a penthouse fan unit or a key piece of manufacturing equipment with ease. After the equipment has been in operation for the period stipulated in the manufacturer's recommendations, the facility control system will automatically generate a work order for maintenance management.

Work Order Generation

Let us assume that the manufacturer's recommendations call for a penthouse fan unit to receive a special lubrication after 500 hours of actual operation. In

Preventive Maintenance Work Order

WORK ORDER : 10-19-86-# 1124 (October 19, 1986 WO # 1124)

Job Description : (i.e., FAN UNIT #37)

Job Location : (i.e., PENTHOUSE 26, SOUTH BUILDING)

Problem : (i.e., 500 HOURS OF OPERATION, REQUIRES OIL CHANGE)
_____
_____

Service Required : (i.e., REPLACE LUBRICATING OIL)

Technician(s) Required: (i.e., CLASS 4 LABORER)

Expendables Required: (i.e., TWO (2) QUARTS 20-90 SILICONE
LUBRICATING OIL, STOCK NUMBER SL-20-90, 1987-3482-2-9.))

Equipment Required : (i.e., ACCESS CONTROL CARD VALID FOR
SOUTH BUILDING , ONE (1) SIX-FOOT STEP LADDER, ELBOW LENGTH GLOVES
FULL-FACE PLASTIC SHIELD WITH HARD HAT, RUBBER-SOLED FOOTWEAR
1 INCH SOCKET WRENCH, 12 INCH BLADE SCREWDRIVER AND PLIERS.

Time Required : (PORTAL TO PORTAL) (I.E., 90 MINUTES)
++

WORK COMMENTS :

Work Order # : (# 1124) **Date** : (10/19/86) **Time** : (60 MINUTES)

Problems Encountered : (i.e., UPPER LEFT-HAND HINGE LOOSE
ON PENTHOUSE #26 DOUBLE DOORS. POSSIBLE LEAK SOUTHWEST CORNER
OF PENTHOUSE ROOF.)

Technician Completing Work: (Signature Required)

Reason for Non-Completion: (i.e., NO CLASS 4 LABORERS)

Supervisor : (SIGNATURE REQUIRED FOR WORK NOT COMPLETED)

Figure 10.6

this situation, as soon as the system has recorded 500 hours of operation, a work order would be generated by the FCC central processing unit based on information automatically received and processed. At a minimum, that work order would include the information contained in Figure 10.6.

After the task described on the building management system work order has been completed, the maintenance staff will enter the appropriate information into the system (i.e., completed 10/19/85 by Technician I.B. Brown in 60 minutes). The system will note that the 60 minutes required for this task was less than the 90 minutes allotted on the work order. After the next 500 hours of fan operation, the work order will indicate 60 minutes in the time required portion of the instructions.

Maintenance Management Techniques

Should the task not be completed, the work order will be repeated again the following day as a Delinquent PM Task Requiring Priority Action. Management will also automatically receive a daily PM Delinquent Log Report. In addition to reporting a delinquent work order, this management report log also indicates the priority of the items to be serviced and the number of days each has been delinquent.

This type of preventive maintenance program can be a powerful management tool ensuring efficient servicing of equipment. Time and money will be saved while utilizing personnel more effectively. Instead of cleaning up after breakdowns, maintenance personnel can prevent problems from developing.

Expendable Supplies Control

Once a facility control system is in place, there is a broad spectrum of subsystem controls that may be implemented. One example that cuts across all types of facilities is the problem of controlling the use of expendable supplies and maintaining bench stocks. This can be accomplished efficiently when managed by the CPU of the FCC.

Control of expendable supplies is essential to efficient and cost-effective building operations. Management of any supply area starts with regulating who is allowed to enter an area. Limiting individual admission to a supply center can easily be accomplished by the access control system. The access control cards of authorized personnel will permit entry based on a predetermined day of the week and time of day.

Bench stocks may be monitored by a supply clerk who enters each withdrawal from the supply center into the FCC system. Properly programmed, the system records the depletion of each item entered. When the bench stock has reached an assigned level, the system issues an instruction for reordering, taking into consideration normal delivery time for that article.

Personal accountability for tools can be managed on a daily or long-term basis by the facility control system. This technique permits management to receive a complete listing of all tools currently signed out, on a periodic or on-call basis. When a worker terminates employment, the supervisor can call for a complete listing of all tools signed out to that individual. When used in such a manner, tool losses can be cut to nearly zero.

EQUIPMENT MONITORING AND TOTAL FACILITY CONTROL

Automatic monitoring of equipment throughout the facility will permit more efficient use of equipment and reduction in the number of personnel required to service the equipment; it will also preclude many breakdowns and permit smoother running of the building.

There is a real possibility for reducing insurance premiums and for increasing the safety and morale of personnel when the FCC is capable of effectively monitoring and controlling the potentially dangerous handling of dust, vapors, and explosive situations.

Production line breakdown and subsequent backup of raw material in feeder lines can be virtually eliminated through timely maintenance, close monitoring of ongoing activity and event initiated programming to shut down operations in a predetermined manner.

Understanding and implementing event initiated programs can readily save time, equipment, buildings, and even lives. The intangible returns of lower personnel turnover and higher morale from increased safety become tangible facts.

Preventive equipment monitoring programs permit more effective use of maintenance department personnel, reduce equipment breakdowns, increase the life span of equipment, and identify pieces of machinery that have become excessively expensive to operate. The increased capability to monitor and control expendable supplies, tools, and similar items can be important in cost reduction.

These system-monitored techniques can be applied to many problem situations. The effectiveness of this type of control capability is only limited to the nature of the problem and the inventiveness of management. The power of the CPU in the FCC should be utilized to manage the building complex as efficiently as possible.

11

The Human Factor

MAN-MACHINE INTERFACE

Security personnel are an essential part of any facility control system. They are required for making periodic tours of the buildings and grounds, collecting and interpreting information, making decisions, and taking action.

All emergency or hazardous observations noted by personnel are channeled to the Facility Control Center (FCC). Examples include reporting of a fire, an oil or waste spill, torn carpet, broken fence, fire lane parking, unusual odors or smoke, loiterers, or other factors that might impinge upon the safety of personnel or protection of the building. It is the human operator in the FCC who will digest this information along with electronic inputs from the building's sensor systems and respond accordingly. It is the function of the central processing unit (CPU) to keep the system operator informed of the status of all building systems. In like manner, roving protection personnel provide their observations and analyses to the central control point.

The flow of information into the CPU must be rapid, accurate, and understandable. Equally important is the flow of information and instructions from the FCC. Sensors and systems can be programmed to react to certain inputs in a predetermined manner, such as smoke doors being closed automatically if a fire zone goes into alarm.

Personnel may be instructed in a similar fashion. A fire alarm may trigger an outside beacon to indicate appropriate access points for entry of the responding firefighters. Protection personnel may have predetermined actions that they are to take at a given signal, such as evacuating workers, directing traffic, or reporting to a specific control point where they know exactly what their function will be.

The skill of the system operator comes into play during an unusual or unexpected occurrence. FCC operators have a tremendously powerful tool at their disposal. They can manually override the building's electrical and mechanical systems. They can control doors, lighting, airflow, and a whole myriad of situations through the FCC console. The shortest route to a point of intrusion may be relayed to personnel responding to an emergency (Figure 11.1, p. 222).

The automatic internal actions of the CPU in the FCC record all incoming alarms and sensor-derived information. With the initiation of an alarm, all ver-

Man - Machine Interface

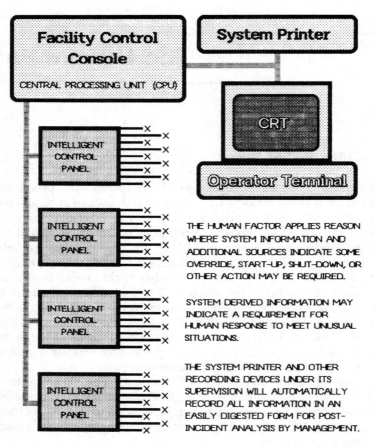

Figure 11.1

bal directions transmitted over the FCC telephone, radio, or audio systems are automatically recorded. The FCC recording systems remain in the record mode until manually turned off by the FCC operator. The information recorded at the time of an incident is valuable in reviewing and analyzing any occurrence.

The human being is the X factor who puts common sense into the facility control system. The system can check doors, report fire, read temperatures, and make calculations with a speed and accuracy that humans will never approach. However, the human being is essential for value judgments, reasoning, and decision making to cope with unforeseen problems. The person controls the system; the system does not control the person. Human beings provide that invaluable service called "effective response." The CPU reacts to the information it receives, but a person can respond with information, tact, understanding, and intellect.

PROTECTION SERVICE

The question of proprietary security for security officers who are company employees or contract security for outside guard services has been widely debated. The truth is that both are valuable assets and only corporate operational differences can determine which will be best for any given situation. The important point is that these are the people who will be charged and trusted to protect the facility and its occupants.

Whether the building is commercial, industrial, or institutional, security personnel are widely used in a variety of protection programs. Generally speaking, more than 85 percent of commercial establishment protection officers are employed by the company whose property is being protected. That figure drops to about 75 percent for industrial plants and roughly 50 percent for financial institutions, major medical centers, and large colleges.

More than half of all security officers are not equipped with firearms. This is generally due to state and local statutes that require training and routine proficiency examinations for security officers who carry guns. A higher number of armed security personnel are found in commercial and institutional areas. It is important for key facility officials to know and understand the state and local requirements that will affect their operations.

PATROL TOUR MANAGEMENT

Most facility managers are content with stationary guard posts or patrols roving about the buildings and grounds. Generally, this is a poor use of available personnel. To receive a full shift of performance from protection personnel, measures need to be taken to ensure that they are able to cover the entire facility and still be readily available in the event of an emergency.

The facility control system provides the software to make this type of protection control possible. The CPU in the FCC can perform the scheduling, timing, and sequence control for the patrolling protection elements. The FCC printer also provides an automatic hard-copy record of the progress of protection personnel through patrol tour stations (Figure 11.2, p. 224).

Management of a **patrol tour system** should provide flexibility, permitting the system operator to readily reschedule patrol tours, change tour intervals, and communicate with patrolling officers directly from the FCC console. Without the capability to run random patrol tours, potential intruders would only have to observe the clocklike movement of the patrolling officers to determine the most advantageous time to attempt a penetration. Any facility large enough

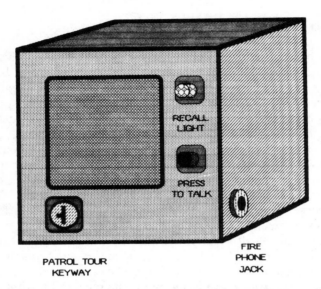

Warden Station

Emergency Call Box

PATROL TOUR
KEYWAY

FIRE
PHONE
JACK

This is a combination: EMERGENCY CALL BOX, PATROL TOUR STATION, and FIRE FIGHTER COMMUNICATIONS System. These Warden Stations terminate in the Facility Control Center (FCC).

Figure 11.2

to have an integrated protection system will probably require multiple, separate, and varied patrol tours.

To run an effective patrol tour operation, the system must be capable of having random starting points and of running the tour in either direction. Other capabilities include automatic logging of the tour's progress, recall and communication network, and delinquency alarms coupled with automatic recording of all occurrences. It should be possible to make all programming changes right from the operator's control console.

The forward and reverse patrol tour option simply means that the FCC operator has the option of running any of the ten or more patrol tours in a forward or reverse sequence by a simple input at the operator's central console. The random starting point is where any station on the patrol tour can be used as a tour starting point. The software in the FCC central processing unit will

Patrol Tour Organization

PATROL TOUR STARTS WITH THE ACTIVATION OF ANY OF THE 13 STATIONS.
ILLUSTRATED IS AN OUTDOOR TOUR OF THE GROUNDS. THIS TOUR
REMAINS INSIDE THE FENCE LINE AND DOES NOT ENTER ANY BUILDINGS.
TOUR MAY BE RUN FORWARD OR IN REVERSE AND START AT ANY STATION.

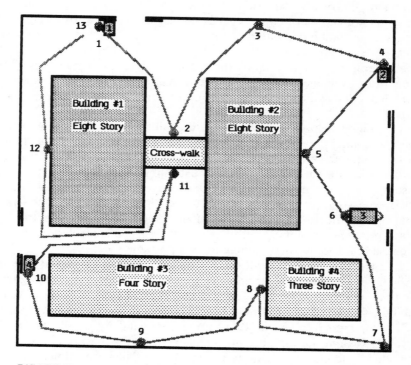

FAILURE TO MEET A TOUR STATION "WINDOW" WILL RESULT IN AN ALARM.
(See Figure 11-4, Patrol Tour Windows)

Figure 11.3

automatically determine the new patrol sequence when the first station is activated, whatever number in the sequence it might be. These are key capabilities
that help to avoid fixed security patrolling activity patterns (Figure 11.3).

It is important for management to receive pertinent patrol tour information
in either abbreviated or full detail. This can be accomplished through a properly
designed facility control system. Activation of the first patrol station on a tour
prompts reporting of a "tour start" printout that includes location and starting
time. This tour activation also causes an audible signal at the central console
to alert the operator. When the last station on the patrol tour is activated, there

will also be an audible signal indicating the time and the end-of-tour printout. At this point, the console operator should be able to select whether a full record of the patrol tour will be printed out or only a short report to indicate the beginning and ending of this specific tour.

Patrol tour delinquency reporting ensures management that the patrolling personnel have successfully completed the tours and have not been disabled or detained. Patrol tour software provides the FCC with audible and visual alerting, as well as hard-copy records of alarms resulting from any out-of-sequence tour station activation or time delinquency (too long or too short an interval between the touring officer's check-in at any tour station). A tour halt can be generated automatically by three delinquencies or manually by the console operator. Management needs this information in order to be informed of any incidents that could affect the safety of the personnel, assets, or the building (Figure 11.4).

The added feature of being able to recall or communicate with the patrolling personnel greatly enhances the value of security patrol tour function. With the communications capability at every patrol tour station, the facility control system operator can signal the patrolling security officer to check in by issuing a single command at the central console. This command turns on a **recall lamp** associated with the patrol tour station. With most good systems, the patrolling officers are provided with an immediate, direct, electrically supervised private communications channel between each patrol tour station and the central console by simply plugging in a portable hand-set.

In a patrol tour system all the patrol tour parameters should be entered into the CPU at the central console. This enables the operator to assign a start time, tour interval, stop time, and station interval for each tour. With this capability, special tours or infrequently used tours can be set up and stored in the CPU's memory to be activated upon command by the operator. When selecting a system, it is important to ensure that new or special tours can be easily added and changes made to accommodate daily operations.

Figure 11.5 (p. 228) illustrates a typical vertical patrol tour of a single building. In this case the patrolling officer enters the building, takes the elevator to the top floor, and proceeds up the stairs to the penthouse where patrol tour station 1 (PT-1) is located. Once the first station has been activated, the security officer has a predetermined amount of time to reach the next station on the tour, and so on. As illustrated, the officer would proceed down the steps from the penthouse location of PT-1, diagonally across the tenth floor and up the steps to the location of PT-2, where that station would be activated within the predetermined time window for activation. To reach the next station on the patrol tour, the officer would proceed down to the ninth floor where PT-3 would be activated before moving diagonally across the ninth floor and down to the eighth floor where PT-4 is located, and so on.

Note that by following this procedure, all levels of the building are traversed from end to end. While this may not work with all building configurations,

Patrol Tour Window

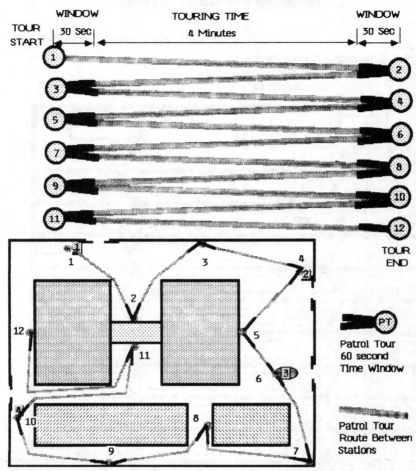

FAILURE TO MEET A TOUR STATION "WINDOW" WILL RESULT IN AN ALARM. SYSTEM OPERATOR WILL KNOW EXACTLY BETWEEN WHICH TWO STATIONS THE PATROLING OFFICER IS AT ANY GIVEN TIME. THE SYSTEM WILL PRINT-OUT THE LOCATION AS EACH STATION IS ACTIVATED.

Figure 11.4

it can serve as a guide to the typical approach for laying out patrol tours that provide necessary building coverage, records for insurance savings, and protection staff visibility for the building's occupants. All these points are important assets in the development of a total facility control and protection plan.

228   *The Human Factor*

Building Patrol Tour

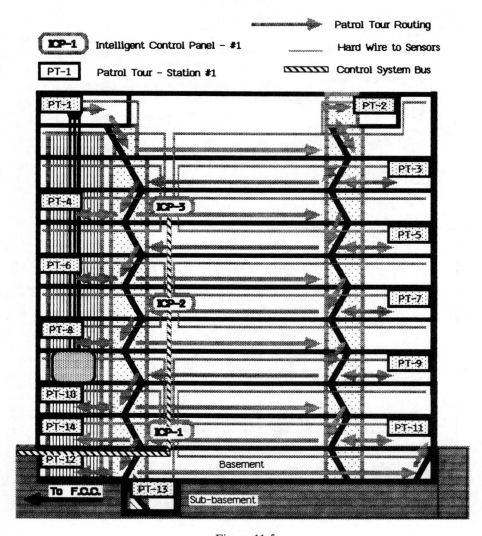

Figure 11.5

THE HUMAN FACTOR AND TOTAL FACILITY CONTROL

The end result of the implementation of a total facility control system is the efficient and effective use of personnel. Maintenance personnel can perform preventive maintenance programs based on work orders generated by the system. Safety personnel are constantly aware of the status of each protective sensor. They also have a secure emergency communications system geared to provide immediate information, as required by the situation. Security personnel are able to monitor the facility more completely with fewer people while improving the overall protection of occupants, buildings, and assets. Operations personnel can monitor production equipment with greater reliability, have more accurate control over process equipment, and reduce the number of production stoppages resulting from accidents or breakdowns.

Building management can reduce the number of personnel required to operate building systems and reduce the cost of building operations while increasing overall safety, protection, and facility control.

12

Audio Control

AUDIO CONTROL APPLICATIONS

To most people, an audio system is something over which we hear subdued music and paging announcements. However, in the context of total facility control, audio control is an emergency communications network functioning as the voice and ears for the building. It is a relatively inexpensive communication system that operates in support of the security, fire, closed circuit television (CCTV), and equipment monitoring systems. It provides a valuable service at all times of the day or night, working indoors and out, and can even be used to monitor unmanned locations.

MAINTENANCE AUDIO APPLICATIONS

Routine application of the facility audio control system would permit emergency calls for key personnel just as public address systems do. Audio management systems also permit maintenance personnel to monitor remote rooftop air-handling units and mechanical equipment rooms for unusual sounds. This can be accomplished in a fraction of the time that it would take a person to make the rounds of the many remote locations throughout the facility. At the first indication of trouble in any of the mechanical equipment rooms, the audio management system automatically switches the audio system to the listening mode. This permits the maintenance department facility control center (FCC) operator to listen to the sounds coming from the area in alarm and possibly receive some indication of the problem. Personnel working in remote locations can easily call the maintenance department for assistance or equipment. It is also possible for the maintenance department to contact personnel working in these remote areas without the expense of telephones (Figure 12.1, p. 232).

SECURITY AUDIO APPLICATIONS

Security personnel utilize the audio control system to monitor closed areas of the facility as a backup to the automatic sensors. When used in conjunction

Audio Control

Maintenance Audio Applications

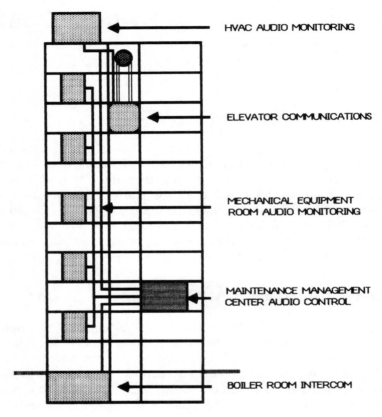

HVAC AUDIO MONITORING

ELEVATOR COMMUNICATIONS

MECHANICAL EQUIPMENT
ROOM AUDIO MONITORING

MAINTENANCE MANAGEMENT
CENTER AUDIO CONTROL

BOILER ROOM INTERCOM

Figure 12.1

with the patrol tour, an audio system provides a verbal addition to the patrol tour circuit station boxes. The patrol officer can also verbally report safety, security, and housekeeping problems for immediate or next-day response. The record-making capability of the audio system within the FCC provides management with firsthand reports of the findings discovered during routine patrol tours. In an active security role, the audio control system automatically responds to security-sensor-generated alarms, permitting the system operator to listen in on the security **zone in alarm**. A cashier being robbed could activate the audio control system by removing cash from a **money clip** sensor. The central console operator would be informed via the facility control system CRT

Audio Control

Security Audio Applications

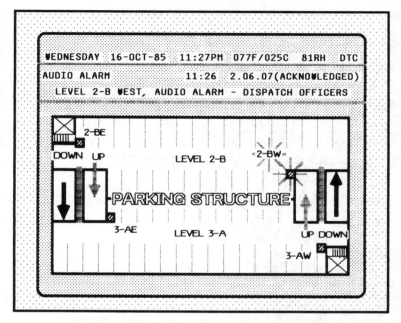

WEDNESDAY 16-OCT-85 11:27PM 077F/025C   81RH   DTC

AUDIO ALARM   11:26   2.06.07(ACKNOWLEDGED)

LEVEL 2-B WEST, AUDIO ALARM - DISPATCH OFFICERS

2-BE
DOWN UP   LEVEL 2-B   2-BW

PARKING STRUCTURE

3-AE   LEVEL 3-A   UP DOWN

3-AW

Facility Control Center CCRT

CONTROL CENTER GRAPHIC CCRT ILLUSTRATING PARKING STRUCTURE
AUDIO DEVICE IN ALARM. DEVICE 2-B WEST IS FLASHING IN RED.
INSTRUCTION INDICATES OFFICER RESPONSE IS REQUIRED.

Figure 12.2

exactly where the incident was taking place and what type of sensor (active, passive, or manual) generated the alarm. By listening to the sounds originating from the scene, the operator can judge what course of action to take.

An integral part of the audio control system is its ability to make automatic recordings of all transactions that take place on the system. Daily review of these tapes will preclude human oversight or failure to report situations noted by protection personnel during their rounds.

An audio call station in a parking structure can bring assistance for the driver of a disabled vehicle or immediate help for a person being harassed. The system **graphic CRT** automatically identifies the activated call station and displays a floor plan of the area where the sensor in alarm is flashing. With this information, the system operator can direct mobile protection officers to the

Audio Control

Grounds Audio Applications

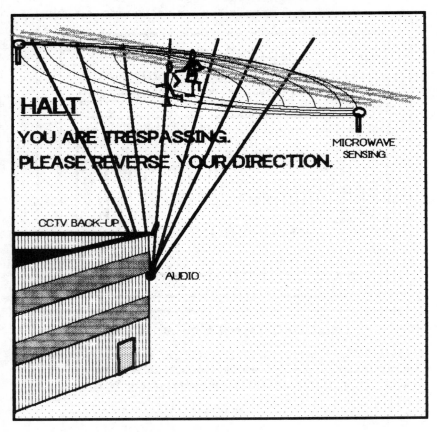

HALT

YOU ARE TRESPASSING.

PLEASE REVERSE YOUR DIRECTION.

MICROWAVE SENSING

CCTV BACK-UP

AUDIO

Figure 12.3

scene by the most direct route and, by using other system sensor information available through the FCC, can provide the responding officers with updates while they are enroute. This radioed information, as well as the sounds from the active audio device, are being automatically recorded in the FCC (Figure 12.2, p. 233).

In the event of an **intrusion alarm** at a perimeter, the facility control system, either automatically or through operator intervention, can inform the individuals that they are trespassing and thus turn back accidental intruders. Even intruders intent upon foul play may be deterred just by knowing that they have been detected and are possibly under observation (Figure 12.3).

Audio Control
Automatic Audio Applications

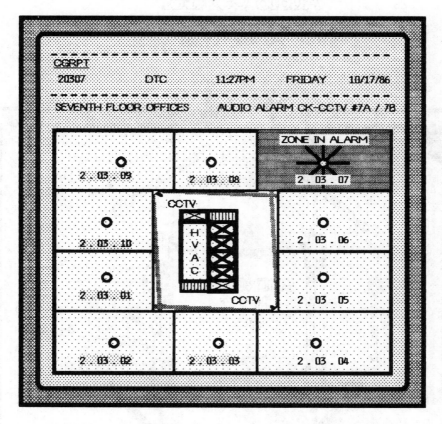

AUTOMATIC AUDIO MONITORING OF CLOSED AREAS. CLOSED CIRCUIT
TELEVISION IS USED HERE AS A BACK-UP, BUT INFRARED OR ULTRA
SONIC SENSORS MIGHT WORK EQUALLY WELL.

Figure 12.4

An audio system aids in reducing false alarms that occur after hours in closed areas. When a security sensor in a closed or compartmentalized area initiates an alarm, the audio system can be used to listen for unusual sounds. When coupled with CCTV, the audio system allows for a two-way conversation with any possible **stay-behind** individual in the closed area (Figure 12.4).

When used in conjunction with access control points, audio greatly assists in eliminating problems created by the forgotten entry card. CCTV must also

Audio Control
Portal Audio Monitoring

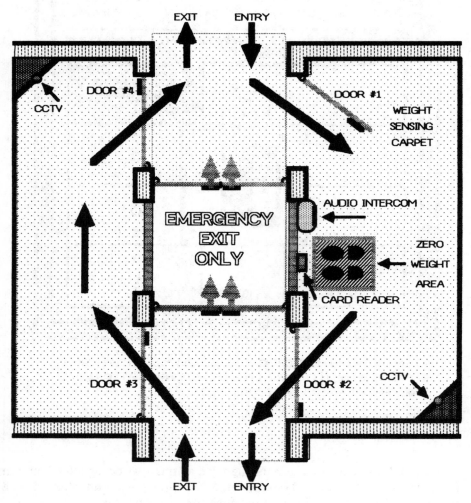

Figure 12.5

Audio Control

Automatic Audio Recording

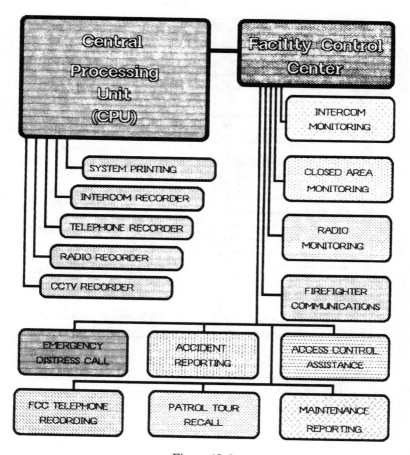

Figure 12.6

be in use for visual identification and as a protective measure against duress entry. Two-way communication and CCTV are essential to man trap access control points, particularly where **weight sensing** or sensing mats are used as identifying functions of **portal control** (Figure 12.5).

Automatic audio recording of listening devices, radio communications, and telephone conversations are all important during periods of alarm. When audio-recorded information is coupled with the printed record of incident reporting, automatic CCTV recordings, documented time of FCC operator acknowledgment, and security officer or maintenance technician response, an

Figure 12.7

accurate record of each audio-initiated or audio-supported security alarm is provided. This information is extremely valuable for reconstructing incidents and for developing protection techniques for the future (Figure 12.6, p. 237).

FIRE MANAGEMENT AUDIO APPLICATIONS

Audio control is particularly important when dealing with fires in high-rise buildings and large industrial plants. At the first sound of the fire alarm, the fire communications audio system initiates a slow whoop or temporal tone for a few seconds to alert the occupants. This alerting signal is a **third priority** signal on the audio system (Figure 12.7).

Audio Control
Priority Emergency Audio

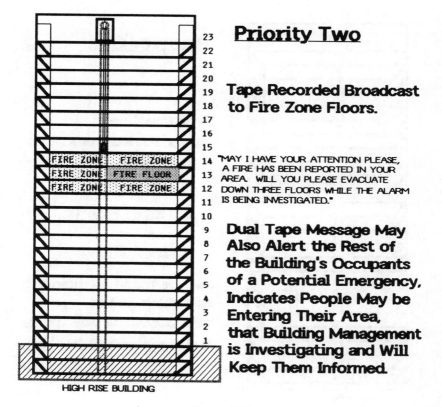

Priority Two

Tape Recorded Broadcast to Fire Zone Floors.

"MAY I HAVE YOUR ATTENTION PLEASE, A FIRE HAS BEEN REPORTED IN YOUR AREA. WILL YOU PLEASE EVACUATE DOWN THREE FLOORS WHILE THE ALARM IS BEING INVESTIGATED."

Dual Tape Message May Also Alert the Rest of the Building's Occupants of a Potential Emergency, Indicates People May be Entering Their Area, that Building Management is Investigating and Will Keep Them Informed.

HIGH RISE BUILDING

Figure 12.8

Following the alerting signal, a **second priority** signal is heard. This is a prerecorded UL (Underwriters Laboratories) listed tape cassette designed for **dual track** announcements. Track 1 on the tape automatically broadcasts to the floor in alarm, the floor above, and the floor below. Generally speaking, track 1 informs the occupants of an emergency and requests that they evacuate down three floors. Track 2 of the fire management tape will automatically announce to the rest of the building that an alarm has been reported and that some people may be entering their area while the cause of the alarm is being investigated. Occupants will also be informed that building management is checking into the cause of the alarm and will keep them informed (Figure 12.8).

The **first priority** announcement capability on the fire alerting audio system is reserved for building management and fire personnel to make live an-

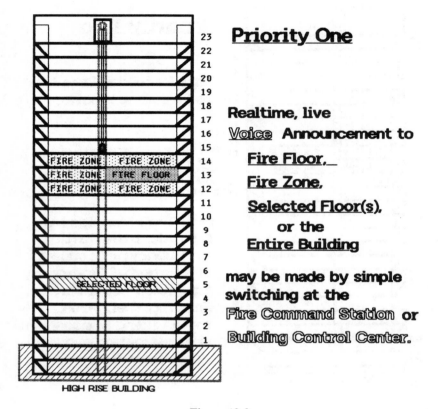

Figure 12.9

nouncements. These announcements can go to the three floors in alarm, to specifically selected floors, or to the entire building. This is usually done via a press-to-talk microphone at the FCC or from a special fire command station (Figure 12.9).

Another key application of audio communications in relation to high-rise fire management is dedicated emergency communications for firefighters. This is a **supervised** private communication system reserved exclusively for emergency or firefighter use. By simply plugging in or lifting the receiver of a pre-positioned fire call station, the individual reporting an emergency or the firefighter is automatically connected with the FCC or the on-site fire commander. This type of dedicated communications system is often mandatory, as the steel

Audio Control

Emergency Communication System

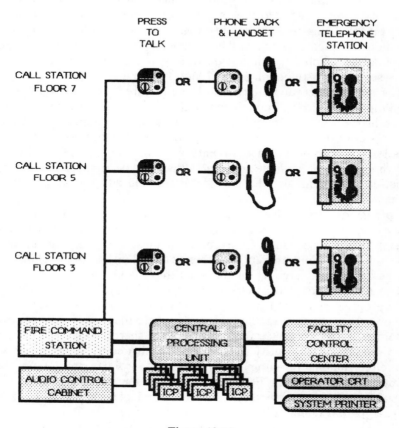

Figure 12.10

masking of many high-rise buildings blocks out the usual fire department hand-held radios. Through this dedicated emergency fire communications network, fire personnel are able to request assistance and to receive instructions. It is essential that these fire call stations, or warden stations, be located in safe-haven areas such as pressurized stairwells (Figure 12.10).

When integrating an audio communications system into the total facility control scheme, it is important to employ a skilled audio specialist. This individual must work closely with the control system manufacturer prior to and during installation and checkout of both systems. This will ensure that the audio system is keyed into the central processing unit to be properly responsive to system activity.

TOTAL FACILITY CONTROL AND AUDIO CONTROL

Audio communication is probably one of the most cost-effective aspects of total facility control and also one of the most important. It is the link which ties the human being into the facility control system with real-time audible information. The audio system will automatically inform occupants of specific actions that they should take in a wide variety of emergency situations. It also protects security personnel on patrol tours.

The maintenance department can save hundreds of man-hours annually through the application of audio listening devices. Audio provides the ears for the eyes of the CCTV, synergistically making both systems more effective. The access control system will be strengthened by the addition of audio communications at each of the access points. When audio is coupled with CCTV at entry points, it will facilitate access to authorized personnel and also provide information to individuals who may be attempting entry at an unauthorized location.

Emergency communication, coupled automatically with the fire detection and alarm system, can prevent panic, save lives, and assist in reducing the damage normally associated with even the smallest fire. This same system can warn of tornados, bomb threats, or other potential disasters by telling the occupants exactly what is going on and what they should do.

The audio system works well with the security system, both indoors and out. Preprogrammed taped messages can warn trespassers to reverse their course or tell **stay-behinds** to remain exactly where they are. Audio control can provide a monitoring service for sounds where there should be only silence and can function as a security sensor. When activated by sound or a security device, either manual or automatic, the audio control can provide unique and real-time information to the FCC operator for proper response action.

Audio devices in emergency stairways and parking structures provide employees with a feeling of well-being just knowing that someone is there if needed. Individuals required to work at remote locations are provided additional protection with the use of covertly activated and automatic response audio control techniques. Audio control is essential to a professionally designed facility control system. No large facility should be without a specialized audio system integrated into the overall building control system.

13

Command and Control

FACILITY CONTROL

Without the ability to command various building systems to meet changes in routine daily operational functions, management can lose control of a building. Command and control of the facility's systems is essential for efficient and cost-effective real estate management. The selection, engineering, installation, and operation of a facility control system that allows management to operate in its own style is the foundation of building command and control. The potential for **modular expansion** to meet corporate growth is extremely cost-effective over the long term. Any control system under corporate consideration should be capable of at least a 100 percent expansion in memory and addressable points beyond the original system design.

Development of an effective command and control function requires full participation of all members of the facility control staff. The first and most natural input is full control of each of the individual building control systems. Only persons directly responsible for a particular system can provide the information necessary for the system to function properly under normal conditions.

Interface with other building systems can begin once the basic system functions have been incorporated into the facility control system and the system consoles of each department are operating properly. This is not as involved as it might seem, but is essential to efficient building management.

EMERGENCY MUTUAL SUPPORT

The two sides to command and control involve automatic and manual operations, actions, and reactions. A few examples will help in understanding these differences, as well as the automatic interactions and manual override capability required from time to time.

The maintenance department must be sure that the building's heating, ventilating, and air-conditioning (HVAC) system operates normally in an automatic mode, but they may also want to manually command certain operations from time to time, as well as change control parameters of some of the individual pieces of equipment.

The safety department must ensure that fire systems are fully supervised and operational at all times. They must also test the system periodically in order to meet building codes, requirements of insurance underwriters, and fire marshall regulations. Routine monitoring of hazardous gas storage, sensing for gas leaks, and monitoring for explosive concentrations of dust and those other areas unique to specialized industrial operations are sometimes overlooked.

The security department monitors the property or fence line, the building perimeter, compartmentalized areas, access control, closed circuit television (CCTV) systems, and those specialty items used in executive protection.

The director of plant operations will want certain pieces of key equipment monitored for maintenance and efficiency. The routine monitoring and control of automatic production equipment shutdown, work order publication, vehicle maintenance, fuel consumption and individual vehicle efficiency, and the scheduling of equipment downtime are important to production managers.

Once these and other unique operating areas have addressed their in-house operational requirements, the task of systems integration begins. All aspects of building control, during both normal and emergency situations, must be considered when planning command and control.

Fire Management

In the event of a fire emergency, occupants must be notified by the audio system, elevators must be captured and returned to the ground floor for fire-fighter use, the HVAC system must stop the flow of air to the fire zone in alarm and send 100 percent air to the adjacent zones for containment, stairwells must be pressurized, security doors must be unlocked, smoke doors must close and transmit confirmation of that closure, the fire department must be notified, and all this must be done automatically to preclude human frailty. Lines of responsibility for building management must be crossed for safety of the occupants and protection of property. This is the automatic portion of building command. The manual part of building control comes into play when facility management intervenes to alter or change actions that were set into motion automatically.

Security Interface

Security problems present a completely different set of requirements for building management. The capability for manned response and manual override of various pieces of equipment on a real-time basis is mandatory. Where applicable, security sensors must capture the CCTV system, turn cameras and point them at the area in alarm, switch the affected camera to a master monitor, and initiate a video recorder with a date-time generator (DTG) to record the scene. The audio system must also be captured, as appropriate, to allow the operator to listen in to the area involved without flipping switches, and the audio system recording device must be activated to record any audible activity at the area in alarm. Where applicable, the access control system must go fail-safe or fail-secure as predetermined by management, while still preserving the capability of manual override from the facility control console. Of course, the system printer would provide **hard copy records** of all system transactions concerning the event and indicate when specific actions took place, including the operator's response.

HVAC Integration

The maintenance department must be capable of coping with other considerations in the event of trouble signal, fire alarm, or emergency situation. The ability to control power stations throughout the facility in case of fire is an important command and control function. The automatic shutdown of ancillary pieces of equipment as the electrical demand limit is approached is equally important if excessive demand charges are to be avoided. The capability to take additional equipment off-line manually will further assist building officials in their attempts to prevent their facility from exceeding the demand limit set by the power company.

Manufacturing Equipment Monitoring

Plant production managers may want to program assembly line shutdown for specific reasons, on a daily or shift basis. Unforeseen equipment shutdowns may be required at any time for a number of reasons. Preprogrammed arrangements for handling that type of action, when coupled with an event-initiated program in the central processing unit (CPU), can shut down upstream affected operations and keep them from jamming. The **override** capability is necessary to remedy special cases, but when coupled with the total facility control system, there is much less opportunity for something to be left undone that could easily create a major problem, hazard, or even a life-threatening situation.

Subsystem Interface

It must be stressed that an integrated facility control system is not just a reactive protection program. It is a tool which actually works around the clock to provide an efficient, cost-effective, and safe place in which to work. Personnel can be used more judiciously. Time, money, and lives can be saved by constantly monitoring the building's environmental control, manufacturing equipment, and emergency protection systems. By being totally integrated, the var-

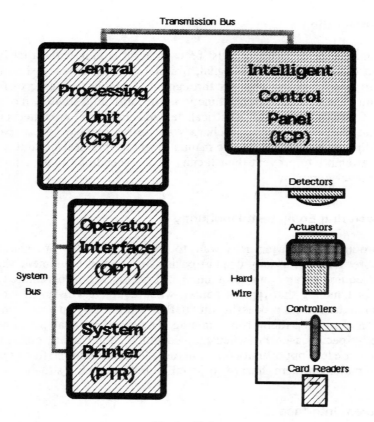

Figure 13.1

ious building systems are actually worth more as a whole than when operating and standing alone. The facility control system is designed to address a wide spectrum of sensor points within the facility. It must be able to read and present this data in a meaningful, understandable, and timely manner. It should also be capable of effectively responding to the monitored information.

The command and control capability of a facility control system can be used in almost every facet of building operation (Figures 13.1 to 13.5, pp. 246–250).

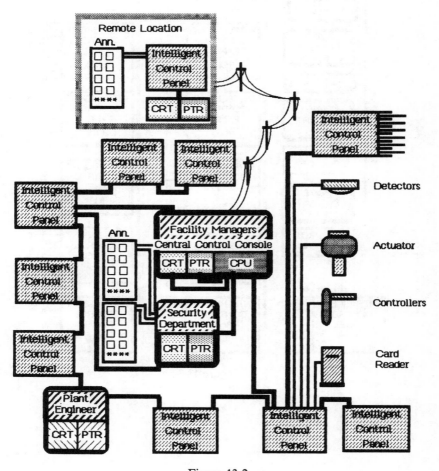

Figure 13.2

Total Facility Control

Expanded Configuration

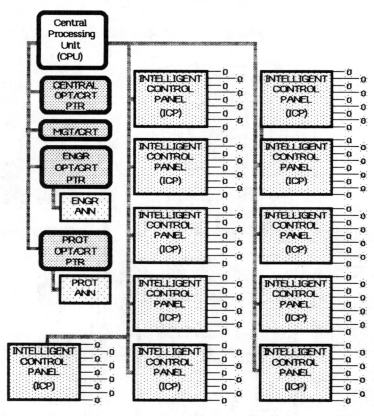

Figure 13.3

Integrated System Control

System Growth

First Year	Third Year	Future
Facility Control Console/CPU	Color CRT Terminal	Operating System Save
Start/Stop Programs	Chiller Optimization	Off-Line Memory Access
Reports & Logs	Load Reset	Enthalpy Control
Event Initiated Programs	Data File Logs	Memory Diagnostics
Command Language Interpreter	Peripherals Exerciser	Perimeter Security
Optimum Start/Stop	Operating System Verify	Pump Control
Access Control	Closed Circuit TV	Remote Building Control
Duty Cycling	Compartmentalized Areas	
Power Demand Control	Equipment Monitoring	
Patrol Tour		
Building Perimeter Security		

Figure 13.4

Integrated Facility Control
Special Data Transmission Options

Fiber Optics

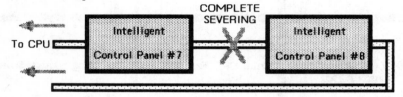

Satellite Communications

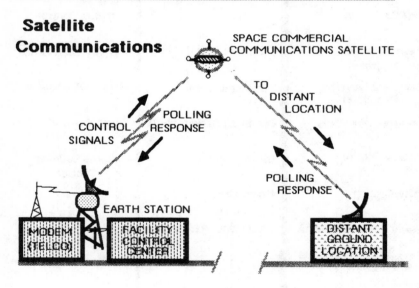

Figure 13.5

14

Integrated System Design

FACILITY CONTROL DESIGN APPROACH

Design is more than just being sure that a system works. Design includes a practical approach to long-term survival, mutual support between the systems to cope with alarm or emergency situations, and cost-effective maintenance.

In the assessment of the *WHAT, WHICH, WHERE, WHEN,* and *HOW* of facility acquisition, nothing must be overlooked. Failure to consider any aspect of the building's comfort, protection, or control of process equipment can be costly. To preclude this possibility, a team of experts should be assembled to provide the leadership necessary for a successful project. The goal of the planning team and the design team should be to achieve the most effective and efficient facility control system possible.

Members of the planning team must have solid familiarity with applicable concepts of energy management and facility protection. This team will also provide the project manager with the technical knowledge to understand and evaluate proposals that will eventually be submitted by various vendors. Very large corporations may have staff personnel with skills necessary to perform the total planning function. However, if there is any doubt, qualified outside experts should be sought. Architects and consulting mechanical and electrical engineers are valuable team members during this crucial stage. Advice from protection professionals skilled in fire safety and security systems can be helpful in devising the best possible system to meet the requirements of a particular facility.

Facility Survey

Total facility control is a specialty which spans many disciplines. Corporate managers should not expect their maintenance, safety, and security chiefs to be able to design systems for their areas of responsibility. This is a major undertaking and requires professional assistance from experts in each discipline (Figure 14.1, p. 252).

Facility Survey

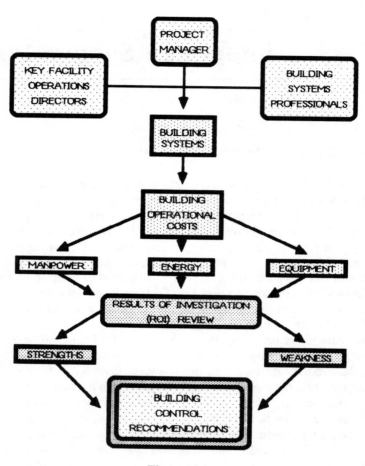

Figure 14.1

Few individuals possess the skills and experience necessary to perform an adequate energy survey for a large facility. This is also true in the area of facility protection surveys. Numerous security professionals are competent to do physical security surveys, but they may be totally unfamiliar with fire systems and their applications. Experts in heating, ventilating, and air conditioning (HVAC) are equally hard to find, but are essential to a satisfactory project. A check with the local chapters of the American Society for Industrial Security (ASIS), Building Owners and Managers Association (BOMA), the Construction Specifications Institute (CSI), or the Association of Energy Engineers (AEE) will go a long way toward finding the type and level of professional assistance required.

The energy portion of the survey covers the interior areas, occupancy, and equipment of the facility. A walk-through of the buildings will indicate the general nature of the energy-consuming devices and systems involved. With this knowledge, the survey team can prepare the necessary forms for collecting complete and compatible information.

It will be necessary to obtain records from accounting and maintenance departments that reflect energy use in order to develop an overall picture of gross energy consumption and costs. During this process individual **fixed rate** and **variable rate** energy consumers must be noted for future close monitoring and control.

Generally speaking, the information to be collected will include:

- Data documenting overall energy consumption
- Daily energy demand peaks
- Utility rate schedules
- Power factor changes
- Physical data on the building's envelope
- Building occupancy and use
- Interior design conditions
- Actual interior conditions
- Equipment size rating
- Hours of HVAC usage
- Lighting arrangement
- Hot water consumption
- Elevator activity
- Special equipment
- Computer operations
- Food service equipment

In determining just how detailed the energy portion of the survey should be, the following questions must be considered:

- What is the present energy bill?
- What annual savings should be predicted?
- What time frame does the energy survey cover?
- Are current drawings of the facility available?
- Can high-energy consumers be identified?
- Can all major energy consumers be measured?
- What types of equipment contribute to peak demand?
- Is the facility large enough to warrant sophisticated control?
- Is funding available for an effective system?

The protection portion of the survey includes the physical security of the facility from the property line inward. Areas of protection coverage to be considered should include:

- Perimeter and grounds physical protection
- Fire detection zoning
- Fire annunciation requirements
- Specialized fire and explosion suppression systems
- Fire and explosion venting
- HVAC fire defense applications
- Smoke control
- Emergency communications
- Control of personnel movement around and within the facility
- Vehicular movement control
- Parking area compartmentalization control
- Vendor access control by time and location
- Restricted access areas
- Afterhours area compartmentalization control
- Object protection
- Protection of proprietary information
- Shredding of sensitive materials
- Compartmentalization of research and development equipment and data
- Closed circuit television (CCTV) applications
- Remote area monitoring

Facility requirements vary from location to location. Some facilities may have specialized needs which definitely require outside experts in determining the present status of existing equipment and the steps necessary to reduce a particular hazard.

The only way to understand the strengths and weaknesses of a facility is to have a thorough survey conducted by professionals working closely with internal department heads and system technicians. The findings of the outside group may or may not substantiate earlier requests for facility operational improvement funds. A fresh look at the weak spots, followed by knowledgeable recommendations, will save money in the long run.

If all the factors that effect a building's controls are considered, it is little wonder that energy consumption continues to climb, utility bills are so erratic, security incidents continue to increase, little fires become big fires, personnel requirements continue to climb, and there seems to be no end to equipment breakdowns. Fortunately, today's technology can provide the solutions and actually permit management to regain control of facilities.

Control features such as optimum start/stop, duty cycling, outside air control, chiller optimization, supply air control, enthalpy control, monitoring of unoccupied periods, and demand limiting are but a few of the techniques available to the skilled practitioner of HVAC controls.

Fire systems that can capture elevators, control HVAC systems, open locked security doors, and provide verbal instructions to occupants automatically are available in today's market.

Security systems that, when activated by an intrusion detection, will automatically select the appropriate CCTV camera, pan and tilt the camera to the point in alarm, and activate a video cassette recording, date-time generator, and audio commands can be installed to provide professional security protection.

Access control systems are available to control the movement of people by time and space, permit card information change and deletion, provide for tracking of individuals within the facility, control parking, and monitor duress signals.

There are also closed circuit television systems that operate in total darkness, serve as motion detectors, or work as a visual subsystem to a larger integrated facility control system. CCTV can also provide increased safety by monitoring the internal workings of equipment and volatile or toxic areas. Only a detailed survey and careful planning can meld the available technologies to fit the needs of a particular facility.

Financial Survey

A financial survey should be done concurrently with the facility survey. They intermesh as time moves forward. It is from the facility survey that the pricing and savings information will be derived. The financial survey will check into the availability of capital expansion funds and determine the depreciation schedule for the proposed expenditures (Figure 14.2, p. 256).

The results of this investigation are fed to the funding survey group for a financial feasibility analysis. This analysis is then incorporated with the operational feasibility study derived from the facility survey. The end result of the financial and operational feasibility studies is a facility Building Management Systems (BMS) Feasibility Statement.

As a result of the facility and financial surveys, senior managers will be better able to understand the facts bearing upon the project and thereby make a valid decision on how best to proceed. After these steps have been taken and the analysis completed a Request for Proposal (REP) is prepared. The end result of this investigation will lead to a quantified system development and a qualified functional system.

To do anything less can only result in a series of decisions based upon ill-conceived or narrow thinking. While this single-thought system may, in fact, solve the problem at hand, it may also be ineffective or excessively expensive in the long run. Any facility control effort should be well conceived and backed by sound financial considerations before being implemented.

Financial Survey

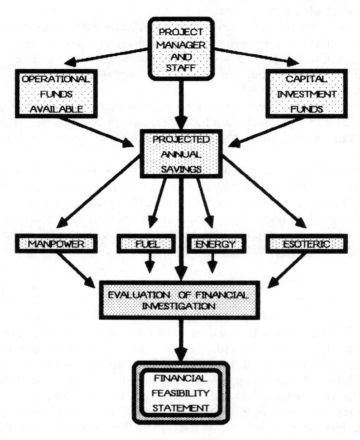

Figure 14.2

Prioritization of Requirements

The ideal time to acquire an integrated building control system is during the initial design of a new facility. By working closely with the architect, the best possible building effectiveness and efficiency can be obtained. Even then, building operators should deal directly with the architectural staff to ensure total protection and total control of the building, its occupants, and its systems.

It is expensive and impractical to retrofit an integrated system all at one time. When faced with a retrofit project, the first step requires full knowledge of the existing systems and which of them will be retained. Next would be the prioritization of requirements. When the actual retrofit installation begins, the control center should be put into place and started up. Then one at a time the remote data gathering panels should be brought on-line and, with them, their individual sensors. In this manner, any problems will be discovered as they are activated. It is also expensive and impractical to install a variety of systems without an overall plan to completely control the facility's systems step by step.

Several key factors are necessary in developing an effective and efficient building management system. Whether the plan is for a new structure or a retrofit of an existing building, the central hardware and software must be adequate for the initial integrated system master plan of the entire facility. Unless that factor is included, along with a 100 percent expansion capability in both memory and addressable points, it probably will be an inferior system.

THE PLANNING TEAM

Members of the planning team need a solid understanding and familiarity with the applicable concepts of facility control before conferring with vendors' representatives. This will give the project manager a definite edge in dealing with vendor sales representatives and will allow for a clear definition of the company's requirements. This combination of technical background and practical experience also permits a more concise evaluation of proposals from the various vendors (Figure 14.3, p. 258).

The planning team must go through several steps to ensure a thorough understanding of the overall situation relative to the facility and its existing control systems. All existing building systems should be reviewed. The effectiveness of each system must be determined so that decisions can be made about their continued value.

A determination of the total facility control requirements should be made without consideration of cost. Coupled with this will be a method for interfacing the various building control subsystems.

It is important for the planning team to become familiar with the major manufacturers' systems. Although time-consuming, understanding the overall system capabilities, service, maintenance, training available, replacement parts, cost, and potential growth is essential in making a wise selection.

The foundations for the preparation of a **performance specification** are knowledge of the company's facility control requirements and familiarity with **standard equipment** readily available to meet those requirements. While outside assistance may be required for final specification preparation, the planning team should be able to indicate its requirements as to how the facility will operate when under the monitoring and control of the selected system. A performance specification tells the vendors how the system is to perform after the installation has been completed and outsiders have left the scene.

When the performance specification has been completed, the planning team will have to decide who the potential vendors might be. Once the spec-

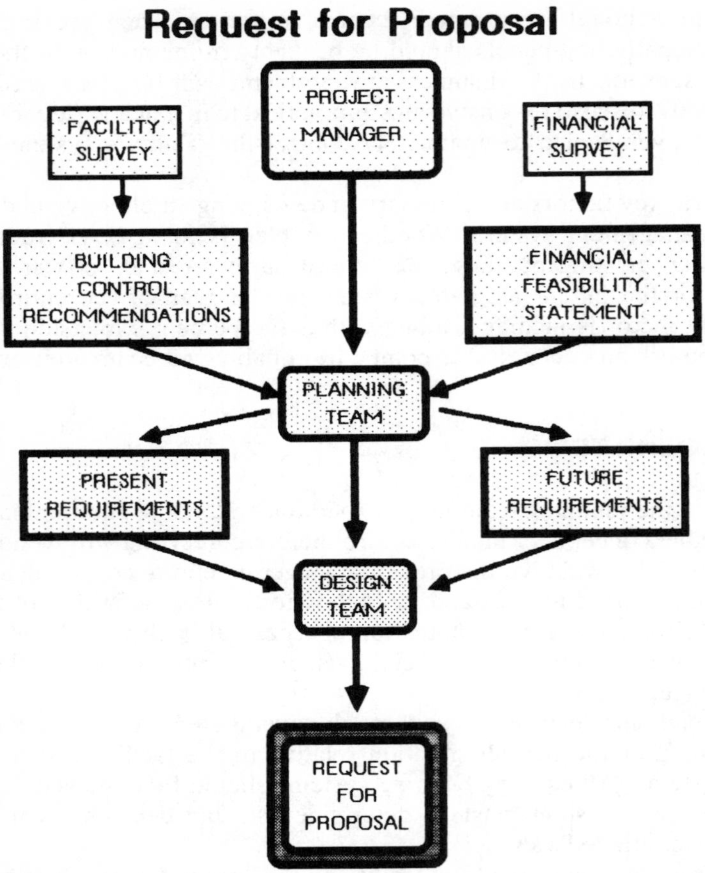

Request for Proposal

Figure 14.3

ification has been put out for bid, the planning team interviews individual vendors. At this time the vendors will explain and, when possible, demonstrate the performance of their respective systems. It is important to differentiate between future capabilities and actual performance.

If a vendor wishes to submit a bid, it must be understood that the project manager will review it within a reasonable time. Members of the planning team need to be available for response to vendors' questions. All team members should make every effort to establish good working relationships with vendor representatives; this will pay off handsomely in the long run.

Adequate time should be allowed for each vendor to make a presentation. This is an educational phase for the planning team and, even if a vendor is not selected, much can be learned from the presentation. A thorough understanding of each vendor's system approach, hardware, software, and method of protecting the facility is essential.

Following the initial vendor interviews, the planning team will need to develop a **short list** of two or three finalists. A formal letter should be sent to these bidders requesting a technical proposal explaining exactly how the vendor would go about assembling a system to meet the performance specification.

Each technical proposal must be carefully reviewed. The planning team must check every aspect of the proposals to ensure that the performance desired will be met in the final analysis. In measuring these technical proposals, every questionable point must be resolved to ensure complete understanding. For full understanding, an actual demonstration should be requested.

During the process of vendor selection, other building control potentials will probably surface. These may be used as bidding chips in the final selection of the vendor. The vendor should cover complete installations, support services, technical support for the system, and specifics concerning cost. At this point, after all questions have been answered, a vendor can be selected and the contract awarded.

For the project manager and the planning team, the time involved in these activities has been well spent. Their informed understanding of various subsystems and system applications are essential for evaluating technical proposals.

THE DESIGN TEAM

The design team should include most of the members of the original planning team plus system experts from the vendor's technical staff. This team should develop an approach to provide a system that is flexible, modular, changeable, and efficient—one that blends personnel and electronics to work as an effective man-machine system. Overlapping, duplication, and improper application of equipment must be avoided. Electronic monitoring and control are possible everywhere at once, but intelligent human response is essential for the facility control system to be effective.

The design team must develop plans for a monitoring and control system engineered for today. Microcomputer technology has been developed to integrate multiple building functions into one control system that is easy to operate. The facility control system will link the life-support, safety, and protection systems with the normal building comfort control systems. For industrial purposes, the system must also be able to monitor and control manufacturing process equipment from both energy consumption and safety points of view.

Design Innovations

The ability to reach across the miles to monitor and control remote locations via standard telephone lines, microwave relay stations, and even satellite trans-

System Design Innovations

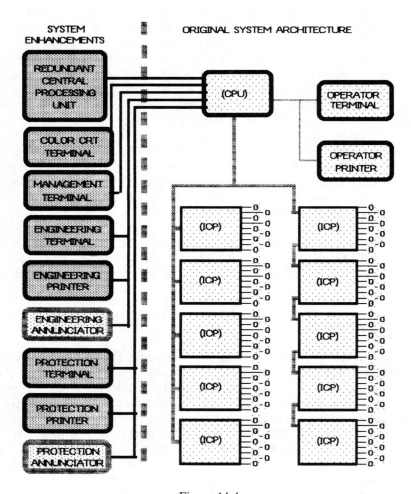

Figure 14.4

mission may be important. **High-line security**, with random-generated coded signal generation, will be a requirement in some cases. Ready adaptability to **fiber optics** will be extremely important in a number of situations. The final system must be capable of providing a wide variety of transmission techniques to meet present and future situations, and the design team needs to look ahead to meet future facility requirements (Figure 14.4).

Uninterrupted power source (UPS) and **battery backup** should be an inherent capability of the system to readily cope with a main line failure. A

redundant central processing unit (CPU) to reduce the mean time to failure should be a routine installation. It should also be possible to draw certain designated data from the system for historical storage and future retrieval.

It must be possible for multiple and segregated operator terminals to be installed at any point along the transmission bus. These terminals should be capable of being relocated to accommodate changing corporate requirements. This same capability should also hold true for the system's printers and annunciators.

The possibility of installing an expanding matrix of intelligent monitoring and control panels to include special-purpose panels at any point along the transmission bus should be a routine system option. The individual, sensor loops, and stand-alone systems report their condition to these panels. Therefore, where appropriate, these control panels must be capable of operating on battery backup power for predetermined periods of time in the event of a power failure.

The Custom-Designed System

Don't be fooled by the "custom-designed just for us" syndrome. In the realm of facility control, that is just not cost-effective. Even a relatively small control system may require as many as 100,000 programming entries. Who is going to perform service, provide parts, and make repairs when your one-of-a-kind system goes down?

A custom system may not have the necessary Underwriters Laboratories (UL) listings. Even in the most unique, one-time situation, a custom-built facility control system will turn out to be relatively ineffective, inefficient, and, above all, costly. Considerable planning must go into such a long-term project. These questions need to be asked: Where does additional equipment come from? Assuming we can acquire additional equipment, what will it cost and who will do the installation and checkout?

The Standard Modular-Designed System

This approach to resolving the total facility control problem is an efficient, cost-effective, reliable, and expandable method. Initially this type of system may be more expensive, but with proper design, installation, and maintenance, it will readily pay for itself within three to five years. Simple systems devoted to energy-saving programs give a return on investment through cost avoidance in usually less than two years. A decision to purchase based on the initial cost differences between systems is short-sighted and expensive in the long run.

The standard modular-designed system begins with a CPU with memory and executive programs to perform the basic functions. There is an operator's interface with the system via a system output terminal and usually a printer to record the transactions and alarms. Attached to this central hardware and software, usually by a single twisted pair of wires, are one or more intelligent control panels. These intelligent control panels are hard-wire terminals for sensors and devices that are located nearby.

TOTAL FACILITY CONTROL SYSTEM DESIGN

The control system selected must meet the requirements of the facility it is to serve. This may seem trite, but any number of facilities have changed the way they operate in order to conform to the "set" program of a particular system. Still others have fallen into the trap of having a system custom-built just for their organizational requirements. Simply stated, both approaches are wrong.

The single program system designed for only one function will not be able to grow with corporate expansion. A facility that changes its modus operandi to conform to the way a particular computerized program works will only end up with gaps and overlaps in information and performance. As requirements change, the predetermined operation simply cannot cope with the additional requirements. Since the problems of growth do not go away, the typical response is to add additional systems to manage the new requirements.

Unforeseen developments in fire protection or security areas call for specialized control systems specifically designed for fire protection. To satisfy underwriters and fire officials, the fire monitoring, detecting, and alarm system must meet Underwriters Laboratories Standard, UL 864, Control Units for Fire-Protective Signaling Systems.

Present and future requirements for security protection can be quite different. What is now a peaceful surrounding for the building complex can change drastically over a short period, necessitating unusual security precautions not even considered at the outset. Proprietary systems must meet Underwriters Laboratories Standard, UL 1076, Proprietary Burglar Alarm System Units.

Advances in the organizations's research and development may require increased control to protect valuable new ideas. Perhaps the sheer size of the work force will require developing compartmentalized areas to control the movement of people within the facility. For a truly effective system with competent design, the access control system must meet the basic requirements of Underwriters Laboratories Standard, UL 294, Access Control System Units (Figure 14.5).

These are only a few examples of what might be encountered in the future if initial design requirements for the basic system configuration are not well planned. Any system being considered should be capable of managing present requirements, be of modular design for future expansion, and already be listed with UL for all possible future requirements.

Beware the salesperson who tells you that their system is UL listed. That may mean it carries a UL listing for fire alone but does not meet the standards

Codes and Standards Considerations

NFPA - 101 LIFE SAFETY CODE

UL Standard - 864 CONTROL UNITS FOR FIRE PROTECTIVE SIGNALLING UNITS

NFPA - 72A-F STANDARD FOR INSTALLATION, MAINTENANCE, AND USE OF LOCAL PROTECTIVE SIGNALING SYSTEMS, VOICE/ALARM COMMUNICATIONS SYSTEMS

UL Standard - 1076 PROPRIETARY BURGLAR ALARM SYSTEM UNITS.

NFPA - 12 STANDARD FOR CARBON DIOXIDE EXTINGUISHING SYSTEMS.

UL Standard - 294 ACCESS CONTROL SYSTEM UNITS.

NFPA - 13 STANDARD FOR INSTALLATION OF SPRINKLER SYSTEMS.

UL Standard - 639 INTRUSION DETECTION UNITS.

NFPA - 110 STANDARD ON EMERGENCY POWER UNITS.

UL Standard - 873 TEMPERATURE-INDICATING AND REGULATING EQUIPMENT.

Figure 14.5

for UL 1076, UL 294, or all of the other standards that might be in your best interest to know about, prior to purchase.

Immediate Applications

Once the overall requirements for the facility have been established, a careful selection of the central hardware should be made, without consideration of cost. This central hardware, with compatible and expandable software, must be capable of meeting immediate system requirements and have the growth capability to meet future demands upon the system.

The basic system will commonly optimize HVAC operations to maximize energy savings, while maintaining adequate building comfort. Standard functions should include **optimized start/stop, night setback, enthalpy control, demand limiting,** and **duty cycling.** Computerized **lighting controls** should be included in the original arrangement. They save energy by powering down or turning off lights when not required or during unoccupied periods.

Facility security requirements, present and future, must be accommodated in the basic central system design. Depending upon the facility's specialized present and future requirements, the security arrangement should be developed to provide initial general protection. Future additions to the security system must be easy to add to the basic system.

It is important that the basic central system be able to accommodate **access control software** for immediate or future application. **Access control** is an extremely important function for overall facility protection and it must be responsive to other building systems in the event of an emergency.

Fire detection and alarm should be a major function of the initial facility control center (FCC). Careful attention to building zoning and close monitoring of specialized stand-alone systems is essential. The ability of the FCC CPU to control the HVAC systems, capture elevators, and unlock security doors should be inherent in the initial installation.

An important asset to the basic installation that is often overlooked is the ability to command a CCTV system for facility control and personnel efficiency.

The ability of the basic system to accommodate a **patrol tour management** system is equally important. This might not be used initially, but care must be taken to ensure that additional patrol tours can be added at future dates.

The basic system should have an audio capability to each of the intelligent control panels. An open-ended capability to install additional transceivers should be an inherent part of the initial **FCC audio system.**

Secondary Options

Secondary options in the maintenance area, if the funds are available, include **variable air volume** fan control, **boiler optimization, chiller optimization,** and **night cooling purge cycles.** These options may or may not be standard but their future addition to the standard system is important. Generally speaking, a quality HVAC energy management system can perform the lighting control functions. If lighting control is not a standard part of the initial system software, it should be a major secondary consideration.

Security additions should be made as funds become available and should follow the original master plan. After high-priority security items have been covered in the initial installation, additional security requirements should be prioritized.

Access control may or may not be part of the initial installation, but if the software is inherent in the basic system it should certainly be considered for activation as a secondary option. Access control is a powerful tool in controlling the movement of personnel and vehicles.

Additions to the fire system include stand-alone suppression systems, emergency voice alerting, and firefighter warden stations. While the individual suppression systems may be expensive, the addition of a monitoring and alarm function to them is not.

Other Options

Many of the basic HVAC functions may, of course, be managed by personnel, but there are still many valid reasons for handling these items through the system's microprocessor. Computer-programmed energy management strategies are stored in the system's software and are thus indifferent to the drifts that normally plague manually-controlled pneumatic systems.

When new lighting is added to the facility, consideration should be given to the type of lighting, wiring, control panel arrangement, and ballast. It is less expensive to add high-quality lighting control at this stage than in a retrofit situation.

Just as there is no such thing as a trouble signal on a security system, there is no such thing as a low priority security point. There are, however, high-security areas that may need to be considered as a secondary priority due to the expense involved in providing maximum security during initial installation. This refers to the installation of additional space protection within a perimeter-protected facility. It may also include addition of object protection within a compartmentalized space that is enclosed within a perimeter-protected building.

Lower priority access control functions may be added with only the expense of door hardware, if the system software contains an access control option. There are many access control applications that go beyond controlling doors and parking areas. They can also be used to control use of computer terminals, copying machines, and fuel disbursement, to name but a few. These should all be considered as additions to the system.

Additions to fire systems will probably be in the form of more finite zoning, roof venting, and application of explosion suppression systems. Monitoring of the water flow to emergency showers and eye-wash basins can summon help by activating the body or eye-flooding device. Each area will require only a single point or two and will certainly be worth the slight cost.

Future System Expansion Configurations

Once the basic configuration of the facility control system is in place and performing well, a system expansion plan should be developed. The major expense has already been covered in the system's central hardware and software. The more points added to the system, the more cost-effective each point in the entire system becomes.

Following are a series of control system growth configurations. The paramount decision to be made is the initial one to install a fully capable central control system. With this in place, all the configurations described are possible. The important consideration is to develop the initial installation with the potential to grow and cope with future expansion, as Figure 14.6 shows.

Basic Facility Control System Configuration

Basic configuration for a facility control system must have a CPU to provide the hardware and software for the system to operate. It also must have an input terminal so that the system operator can acknowledge alarms and tell the system what to do. There should also be a printer to provide hard-copy records.

The facility control configurations illustrated here show a basic format with only the central processing unit (CPU), operator interface terminal (OPT), system printer (PTR), and one intelligent control panel (ICP) (Figure 1.1).

Expanded Facility Control System Configuration

The difference between the basic and the expanded systems is that the latter is much more efficient. Refer to Figure 13.3, Expanded Configuration, in the previous chapter, which illustrates the same central hardware, but adds an additional CRT for management and provides an operator terminal and printer for the plant engineer, and a similar arrangement for the protection department.

Under this arrangement the management CRT permits top-level system changes, provides for system terminal redundancy, and allows immediate reporting of alarms to senior management. The maintenance terminal is dedicated to plant operations and similar functions. All fire, security, access control, and protection sensors are directed to the protection department terminal. System flexibility permits any of the terminals to serve as an alternate should the situation require, but terminal segregation eliminates needless report duplication.

The expanded format illustrated in Figure 14.4 shows a more typical arrangement with the single CPU monitoring a number of ICPs providing segregated control to maintenance and protection areas via their own operator terminals, printers, and annunciator panels (ANN), and to remote locations via telephone lines.

Near Remote Facility Control Configuration

The difference in the case of near, but remote, facilities lies in the transmission bus. In the case of nearby buildings on the same property perhaps buried cable to the remote building will suffice. Should those nearby buildings be separated from the main complex by a river or freeway, a buried cable may be impractical and dedicated telephone lines too expensive. In this situation microwave transmission of data, video, and voice might be the answer.

The near remote facility control system is capable of reaching across bodies of water, freeways, airports, and similar obstacles that permit line-of-sight. For buildings closer, but still removed from the primary complex, the ability to use buried cable is important (Figure 14.6).

Near Remote Configuration

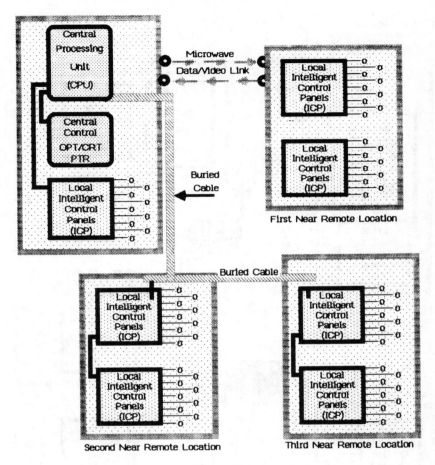

Figure 14.6

Far Remote Facility Control Configuration

Due to the distance involved, far remote locations are most effectively controlled over a standard RS232 voice grade telephone line used in a leased line mode. Depending on the nature of the facility, it is possible to monitor the entire second control system operation or just the control panels. In the first case the size and importance of the far remote facility may justify its own complete system, in which case the central location CPU would exercise only limited control or a monitoring function. This would be most effective when

Far Remote Locations Configuration

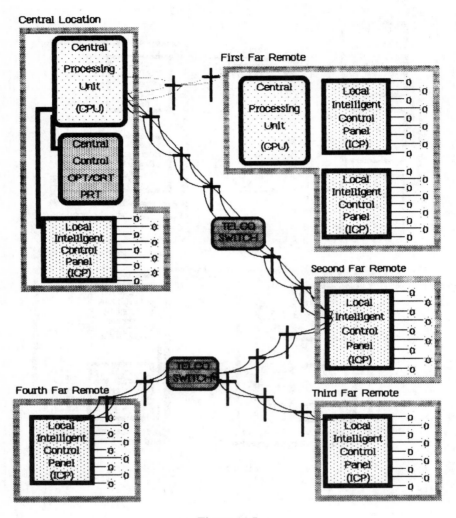

Figure 14.7

the central location is a twenty-four hour operation and the far remote a five-day week facility.

For smaller far remote locations, the RS232 telephone line is merely an extension of the transmission bus, and the control panels respond just as if they were on the central location premises. This far remote configuration is illustrated in Figure 14.7.

When dealing with far remote buildings, the facility control system is capable of data transmission over standard RS232 (voice grade) telephone lines even if required to go through one or more telephone company switching centers. It is desirable to have far remote buildings totally self-sufficient with their own CPU, reporting only alarms and other specifically desired information to the central location. A far remote location may be of such a size that an independent CPU would not be cost-effective. In such a case, all that is required is an ICP to monitor and control the far remote location's functions using the power of the centrally based facility control system. At a minimum, it would be advisable to have an annunciator panel ANN at the far remote location to provide responding emergency personnel with some indication of the source of a reported problem (see Figure 14.7). Each remote and far remote location must have its requirements carefully analyzed and these requirements must be designed into the initial facility control system.

Far Distant Facility Control Configuration

Far distant locations should have a stand-alone facility control system as a first criterion. If worthwhile, commercial microwave or satellite transmission service is a relatively inexpensive communications technique to monitor alarms, on-site equipment, and personnel movement. This technique is important to petrochemical corporations wishing to monitor offshore locations or critical processing facilities for problems (Figure 14.8, p. 470).

Far distant facilities must have a stand-alone capability, using the central system as an emergency backup. In this configuration, senior corporate management is kept informed concerning the status of the far distant location. The far distant facility should have the memory, hardware, and software capability for the central location to draw upon, and the local far distant management should have the capability for making necessary changes to enhance their location's protection and control activities.

Large corporations with multiple operations in a wide variety of locations can capitalize on an independent facility control system. Tremendous financial and control advantages accrue from the ability of the smaller remote installations to operate on their own, while still reaching back to the central location to tap the power of an enhanced CPU.

Each of the larger remote locations will have resident computer power to provide energy management through the monitoring and control of their pumps, chillers, boilers, fans, dampers, temperature sensors, and other control functions. With the information provided from the sensors, the primary energy management system will provide optimum start/stop, load reset, chiller optimization, duty cycling, enthalpy control, and power demand control for the most efficient energy consumption.

Large remote locations may also have a requirement for monitoring air compressor pressure, air handling system start-stop status, burner failures, freeze alarms, heating water circulator pump failure, high water level on sump

Far Distant Locations
System Configuration

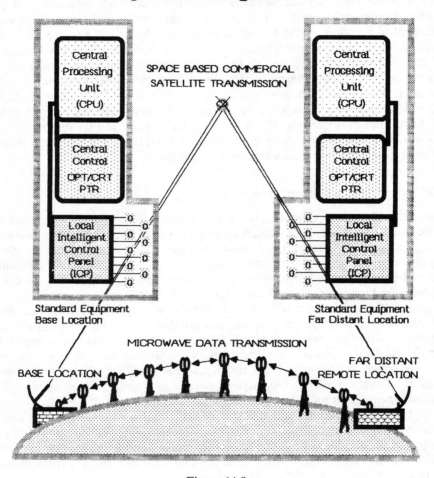

Figure 14.8

pumps, hot water boiler temperature, pump pressures, pump vacuums, and steam boiler pressure and water level. Thus the CPU power must be there for effective use.

All locations, large and small, local and remote, require fire and security monitoring. These activities include not only life safety and the protection of property, but also a security alarm system, compulsory patrol tours, access control that manages movement by time and area, audio communications, and various command functions.

Redundant Central Processing Unit

One of the efficiencies of a centrally managed facility control system is a redundant CPU that will normally provide a mean time to failure in excess of thirty years. An additional benefit is the provision of a corporate-wide equipment preventive maintenance program, top management interface with remote locations via system-derived reports, emergency notification of remote alarms and the efficiency such a system will provide in personnel savings. Why have people performing duplicate tasks at multiple locations when it can be done once at the central location by a single staff of dedicated personnel?

All major locations should have a stand-alone facility control capability. Multiple lines of system communication are available and can be automatically routed over a secondary method should the first signal carrier fail. The redundancy of the second main CPU and the fact that each of the control panels are in themselves intelligent provide continued service. Severing of the **transmission bus** between the main CPU and the ICPs would still provide system functions, but in a degraded mode and without system reporting. Additionally, the facility control system should be self-diagnostic, reporting trouble, grounds, and alarms in the transmission bus as well as internal CPU or peripheral equipment malfunctions.

Large Operations

Problems arising from large, multifaceted installations, contracted by large corporations or government, come from trying to make everyone happy. One example is a very large, $500 million federal project. In order not to show favoritism, spread the work around, or for financial considerations, four general contractors, and later a fifth, began work on the project. Each general contractor had his favorite subcontractors, and they in turn, their favorite suppliers, distributors, and installers.

On this project, the four prime construction areas were installed by the four initial general contractors. The fifth area is a specialized, design and build, one-of-a-kind, movable structure. To further complicate the problem, the governmental agency overseeing the installation will not be the final operator. In all fairness, this installing agency interfaces with a second governmental agency that is charged with the activation of the project. This second agency will operate the location for additional third-party users. Does this sound confusing?

In the final analysis, the completed project will require the five major installations on location to interact with each other on a real-time basis and be responsive to one primary remote location seventeen miles away and one, or possibly two, secondary remote locations hundreds of miles from the project site. The different locations feed information into a central location at the project site, but there is little or no capability to rectify a problem at the four outlying facilities short of physically going to the individual buildings. Even if that were always possible, which it is not, location of information concerning the system-reported problem, much less its resolution, can be difficult to reach and retrieve.

This is a dramatic and expensive project where the four major facilities were practically designed in a vacuum, as far as total facility control was concerned. The individuals involved in the construction of the project are extremely well qualified, if not the best in the business. The end user is depending on the group overseeing the installation to give them a quality finished product. The group overseeing the installation is working closely with the agency supervising the installation on a firsthand basis. The five general contractors are following closely the contract documents and the specific directions of the supervising agency. Only the best material and equipment are being used. The quality control along each step of the way is outstanding and the personnel working on the project are devoted to the task. Nothing can go wrong—go wrong—go wrong!

Steps have been taken to ensure that each part of the assembly will work exactly as designed. Unfortunately, little has been done to ensure that the five major parts will work in unison, provide a cross-flow of building function information, be mutually supportive in event of trouble, or take automatic corrective action to cope with local or remote problems.

For instance, if there is a fire alarm initiated in complex 3, complex 1 and the remote monitoring sites will know immediately of the alarm, but they will have no way of knowing if it is a false alarm or not. If there is a breakdown in the building's HVAC control system, an indication will be received, but there is no capability to remotely control, start/stop, or open/close the problem. In short, control systems of this five-building complex do not work as one. They work as five separate operations that tell a central location when there is a problem, but the centralized command and control function is missing.

There must be a transmission line from the control center to the various remote panels so that system sensors and control points may be polled, alarms received, and commands transmitted. Sophistication of the transmission line, or bus as it is commonly called, will generally be a function of the caliber of the system and the priority given to facility protection requirements. This transmission bus can be a simple twisted pair of wires, fiber optics, or a randomly generated signal transmitted over a series of wires to and from the control panel.

The third part of a basic system is the remote control panels. A broad variety of sensors are connected to these panels by normal electrical hard-wire techniques.

FACILITY CONTROL SYSTEM EVALUATION

The key to effective system design, support, and service is careful, intelligent advance planning. There can be no doubt that a well-designed facility control system will quickly pay for itself. The trick is to write a tight **performance specification,** select a quality vendor, closely monitor the system's installation, and maintain it with in-house personnel.

Owners are more or less at the mercy of vendors or general contractors when they seek information on facility control systems. No vendor is going to say that another vendor has a superior or more capable product. To assist those who might be considering a total facility control system, an Integrated System Evaluation Checklist is given in Appendix A. This is not a complete list, but it will help eliminate firms that do not meet basic requirements. Measuring the three or four potential suppliers against the checklist items and rating each will help an owner find the supplier best qualified to fulfill specific present and future requirements. This checklist is intended to provide the owner with questions that should be satisfied prior to system selection.

15

System Hardware

System hardware consists of the basic and sophisticated pieces of equipment that provide the nucleus of the visible part of the system. The individual pieces of the system's hardware perform a variety of functions; they are the physical items that house the software and inner workings of the facility control system.

CENTRAL HARDWARE

Central hardware consists of those pieces of equipment which are normally housed in the Facility Control Center (FCC). Remote hardware items are those pieces of equipment which generally lie outside the FCC. The essential items of central hardware consist of the central processing unit (CPU), an operator's terminal, and a system printer.

The central processing unit (CPU) houses the microprocessor that drives the entire system. The operator's terminal permits the operator to respond to and provide instructions for CPU execution, and the printer provides a record of all activity taking place on the system that management chooses to retain (Figure 15.1, p. 276).

Central Processing Unit

The brain of the system hardware resides in the **central processing unit (CPU)**. In most cases the CPU is a general-purpose, 16 or 32 bit microprocessor programmed to provide central control and monitoring functions. Inherent in the CPU is an **operating system (OS) function** that controls the internal data transfer and processing functions. Coupled with these internal activities, the CPU also communicates with pieces of man-machine interface equipment, directs the sending and receiving of data from remote information collection points, and supervises the functioning of the system.

Normally some sort of transmission power supply equipment that provides the **direct current (DC)** source for the DC transmission loops is associated

Basic Central Hardware
and Remote Control Panels

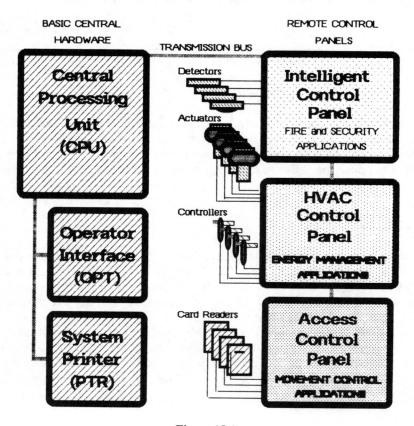

Figure 15.1

with the CPU. This element also furnishes the static discharge transient protection for both the DC and **tone transmission** lines.

Operator's Terminal

The operator's terminal is a man-machine device, usually modular in design, that provides for two-way communication between the operator and the system. The individual terminals available range from a relatively simple wall-mounted terminal, to a desk terminal, to a console terminal with self-prompting CRT screen. More advanced and efficient systems have color CRTs which actually lead the operator through a series of instructions with dynamic displays in a color-coded format.

The terminals may be dedicated to a specific building function such as energy management, building management, fire detection and alarm, security system functions, and patrol tour management. Conversely, one operator's terminal may be used for all these functions. Depending upon the physical arrangement of a facility, one operator terminal may perform management of a given physical area through monitoring and control of the systems and devices within the area controlled.

The only difference between a wall-mounted operator's terminal and a desktop version is cosmetic. The wall-mounted version is usually a self-contained terminal while the desktop models have an umbilical cable between the keyboard and the bulker electronics that is normally stored within a container inside the desk or console.

A carefully designed integrated system allows the various operator terminals to operate in a segregated mode, servicing only energy management or fire or security, during day-to-day operations, while operating from a single central processing unit. In the event of a problem with a terminal or within a terminal area where the terminal cannot be used, management should be able to transfer any terminal's activity to another on the system. This technique provides for inexpensive redundancy within the system.

Several manufacturers provide a relatively inexpensive but very effective CRT operator's terminal. In addition to the normal operator terminal functions, this CRT terminal provides a conversational, self-prompting technique for system penetration. Through such a terminal, an operator may request and display data concerning the system, issue commands, and retrieve stored programmed information. These CRT terminals are generally easy to use and require no computer training. A wide selection of logs, software-controlled formats, full English language alarm, and descriptions of the various points monitored and controlled by the system are stored internally for call-up on the CRT.

The CRT terminals should also be segregated by specific function. This means the maintenance department will have its own terminal and printer, segregated from the main system to provide only that information necessary for the maintenance department to perform its responsibilities. Likewise in the protection department, fire and security items will be reported on the system, leaving it free of maintenance logs and alarms. Of course, information vital to both functions will be duly reported by the system.

Multiple CRT terminals and printers on a single system, and data segregated so that each CRT monitors specific groups of designated sensors enhance the system's capability. To be fully effective, the CRT terminals should be self-instructing and provide interactive operating procedures. Speed of intelligent response requires a full English language method for message descriptors, alarms, and points associated with the system. Special capabilities to look for prior to selection of a CRT terminal include the ability to field program system points and descriptors, data segregation for use of multiple CRTs, and the ability to use telephone leased lines to monitor remote locations.

System Printer

The basic function of system printers is to provide a hard-copy record of what has transpired on the system—whether a routine event, trouble signal, or an alarm. Printers are nothing more than a hard-copy device used in conjunction with the CPU to provide the system operator with a record of alarm and log printouts.

When selecting an integrated system, it would be wise to choose one which not only allows for multiple printers to be attached to the system, but also permits the assignment of different types of information to flow to the designated printer. With this capability of dedicated printers, they may be assigned to individual fire, security, building automation, or patrol tour functions or any combination.

One printer may, of course, be used for all integrated functions for the entire complex. If desired, individual printers may be segregated by function or location of the facility being monitored and protected. The selected integrated system should permit printers to be added to the system at any point along the **transmission bus** as well as permit their movement from time to time to allow for changes in managerial or production requirements.

Basic Printers

The simplest printer is a wall-mounted strip printer. Such a printer provides automatic printouts covering change-of-state information, such as additional alarms, restoration points in alarm, and operator acknowledgments. It should also provide log printouts to the operator, upon demand, for all points, a summary of point status, and a summary of alarms for a given period of time.

These wall-mounted strip printers normally use an **alphanumeric** format to conform with a twenty-one-character line on the 3.5-inch paper roll. This permits a concentration of reporting information in a compact space. Such a printer usually has an **audible alarm** with a **silencing switch** to provide an hourly test printout and possibly a red or bold face printout indicating an alarm. There is usually a manual reset which must be made at the termination of a log or report run. This printer provides good backup for a more sophisticated system printer.

Intermediate Printers

Intermediate system printers may also serve as the principal man-machine interface when a keyboard has been added. When the printer has no keyboard, it is used as a **read-only** device for alarm printouts and logs. With a keyboard, the printer is capable of functioning as a complete operator's terminal and as such allowing a conversation-mode of system penetration for requesting data, issuing commands, and entering specific program data.

Printers of this type may be segregated by type of data flow, allowing for exclusive operation of building environmental controls or the fire and security systems. Such printers can be located at any point along the transmission bus or in remote buildings by use of leased telephone lines. On these printers the alarms are usually printed out in elongated or boldface headings in full English language format, simplifying action-taking responses and making them easier for the operator to understand, Logs on generic printers of this type include: All Point, Single Group, Alarm Summary, Status Summary, Trend, Access Control, Energy Management, and Programmed Data Logs.

Advanced Printers

The more advanced system printers are a combination printer and operator terminal. Printer features are interactive and provide a conversational mode of operation. They offer a wide selection of logs with software-controlled formats in full English language. Of course multiple printers may be used on a single system to permit complete data segregation and reporting features.

Advanced printers offer multisystem compatibility and self-instruction, and interactive operating procedures that make them relatively easy to operate. Depending upon the requirements of the facility, ease of use, clarity of reporting, and functional capability are important features.

System Logs

System logs go a long way in providing expanded control over a facility. As many as seven different logs are available on the more advanced systems. Advanced printers feature over 120 characters per line, 40 lines per page, automatic heading and column layout, and a complete ASCII character keyboard. Printers should have at least the following logs inherent in the system to be acceptable.

- Single group
- Card access control
- Print program
- All point
- Status summary
- Alarm summary

Additional assets to look for in system printer capability include automatic formats for all logs.

- Automatic formatting eliminates the requirement to sort through unnecessary information to find critical management data.
- A full English language capability provides optimum user interface with a minimum of programming effort.

- Management-oriented trend logs provide periodic reports for a wide variety of owner-selected points. The trend log recognizes and exhibits a trend before a given point becomes a problem.
- Instantaneous printouts can save precious seconds. With this capability, the system will recognize the log being requested after the first two or three letters of the log title have been typed into the system and immediately start the printing process. The faster a problem is recognized the sooner it can be remedied.
- User-customized print programs allow a status printout of selected groups of points. This type of printout is generally requested manually, but might be initiated automatically by an event. This type of feature permits a mixture of point types to be included in the print program. User-customized logs are handy for resolving unique building management problems.

The system printer is a valuable tool for facility management. The flexibility of the print programs permit maximum utilization of the total facility control system. The reliability of the system printer reflects the professionalism of management by providng routine and critical information in a timely and usable manner.

Specialized Building Management Equipment

Several major manufacturers of building control systems offer color CRTs to display pictorially a wide variety of building functions. These color CRTs, sometimes referred to as CCRTs, combine interactive graphic displays with normal command and data retrieval functions. This provides the system operator with maximum assistance in determining what the problem is and where it is located.

Graphic displays are generated to match the facility's requirements. Generally speaking, over twenty status and log values are continuously displayed at the proper location on each individual graphic. Every point on the display is updated each time the graphic is called up by the system operator. If an alarm occurs, the color will change on the graphic at the point in alarm and the individual point will flash to permit immediate recognition of the alarm or trouble point. There is also an audible alert signal associated with the graphic display when it goes into alarm.

Graphic displays representing remotely controlled and monitored building systems are designed for each specific application. When building heating, ventilating, and air-conditioning (HVAC) schematics are called up for display by the maintenance departments they can actually see changes take place in the graphic following fan or louver operational changes.

Building floor plans are automatically displayed on the CCRT, indicating not only the floor or zone in alarm, but also the device that has initiated the alarm. The initiating device, pull station, or smoke detector, undergoes a color change, the device flashes, and the change-of-status display area will provide written information for the operator.

- Custom-designed floor plans display the floor in alarm and the device which is indicating the fire or security problem.
- A dedicated change-of-status is associated with each graphic display. It provides written information concerning the identification of the alarm, point type, and appropriate engineering information.
- The time of the occurrence, day, and date are continuously displayed.
- Subsequent alarms, in addition to being buffered in the system if required, will override the display. As each alarm is acknowledged by the operator, the next alarm in time reporting sequence will be automatically displayed until the last alarm display has been exhibited.
- As each new alarm is displayed, an audible signal sounds until the **buffered alarm** has been acknowledged.

Grounds layout or a building floor plan display appears to indicate a point of intrusion. The device at the point of penetration goes into alarm and calls up the appropriate graphic. The device in alarm flashes and the change-of-status display area provides the written hardcopy information for the operator.

Overall effectiveness of a graphic display CCRT is limited only by the imagination of the management team operating the system. The larger the facility, the more valuable the CCRT can be in providing a maximum amount of information to the system operator in a minimum amount of time.

REMOTE CONTROL PANELS

A typical integrated building protection and control system has a series of **remote control panels (RCPs)** located throughout the facility. These RCPs act as a communications director for the receipt and transmission of data along the transmission bus. The RCP receives commands from the central processing unit (CPU), sorts the command, and sends the command along to the appropriate sensor or device for the required monitoring or control (Figure 15.2, p. 282).

Standard remote control panels range from only four points or zones to a high of about sixty-four. Some come only in clusters of sixteen points, but they will still perform the processing of data to and from the CPU and the host panel. Coupled with this function, individual sensors, points, or zones are monitored and controlled, depending on the specific function.

A basic remote control panel acquires, processes, and transfers data with the CPU. It also accepts, processes, and executes commands from the CPU. Finally the basic RCP records and evaluates the reported change-of-state and

Remote Control Panels

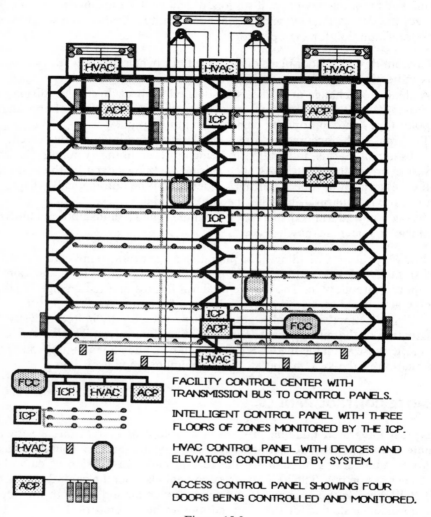

FACILITY CONTROL CENTER WITH
TRANSMISSION BUS TO CONTROL PANELS.

INTELLIGENT CONTROL PANEL WITH THREE
FLOORS OF ZONES MONITORED BY THE ICP.

HVAC CONTROL PANEL WITH DEVICES AND
ELEVATORS CONTROLLED BY SYSTEM.

ACCESS CONTROL PANEL SHOWING FOUR
DOORS BEING CONTROLLED AND MONITORED.

Figure 15.2

values which occur among the digital (binary) or analog (value) points monitored and controlled by the RCP.

More advanced RCPs can also function as a stand-alone distributed processor and programmable controller. In this configuration the RCP can perform
all the basic functions in addition to the following. It can locally generate and
execute commands covering energy management and building operational func-

tions. It can perform local mathematical calculations for the panel itself and evaluate conditions and automatically take appropriate action.

Should the transmission bus between the CPU and RCP be interrupted, this semiintelligent panel continues to execute energy management functions under its jurisdiction and to control the HVAC equipment without interruption. In some cases the RCP continues to monitor certain change-of-state and value information and even retains the most recent readings.

More sophisticated **intelligent control panels (ICP)** provide all these functions and a precise real-time clock, battery backup of the local memory and the real-time clock, high-speed transmission bus capability, and a man-machine interface port for localized operation. In some cases the man-machine interface port might also serve as backup communications with the CPU.

These RCPs house the necessary multiplexing circuitry, analog-digital converters, and termination modules to accomplish the required tasks. With the exception of ICPs, each RCP can generally be fitted with an additional board or card to accomplish the transmission bus extender or telephone modem interface function.

Fire and Security Control Panels

An RCP dedicated to fire detection and alarm will have different names depending upon the manufacturer. The important criteria for a fire panel is that it must have been designed and listed by **Underwriters Laboratories (UL)** and approved by **Factory Mutual (FM)** specifically for fire applications. Where an entire system has been assembled to perform the fire detection and alarm function, that system must, in its entirety, be listed by UL for that specific purpose. Failure to install a UL- or FM-listed fire system may not only result in failure of the system to perform as expected, but also may negate building insurance.

The standard (UL-listed and FM-approved) fire control panel (FCP) will incorporate the necessary fire detection and alarm disciplines. The fire detection and alarm functions of the panel work in conjunction with the HVAC equipment in the panel's area of the facility. The fire panel, through zone monitoring via supervised wiring, provides fire detection and alarm, suppression system activation, HVAC and smoke door control, fire management capability, and property protection. These fire panels are more specialized than remote control panels. In addition to being tested by UL and FM, these fire panels are electronically supervised to ensure a constant state of readiness. They are generally multizone, solid-state, low-voltage panels designed specifically for the purpose of performing the monitoring and control function of fire detection and alarm.

More advanced fire control panels (FCP) are designed to accommodate a variety of specific functional requirements and, as such, can be tailored to individual facility requirements. This advanced FCP is designed to house functional modules to cover the requirements of a facility. These advanced panels are also capable of managing various security functions, as well as those of fire.

Standard modules are available for these panels to meet multiple-zone fire annunciation, security system monitoring and control, **high-security** sensor monitoring, and intercom. The panel also covers necessary coded or noncoded signaling and accessory relay functions, and provides for standby battery operation. The wiring of all **initiating** and **indicating** circuits is electrically supervised for opens, shorts, and grounds. Any trouble on the security circuits will be reported as a security alarm, as there is no such thing as trouble on a security circuit.

There is usually a logic control module for each of these advanced fire control panels that provides the power interface between the central processing unit and the panel. This is the module that generally contains the power supply for the panel and controls the battery charger. Also located in the logic board are provisions for ground fault detection for the panel and **light-emitting diodes** (LED) for panel diagnostic troubleshooting.

Fire and security modules normally come in blocks of four or eight zones that are supervised by internal electronics. They can be independently designated to monitor normally open (N.O.) fire devices and normally open or normally closed (N.C.) contact devices such as manual pull stations, waterflow switches, and intrusion alarms. Accessory relays should be available for each zone to trigger such desired actions as closing smoke doors or activating beacons.

The high-security module is a highly specialized item required only for government work and the protection of sensitive proprietary information and material. This module supervises high-security circuits by sending a pseudo-random digital word to a high-security transponder at the protected point. The high-security transponder processes that word and sends back a masked response to the high-security module. If the returned word is not processed correctly or does not return due to a cross or a break in the line, an alarm is generated.

If for no other reason than ease of system checkout, an intercom module should be included in the original system design. This device will interface with the system intercom trunk line, permitting audio communications with all other intercom stations. This module is usually supplied with a simple push-to-talk activating switch.

Important emergency capabilities to look for in any fire management system include variable tone signaling, public address, and two-way communication with firefighters and with the various floors throughout the building. Automatic features should include fire department notification, recall of elevators, prerecorded tape notification to the zone in alarm and surrounding areas, and buffering of alarms within the system.

Fire command stations provide both emergency public address capabilities and a private firefighters' phone-in system. Not to be overlooked in such a system is the ability to override the associated building HVAC systems to assist, change, and redirect these systems to reduce casualties and property damage.

Another highly desirable feature is the automatic recording of all transactions carried out during the period of an emergency. This should extend beyond printouts of the system's activity to include all voice, radio, telephone, and intercom transmissions. Where closed circuit television (CCTV) cameras provide a view of the ongoing emergency, the building's integrated control system should also capture the CCTV system and automatically record the acitivty.

Although these functions may seem exotic, they merely use all the system's capabilities to record an incident. The information derived may not only prevent a reoccurrence, but also preclude costly litigation.

EXISTING SYSTEMS INTEGRATION

Most existing facilities have a fire detection and alarm system of some sort. If it is an effective system, chances are that it can readily be assimilated into the integrated control system. This is also generally true with existing **proprietary** security systems, but professional consultation is recommended before any major outlay of funds takes place. There are a number of situations where security systems need to be tied in with other functions in order to be responsive to a disaster (Figure 15.3, p. 286).

Whether or not a building presently has a patrol tour system, it is an extremely important function. The patrolling officer provides protection visibility to the staff and provides immediate directions and information to occupants. These individuals also serve as mobile eyes and ears for building management, reporting on potential hazardous situations or items that impinge on safety. Patrol tour management can become an integral part of the facility control system. Through system integration the patrolling officer is constantly in touch with the FCC. As the officer progresses through the tour, reportable situations can be forwarded and recorded in the FCC for immediate or future action. The integrated system makes automatic records of each patrol tour for management review and insurance company requirements. The officers have increased protection through monitoring by the FCC of their progress throughout the tour.

Access control systems, regardless of type, are valuable control mechanisms for any facility. Truly effective systems permit management to determine who goes where and when. As with other independent systems, access to areas must be controlled to prevent losses, accidents, and industrial espionage and to provide safety. However, in emergencies, controlled doors can become a liability. When access control is integrated into the overall building management, this shortcoming can be resolved. Certain doors connecting with the zone in alarm must open automatically to prevent panic. Other doors protecting proprietary information, high-value items, corporate records, and tape vaults should be designed to go to a **fail-secure** mode. This arrangement permits

Existing Systems Integration

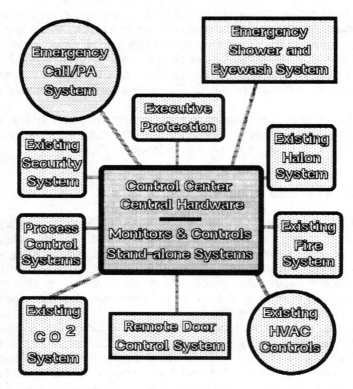

Figure 15.3

individuals inside the fail-secure areas to exit, while preventing firefighters or others from entering the area.

By having the access control system tied into or functioning as an integral part of the facility control system, specific areas may be easily monitored and controlled before, during, and after an emergency. Stand-alone access control systems are inadequate in emergencies if not effectively integrated into the overall system.

Existing building intercom systems should be made a part of any integrated facility control system. In an emergency all types of notification systems might be required. It is important to understand that any alarm or emergency notification system must be electrically supervised to ensure continuous operation. Music systems are seldom considered for this type of warning system.

Annunciators

Remote annunciators are generally an appendix to the system. This means that they need not be supervised. If the annunciator fails to function, it will not affect the primary operation or functioning of the alarm system. Annunciators come in the form of light display panels where pilot lights or LEDs (light-emitting diodes) indicate the normal or alarm status of a particular point.

Custom annunciators illustrating the grounds or a floor plan may be most useful to the operator in quickly grasping an alarm's point of origin. A relay or an input from the CPU would indicate the point of intrusion by illuminating a point. A fire zone in alarm might be illustrated by use of back lighting of the entire area. Manufacturers have a wide variety of standard annunciators to choose from, or a qualified in-house crew may elect to make their own custom annunciator. Annunciators are not a required part of an integrated system, but they ease alarm identification at a time when seconds count.

Projection screen annunciators are available which will pull up a 35 mm slide on a rear projection device. This is usually activated manually to preserve bulb life, but it will provide the user with a file of at least 80 custom-made slides for immediate review. These systems have been bypassed by technology, but should not be cast aside because they may still be useful.

Maintenance personnel can store a wealth of graphic knowledge on fan systems and air handling units for troubleshooting and training. The major drawback of the 35 mm projection annunciator module is not the technique itself, but the fact that the slides depicting the systems become dated. If the user keeps the slides current with the upgrading of each system, this is an effective approach to HVAC troubleshooting.

FACILITY CONTROL SYSTEM HARDWARE

The development of a building operations center requires considerable planning by an informed group of management personnel. Decisions must be made concerning who is responsible for each of the building systems and how each of these functions will be met through the implementation of a facility control system.

FCC hardware is the key to energy efficiency and effectiveness of operating personnel. The central hardware for the system provides the primary man-machine interface point from which access to the system is made. The brain and heart of the system is a minicomputer designed and programmed to perform the complete building management function. The interactive operator terminal featuring English language messages and a self-prompting system penetration procedure is located here.

The man-machine interface takes place through a CRT terminal and keyboard that provides access to the system. The system printer provides hardcopy data automatically and manually upon request. A color CRT, annunciator, or graphic annunciator should be available to assist the system operator.

The system transmission bus reaches out from the control center to the remote panels. This data link connects all the remote control panels on the system either directly, over leased telephone lines at rates up to 9600 **Baud**, or via microwave transmission systems.

System hardware is really more sophisticated than described here, but this simplified explanation is not intended to be highly detailed. However, all this system hardware is completely useless without well-**documented system software** which contains **executive software** that tells the **operating system** software what to do and **data file software** that will allow the facility control system to meet specific building requirements.

Before selecting a system, it is essential to determine the future availability of system growth, replacement parts, and prices. When checking into that future availability, one must be sure that a firm price is determined well in advance of purchase. Even if the exact equipment is not available, the purchaser would be wise to ensure that compatible equipment at a reasonable price will be available for at least seven to ten years following acceptance. There is nothing magic about the time period of seven to ten years because any sophisticated system, no matter how exotic, should pay for itself in tangible dollars in less than five years.

Determination of the payback period is difficult. A straight energy management system will show a "dollar" payback more quickly than a system that also includes fire management, security protection, access control, patrol tour, closed circuit television, and manufacturing process monitoring. Savings derived from these latter systems are not only intangible, but also difficult to identify. How can a price be put on a proprietary secret that wasn't stolen because of good security or the parking structure rape that didn't happen because of proper surveillance?

When determining the availability of replacement equipment, some rationale must be given to the expected useful life of each piece of equipment and its future availability. Some manufacturers will provide spares with the original purchase; others will guarantee stocks of certain equipment through a given date at a set price; and still others will offer no future guarantee at all. Caveat emptor!

16

System Software

System software is the minimum amount of programming software that is necessary to make the system hardware perform its most basic assigned functions. The true heart of any facility control system is the software. System software and the associated hardware are the foundation of building control systems. Regardless of the computer system, the software is the set of instructions that tells the hardware what to do. Systems software should be the simplest to use, the most versatile, yet the most cost-effective way of controlling the facility in order to manage the buildings. No matter how sophisticated the systems hardware might be, the system will fail without good software. It is software which drives the energy and facility management programs that provide the actions and services being sought for optimum building operational efficiency. Attention to the following information will provide the background which facility managers need in order to approach the subject of system software intelligently.

System software will be assigned to scan all the assigned points on the system. It will perform analog-to-digital conversions for sensor-derived information. It will perform localized fault detection, provide the necessary signaling and, where possible, take corrective action. It will schedule other software, handle messages received and transmitted from the operator's terminal, and process all alarm and trouble signals reported on the system. This is only a partial list of software functions. However, without the software to interpret the hardware responses, any system is worthless.

SOFTWARE CATEGORIES

The importance of software documentation can probably best be understood if one becomes aware that even in a small-scale security system, well over 100,000 instructions would be required for it to provide all its functions. These instructions are written by programmers and, thus, this area is most prone to system error and omission.

Software for most systems falls into three categories:

- Operating systems software
- Utility software
- Applications software

The operating systems software is generally a standard set of programs which are available through the system manufacturer. While prone to some error, this is probably the most stable of the software groups. Programming errors here have the potential for being the most serious, for this is where the software interfaces with the hardware. As operating software does not generally report on its own shortcomings, this is also the most difficult area in which to track down a problem. If the vendor has modified an off-the-shelf computer operating system to perform different functions than that for which it was designed, the risk of system error is greatly increased.

Utility programs copy files for backup, catalog alarm, divide the gross input of information for log preparation, and perform other similar functions. They are standard programs assembled for control of a variety of different applications. Generally, utility programs have been subjected to extensive testing and, thus, will probably not develop major problems once the system is up and in use.

Applications software is written to support specific areas of the systems activity on the total facility control system. Unless the system is operational at a number of installations and the initial application software approach has been debugged, this type of software is most likely to develop errors and be prone to malfunctions. The meeting point for man and machine is in the applications software. For this reason it must be user friendly to permit ease of operator training. The quality of the application software is critical when one chooses to upgrade the system or when a special requirement calls for some slight customizing.

Without doubt, the best way to evaluate software is to talk to actual users and to see a system in action. Seeing the system functioning in the real world enhances credibility. A thorough check of the system's functionality, documentation, and manufacturer support in the areas of service, training, and parts availability can be a convincing demonstration that a quality system will function in the way it is intended. Failure to follow this step could result in purchasing an expensive piece of worthless equipment.

SYSTEM FUNCTIONALITY AND COMPATIBILITY

Before functionality can be determined, the owner/operator of the system will need to describe the performance requirements for a system. One of the best ways to determine these requirements is to study the flow of information that will move within the system and to describe what is to finally happen to this information.

Functional requirements must be identified for each situation if the system is to be reasonably evaluated. These functional requirements must be spelled out as accurately as possible to preclude any possible question or margin for error. By finitely describing each function in detail, the evaluation of the system will be much more accurate. Some systems may offer more in the way of additional functions than the basic requirements, but this should not have any bearing on a decision to purchase. Of prime importance is how well the system meets the owner/operator's present and future functional requirements. These functional requirements should be completely described in the **performance specification**.

Even if the facility control system is being considered for a new structure, its compatibility with other equipment also being considered or its ability to interface with equipment in allied facilities should be taken into account. The compatibility and functional interface with other stand-alone or manufacturing process equipment must be considered.

In the overall design of the systems, compatibility with fire, security, closed circuit television, access control, lighting control, energy management, and specialized add-on systems is essential. The basic control system must have the initial and future compatibility to interface with these and other systems if it is not to become antiquated too early. It is extremely important that the issue of system compatibility be settled before any final decision is made on the facility control system.

SOFTWARE DOCUMENTATION

One of the most important considerations for any computerized system is the availability of software documentation. Good system design will require that the user's requirements are documented before the programs are written. This is where all of the system interrelationships are identified and system interfaces are standardized.

It would be foolhardy to deal with a vendor who will write a system for your exclusive facility. That is as bad as having a system designed where "no one else will have a system like this." That is undoubtedly the worst of all situations. Who is going to provide the service, parts, and software upgrading? This type of arrangement is also prone to errors. It also defeats cost-effectiveness, as such custom systems will not have the Underwriters Laboratories (UL) and Factory Mutual (FM) listings that will permit significant insurance premium reductions.

When it comes to system compatibility documentation, all functions that the system is to perform should have some sort of user-oriented documentation that describes its function and operation. This documentation should be readily understandable by a nontechnician with a high school education. Some of the more complicated documentation covering energy management calculations may require some advanced math, but will still be written in an understandable style.

The documentation could include a listing of all system error messages where each is followed by a straightforward step-by-step explanation of the corrective procedures to follow. Remember, system documentation need not be voluminous to be good. As a matter of fact, the simpler the better, so long as the documentation can lead the individual through the procedures in an understandable manner.

Some systems will even include on-line documentation in a menu format to assist the operator. In this instance, the operator would merely request assistance from the system to work through a problem. This usually provides the operator with a series of yes or no questions that work toward the solution of the problem.

AUTOMATIC SOFTWARE UPGRADE

Future availability of parts, equipment, training, and maintenance are extremely important to the success of the system, but none more so than in the realm of software upgrade. A qualified vendor must be ready and willing to provide upgraded software material for their systems.

The manufacturer who offers a full line of equipment and service will probably automatically upgrade their software each time they service a major system. It is beneficial for the owner/operator and also a positive factor for the servicing technician who may be relatively new to the business. In this case, the new system technician might have been trained only on the latest version of the software. The first thing this technician might do upon arrival at the work site is to upgrade the existing system to the most current version with which he or she is thoroughly familiar. This reduces the technicians' time on the job, freeing them for other work. It also cuts system downtime and service call expense for the owner. This automatic upgrade of the system software should be investigated before selecting a system. It is an excellent bargaining chip that the manufacturer should be more than willing to provide.

17

System Supply and Service

Selection of a vendor or manufacturer for a facility control system is critical to successful implementation. There are several major manufacturers of building control systems. They have many years of experience in building control systems and devote a considerable amount of their resources to developing new and improved versions.

These major manufacturers have also gone to the trouble and expense of having their systems tested by **Underwriters Laboratories (UL)** and, where required, **Factory Mutual (FM)** or other similar testing services. Intermediate-sized manufacturers also go through this procedure. Regardless of the manufacturer, the owner should clearly specify full UL listing or similar testing verification in the **performance specification**, and the **Owner's Authorized Representative (OAR)** must verify the testing of all required pieces of equipment prior to accepting each item.

SYSTEM SUPPORT AND SERVICE

Support

System support is not nearly as involved as central control, but it is certainly equally important to the ultimate success of the facility control system. The initial supply of certain spare parts for specific pieces of equipment can and should be a part of the initial contract, but what about next year, or three years, or six years from the time the system guarantee expires?

Responsible planners will know not only where to obtain replacement parts in the years to come but also what the approximate price of each item will be. It is important to know the cost, when the last of a series production will be completed, and how to go about procuring standard equipment from the manufacturer. It is not unheard of for a manufacturer/supplier to guarantee future stocks at a predetermined price through a given date just to receive the initial contract.

If these precautions are not written into the basic contract, owners can find themselves being gouged financially to acquire future spare pieces of equipment and additional software. A supplier of quality hardware and software will not only make these arrangements at the outset of a project, but will also provide a system software update during routine maintenance programs, if properly contracted for from the start. Solid planning and attention to system support will be time well spent. It is not expensive initially, but can be extremely costly later. Failure to attend to this generally overlooked area can result in early obsolescence.

Service

With any quality facility control system, the initial contract generally specifies a minimum time period under which all equipment will be under guarantee. Also during this time frame, service will be provided by the system manufacturer/supplier with the stipulation that such service be performed during normal business hours. For a nominal fee, additional work of an emergency nature can generally be had on four to eight hours notice.

Careful attention should be taken to this aspect of any facility control system contract. It must be remembered that manufacturers are in business to make a profit, and "let the buyer beware" still holds force in the marketplace. Even so, facility management and control systems are well worth their cost if owners and operators do their homework.

A service contract that will continue after the guarantee period for a given number of years can be part of the initial bidding contract. Such a service contract can include replacement or upgrading of equipment and software. This contract may become an automatic follow-on to the initial service guarantee or may be at the owner's option to activate.

Depending on the facility operator's situation, the best of all worlds would be to have their own personnel trained to maintain the full system. This would include both on-site and factory training. Such advanced training may also be a part of the initial bidding document and warrants serious consideration from the start. In-house personnel factory trained to maintain and troubleshoot the system can greatly reduce maintenance costs and expenses for future additions.

Regardless of how well trained, the owner's maintenance personnel will still require assistance from the supplier's technicians from time to time for high-level system changes. This assistance may be had at a reasonable cost, which is far less than the price of repeated outside service calls, should in-house personnel not be factory trained. Assistance must also be sought when contemplating innovative system expansion. When this is done in conjunction with knowledgeable individuals, system costs may be kept to a minimum.

MANUFACTURER'S RECORD

Regardless of the size of the manufacturer, the number of systems installed and operational will generally speak for itself. When the bidding **short-list** has been developed, the owner should not hesitate to request that each short-listed bidder show them a similar installation. There is nothing quite like talking to a satisfied user.

The manufacturer who has a thousand systems in operation will have a stronger base to operate from than one who has only installed ten. The experience factor alone of installing a large number of systems would indicate more than just a passing interest in systems design. Ask for names, addresses, and telephone numbers of individuals you can speak to at selected installations.

INSTALLATION EXPERIENCE

Do not confuse a large number of systems installed with installation experience. Some manufacturers prefer to simply sell their systems and then move on, leaving the actual installation to a local electrician.

The manufacturer who installs, or supervises installation, will offer far better service and the end product will operate with far more reliability. Nothing can replace the care and speed a trained technician can bring in making a satisfactory installation.

PARTS STOCKPILE

Like anything with moving parts, things will go wrong with any control system, no matter how precisely documented and installed. The availability of spare parts is essential. Some spares might be purchased in conjunction with the original installation, but it is also wise to ensure the availability of spare parts for several years into the future.

Look for a vendor who has regional stockpiles of a broad selection of spares. This capability will generally provide twenty-four- to forty-eight-hour service, if required, and possibly even a loaner should a piece of equipment need repairing.

FUTURE PARTS AVAILABILITY GUARANTEE

Be assured, in writing, at the time of contract signing, that a given list of spares will be available at a predetermined price five to seven years beyond the final installation acceptance. This will ensure an operational system well beyond its assumed payback date. Most manufacturers will be happy to set aside a small portion of their present production to fulfill such a requirement if it clinches the sale.

The availability of parts will ensure long-term system operation. Failure to look to the future in this area could cause serious problems. No systems purchase should be entered into unless there is some guarantee of long-term availability of spare parts.

FORMAL TRAINING AVAILABILITY

When looking for a quality facility control system, formal training of in-house personnel is essential. This training may take place at the manufacturer's facility or, if the size of the student group warrants, at the owner's facility on the newly installed equipment. Regardless of where the training occurs, it should be for a specified number of hours and cover training of both operator and maintenance support personnel.

In-house training should be provided in at least three major areas: operator, maintenance, and management. These should be separate training sessions and should include enough hours to provide a thorough understanding of operating, maintaining, and managing the system.

Operator training should include all possible types of signals, trouble, alarm, and condition. Operators need hands-on time prior to being turned loose on the system. They need the confidence that such training can provide to understand what they can and cannot do with the system. For very sophisticated systems incorporating multiple stand-alone systems, the operators need to understand how each subsystem works.

Following training, the individual operators should be continually tested to see how they manage a myriad of situations. This testing should continue as unusual situations present themselves until all operators have been tested against every possible type of emergency situation. This testing sequence might also be used as a measuring device for promotions.

Maintenance personnel need on-site training on their own in-house system and a select few, depending upon the size of the system, should probably attend factory training sessions, which cover all aspects of the purchased system. The owner's maintenance staff should make a point of becoming friends with the manufacturer's technicians. In a great many cases a simple phone call may replace a costly service visit.

Once the in-house maintenance personnel are fully trained, they should be capable of servicing 95 percent of any service problems. This is where a system becomes truly worthwhile. High efficiency and low maintenance costs add to the overall cost effectiveness of a system.

The training program cannot be complete unless key supervisory and management personnel have been specially trained to make changes in the system over and beyond the capabilities of the operators and maintenance personnel. This aspect of key personnel training will truly give management control over their system. They will be able to make high-level changes in their own areas, protection, maintenance, and access control, without calling in the manufacturer's representative for assistance.

The manufacturer should be able to supply self-study training manuals and visual aids for owner training of their own personnel. This need not be an elaborate program, but should be adequate for the indoctrination of new employees who will operate and maintain the system.

SYSTEM GUARANTEE

The system guarantee will usually be for a year, but once a short list has been established, that guarantee can usually be pushed to two years. There will be exceptions to the blanket guarantee for items like chip boards and television camera tubes, but even they will have acceptable, but shorter guarantees. System guarantees should be read very carefully prior to the signing of any system purchase contract.

SYSTEM SERVICE CAPABILITY

No matter how simple the system and how effective the training of the in-house personnel, the time will come when the manufacturer's technical service staff will need to be called to assist in some portion of the systems functioning. This is where the size, training, and location of this technical staff becomes important.

Some manufacturers have "flying teams" that respond directly from the factory to service system problems. Others have a broad-based local service organization of factory-trained employees who supervise installation of systems and make service calls, when required, in their local area. Still other manufacturers provide training, some factory and some not, to electrical contractors and electricians and use them as service personnel.

It will pay to take a close look at each of the short-listed manufacturer's service arrangements. Depending upon each owner/operator capability in servicing the system, a hard decision may be necessary concerning this single aspect of system service.

AUTOMATIC SYSTEM UPGRADE

Asking the manufacturer to provide an automatic upgrade of the systems software is not as involved as it sounds. The manufacturer's technician upgrades the systems software on an as-available basis. All major manufacturers engaged in developing and selling building management systems are constantly involved in an effort to improve their software. As these new **software revisions** become available, most manufacturers will be glad to provide major system owners with this update. These software revisions are a double-edged sword. It pleases the system owner that the vendor is providing this service, generally on a

System Support

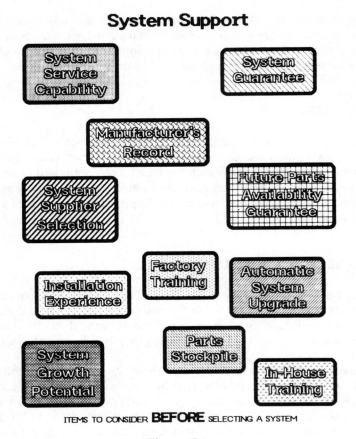

ITEMS TO CONSIDER **BEFORE** SELECTING A SYSTEM

Figure 17.1

routine service arrangement, and it provides the owner with an opportunity to ask technical questions of a knowledgeable factory-trained representative. This upgrading may or may not carry a fee, but regardless, it will improve overall system operation.

The manufacturer also benefits by supplying this automatic software revision upgrade. When done on a timely basis by the vendor, all their service personnel are trained and up to date on the systems capabilities. Younger technicians are not faced with a software package antiquated by the passage of a couple of years and several intervening updates. In addition to being a goodwill gesture, this meeting also provides the manufacturer with an opportunity for sales promotion along with the service visit.

SYSTEM GROWTH POTENTIAL

Failure to investigate the growth potential of each system under consideration could be unnecessarily expensive. Today's technological explosion can antiquate some systems almost before the guarantee has expired. A positive statement, in writing, from a potential vendor will go a long way in keeping the owner from being stuck with an old technology.

No manufacturer can supply technological capabilities that have yet to be developed. However, if the manufacturer has developed modular hardware and software, this modular scheme can be carried out during future development. The physical appearance and size of hardware may differ, but this is immaterial if the connection points are compatible.

Software may be developed in the future which will improve the overall operation of the basic system. This, too, must be compatible with the existing **operating system (OS)** software. Careful examination of the **technical proposal** must be made to assure that this future software growth will be available and compatible with the system under consideration.

To make vendors realize that future system growth is an important item, the owner should spell out specific growth requirements in the initial **performance specification**. Of course, the system's potential growth is only one of several aspects in developing total facility control, but it must be considered if the system is not to become a dinosaur and extinct before its time (Figure 17.1).

18

Integrated System Design and Total Facility Control

The owner/operator will have to live with the building control system that is selected. Early attention to detail will go a long way toward reducing operational expenses through the years to come. A careful and complete facility control design approach is necessary. A thorough physical survey of the facility to be controlled must be made by competent individuals who have a broad understanding of internal problem areas, as well as specific knowledge of commercially available standard equipment. Parallel to the physical survey of the facility, a financial feasibility study must be conducted. This financial survey will have a strong bearing on what can and cannot be done to protect and control the facilities concerned. Assuming that there are limited funds, a system of prioritizing all facility requirements should be developed. This will help ensure that all departments are consulted and that their individual requirements are considered (Figure 18.1, p. 302).

The organization of a planning team, dedicated to effective building systems management, is essential. This team should be knowledgeable in all aspects of building systems, their capabilities, interaction, effectiveness, cost, operation, and future growth potential. System planners must understand the full spectrum of operational requirements. They also need to understand the use of modular equipment in meeting building control demands.

Following broad direction and decisions handed down by planners, a design team should set about to develop a scheme that will meet the building control and protection requirements defined and listed by the planning team. The design team also has a responsibility for meeting time and budgetary requirements, while still providing an effective and efficient facility protection and control system. Designers need to address the immediate and mandatory functions that must be implemented to provide occupant protection and comfort, while still conforming with national and local building codes and standards. Where applicable, standardized testing requirements must be met for specific items of equipment before they can be installed or operated. Secondary options are an essential part of the design team's responsibilities. The design team needs to investigate all secondary options to determine which might be important

Integrated Facility Control

System Architecture

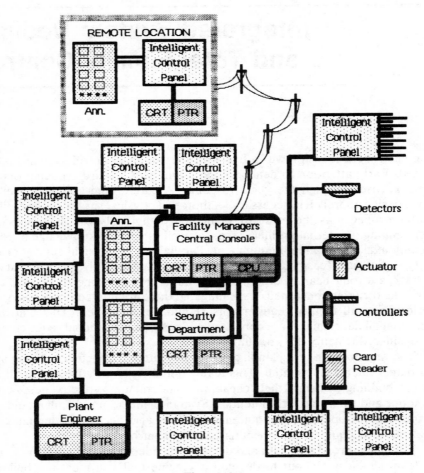

Figure 18.1

additions to the system at minimal additional expense. Options not meeting this criteria should be prioritized for consideration as funds become available. A definitive look should also be taken at lower priority items on the planner's list. Determinations should be made and the most appropriate course of action defined for each, depending upon the system's capabilities and the availability of funds.

Working in conjunction with the original planning team, the design team should also investigate the capability for the system to grow in the future to meet corporate expansion. There are many pitfalls, some obvious and some not so apparent, that present themselves when trying to conceive, develop, design, select, install, accept, and operate building management systems.

Drafting a **performance specification** that spells out in detail exactly how the system should function after all vendors and trade personnel have left the premises is essential. This type of specification describes the end product which the owner desires and, unlike a **proprietary specification**, does not lock out deserving potential bidders. The performance specification permits the owner to say what is desired without telling the vendors how to do it. It also provides an end product with much greater definition than accepting a proprietary manufacturer's definition in attempting to settle a disagreement.

In-house personnel understand operational requirements better than any outsider. Manufacturer's representatives understand their product's capabilities, but generally lack knowledge of problem areas for a specific owner. It is essential that the owner not lose control of the design portion of the project. Independent outside professional assistance may well be the key to success in this area. Great care must be taken in selecting specialists. These specialists should not be in the employ of any manufacturer or have any vested interest in the project other than that of providing expertise to the owner.

The **authority having jurisdiction** may be an office, organization, or individual that is granted this authority by local ordinance or law. In most communities the authority having jurisdiction is the local building inspection agency or the fire department. Sometimes, usually in industrial areas, more than one agency is the authority having jurisdiction and they preside over various aspects of a project. In other cases the insurance underwriter may be the ipso facto authority having jurisdiction if they are to be the company insuring the facility against loss.

This *authority* is essential to the development of a successful facility control system. It is responsible for approving the equipment, an installation, or a procedure, and its approval must be given before any final commitment to purchase or build.

Standardized testing requirements must be met for specific items of equipment before they can be installed or operated. The authority having jurisdiction must be consulted and that *authority* must approve in writing all safety and construction plans prior to installation or construction. The advice and recommendations of an expert will speed the development of a successful project. Directing the general contractor to use only UL or FM approved equipment or systems will facilitate a positive response from the authority having jurisdiction when various system reviews occur.

Just as with codes and standards, the authority having jurisdiction defines the minimum standards, requirements, or procedures for a specific facility. There is nothing to preclude prudent owners from exceeding these minimum requirements in their quest for an even safer work place.

The Owner's Authorized Representative, or OAR, should be a member of the project from the start. This individual has ultimate responsibility for monitoring the installation and final system acceptance. The OAR must not only understand the full range of the owner's requirements and desires as defined in the performance specification, but also must go through the punch list with the installing authorities and officially accept each segment of the overall system as it becomes available for use. To obtain the full range of expertise and authority, the owner may decide to have the OAR be a team of two individuals who will work in close conjunction with each other. The system expertise may have to come from an outside professional consultant, while the ultimate authority would come from a key member of the owner's staff. The owner might even consider having the ultimate facility manager as the staff member of the OAR team. This approach does several things for the owner. It permits tight inside control over acceptance of an expensive capital expenditure, ensures technical professional assistance, and provides valuable firsthand experience to the facility manager.

Careful attention to the development of requirements and specifications for the system will ensure standard system hardware and well-documented software. This is essential to maximize in-house maintenance, provide minimum downtime through modular repair, and ensure availability of spare parts and upgrading of software and long-term supplier support.

There is no question that effective control of facilities is essential for efficient operation and protection of occupants. The refinements available through standard equipment will provide tangible figures concerning the payback of the capital expenditure. Savings derived from protection techniques may not be as evident, but might in fact exceed those savings derived from the control of energy consumption and efficiency of other allied systems.

Total facility control, as described in this text, provides a safer and more efficient work place. Control system growth can readily match corporate expansion for years to come with proper planning, design, and development. Understanding the benefits of initial capital expenditure for a truly efficient facility control system and how that expenditure relates to long-term operational savings will go a long way toward instituting effective total facility control (Figures 18.2–18.5, pp. 305–308).

TOTAL FACILITY CONTROL AND THE DREAM SYSTEM

Management, at all levels, has the responsibility for running an efficient, safe, and secure facility cost-effectively. Far too many facilities are built and operated with no master plan or one where the systems are fragmented. The material presented in this book is designed to be educational and to serve as a guide.

No two facilities have the same requirements; therefore a wide range of

Integrated System Design

System Growth

First Year	Third Year	Future
Facility Control Console/CPU	Color CRT Terminal	Operating System Save
Start/Stop Programs	Chiller Optimization	Off-Line Memory Access
Reports & Logs	Load Reset	Enthalpy Control
Event Initiateg Programs	Data File Logs	Memory Diagnostics
Command Language Interpreter	Peripherals Exerciser	Perimeter Security
Optimum Start/Stop	Operating System Verify	Pump Control
Access Control	Closed Circuit TV	Remote Building Control
Duty Cycling	Compartmentalized Areas	
Power Demand Control	Equipment Monitoring	
Patrol Tour		
Building Perimeter Security		

Figure 18.2

Integrated System Design
Far Remote Locations

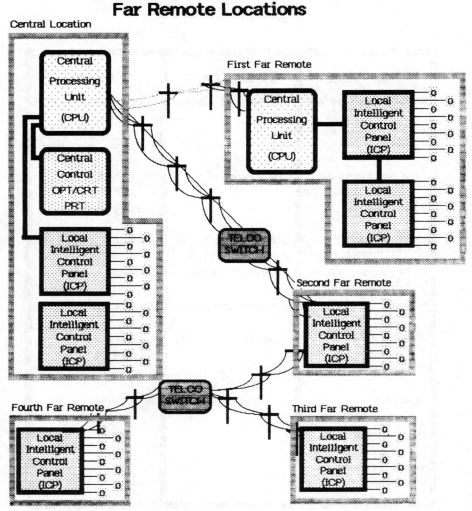

Figure 18.3

Integrated System Design

Far Distant Locations

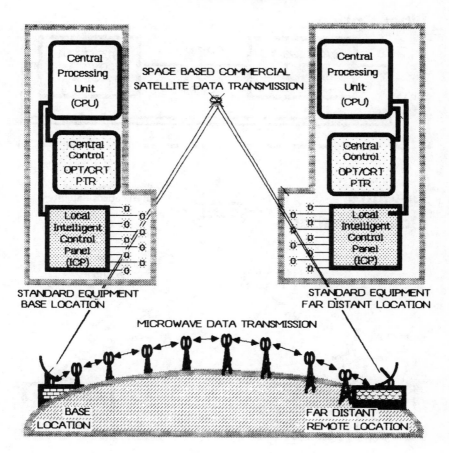

Figure 18.4

Integrated System Design

Special Data Transmission Options

Fiber Optics

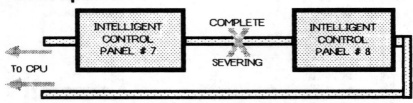

Satellite Communications

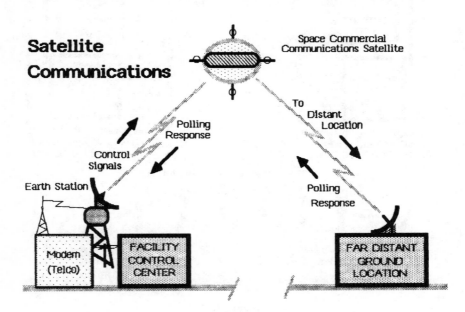

Figure 18.5

options has been outlined. With this information as a starting point, it is possible to develop and implement a facility control system which will meet the needs that have been established for any particular facility. As additional operational requirements are recognized, a well-designed system can be expanded to meet those needs. Whether an institution begins with the most basic system possible or initially opts for the ideal solution, the material presented here can guide those involved in planning and designing to make informed, prudent, and wise decisions.

Total Facility Control is using today's technology to meet the challenges for tomorrow's building control requirements. The challenge to excellence in facility design is here now. Responding to this demand for excellence by using **Total Facility Control** may be one of the wisest decisions you will make.

Appendix A

Integrated System Evaluation Checklist

Area Being Rated Prime Vendors	A	B	C	D
EQUIPMENT FEATURES				
Microcomputer, CRT and printer manufactured and serviced by system supplier.				
Distributed microcomputer architecture.				
Central and remote system powering for intelligent control panels, smoke detectors and indicating devices.				
Smoke detectors powered over alarm circuits.				
Modular system, expandable to 1,000 points.				
Remote operator terminal option.				
Remote printer option				
Intelligent control panels (ICP) battery backup				
Local annunciation (ANN) from ICP				
ICP are similar, simplifying service				
Fire & security points mixed in ICP				
System Alarm Log				
System Fault Log for troubleshooting				
Total this page				
Total preceding page(s)				
Total – Low Score indicates best vendor				

YES = 1,   QUALIFIED YES = 2,   NO = 4

Integrated System Evaluation Checklist

Area Being Rated / Prime vendors	A	B	C	D
MAN-MACHINE INTERFACE				
English language alarms				
English language reporting				
English language emergency instructions				
Standard typewriter keyboard				
Identified function buttons				
Self instructing menus				
Self instructing menus for locations				
Self instructing menus for requests				
Self instructing menus for commands				
All index points addresses in English language				
Special CRT area for alarms				
Separate CRT area for data retrival				
Rapid point addressing numerically				
Associated monitor & control point addresses				
Total this page				
Total preceding page(s)				
Total – Low Score indicated Best vendor				

YES = 1,   QUALIFIED YES = 2,   NO = 4

Integrated System Evaluation Checklist

Area Being Rated Prime Vendors	A	B	C	D
MAN-MACHINE INTERFACE				
Report output via printer				
Report output via CRT				
Black & White CRT graphics				
Four color CRT with graphics				
Eight color CRT with graphics				
Dynamic graphics on alarms				
Operator terminal segregation				
Printer segregation				
Rapid display of individual points				
Alarms prioritized on CRT				
Buffering of alarms				
Operator prompt of buffered alarms				
Hardcopy of alarms as detected				
No alarms are lost in system				
Total this page				
Total preceding page(s)				
Total – Low Score indicates best vendor				

YES = 1, QUALIFIED YES = 2, NO = 4

Integrated System Evaluation Checklist

Area Being Rated　　　　　　　Prime Vendors	A	B	C	D
MAN-MACHINE INTERFACE				
System reports available on demand				
System reports available by point				
All points log report				
All point log report by system				
Fire alarm summary				
Fire trouble summary				
Security alarm summary				
Maintenance alarm summary				
Maintenance trouble sumary				
System status summary reports				
Event command recording by program				
Manual command recording				
Printouts dated & pages numbered automatic				
Alarm printouts different and highlighted				
Total this page				
Total preceding page(s)				
Total – Low Score indicates best vendor				

YES = 1,　QUALIFIED YES = 2,　NO = 4

Integrated System Evaluation Checklist

Area Being Rated Prime Vendors	A	B	C	D
PROTECTION FEATURES				
Multiple transmission systems				
Bi-directional transmission bus				
Two wire fire initiating circuits (Class B)				
Three wire fire initiating circuits				
Four wire fire initiating circuits (Class A)				
Two wire system bus				
Three wire system bus				
Fiber-Optic system bus				
Security circuits meet UL Grade A Reqmts				
Automatic test/reset of ICP's w/printout				
Multiple level system access				
Program modification controlled access				
System access via secret codeword				
System access not via key				
Total this page				
Total preceding page(s)				
Total – Low Score indicates best vendor				

YES = 1,   QUALIFIED YES = 2,   NO = 4

Integrated System Evaluation Checklist

Area Being Rated Prime Vendors	A	B	C	D
PROTECTION FEATURES				
System Executive in non-volatile memory				
Operating System (OS) in non-volatile memory				
Data File in non-volatile memory				
Prioritized command structure				
Automatic fire evacuation signaling				
Fire signaling programmable by zone				
Automatic alarm-initiated commands				
Event-initiated programs (EIP)				
Multi-sensor EIP commands				
EIP command of multiple points				
Automatic Time-Initiated commands				
Automatic Time-Initiated holiday scheduling				
Central Console EIP commands				
Manual keyboard commands				
Total this page				
Total preceding page(s)				
Total – Low Score indicates best vendor				

YES = 1,   QUALIFIED YES = 2,   NO = 4

Integrated System Evaluation Checklist

Area Being Rated Prime Vendors	A	B	C	D
PROTECTION FEATURES				
Supervisor only point alteration				
Supervisor only EIP modification				
Supervisor only printout modification				
Supervisor only holiday schedule change				
Tamper alarms for console equipment				
Tamper alarms for all remote panels				
Cost-effective visual annunciation				
On-site non-volatile program modification				
System meets UL 864 (Fire-Protective Sys)				
System meets UL 1076 (Proprietary Burglar)				
System meets UL 294 (Access Control)				
System meets NFPA 72 D (Proprietary Fire)				
Automatic system switch to secondary power				
Autmatic restart w/primary power return				
Total this page				
Total preceding page(s)				
Total - Low Score indicates best vendor				

YES = 1,   QUALIFIED YES = 2,   NO = 4

Integrated System Evaluation Checklist

Area Being Rated Prime Vendors	A	B	C	D
EMERGY MANAGEMENT				
Energy Management System (EMS) Programs				
EMS duty cycling				
EMS chiller optimization				
EMS optimum start/stop				
EMS enthalpy control				
EMS load reset				
EMS zero energy period				
EMS power demand control				
EMS night cycle				
EMS night purge				
Total this page				
Total preceding page(s)				
Total – Low Score indicates best vendor				

YES - 1,   QUALIFIED YES - 2,   NO - 4

Integrated System Evaluation Checklist

Area Being Rated Prime Vendors	A	B	C	D
COMMAND & CONTROL				
Start/Stop programs				
Event-initiated programs				
Color graphics				
Change analog alarm limits				
Automatic device control				
Trend log modifications				
Temporary scheduler				
Extended service programs				
Run-time programs				
Automatic alarm enable/disable				
Operator assignment control				
Total this page				
Total preceding page(s)				
Total – Low Score indicates best vendor				

YES = 1,   QUALIFIED YES = 2,   NO = 4

Integrated System Evaluation Checklist

Area Being Rated Prime vendors	A	B	C	D
LOGS & REPORTS				
All point log				
Status summary log				
Single log group				
Trend log group				
Access control log				
Energy management logs				
Time-initiated logs				
Event-initiated logs				
Data file logs				
Total this page				
Total preceding page(s)				
Total – Low Score indicates best vendor				

YES = 1,   QUALIFIED YES = 2,   NO = 4

Integrated System Evaluation Checklist

Area Being Rated — Prime Vendors	A	B	C	D
SECURITY REPORTING				
Patrol tour management				
Access control and monitoring				
Closed Circuit Television (CCTV) monitoring				
Security and CCTV interaction				
Security and fire system interaction				
Total this page				
Total preceding page(s)				
Total – Low Score indicates best vendor				

YES = 1,   QUALIFIED YES = 2,   NO = 4

Integrated System Evaluation Checklist

Area Being Rated Prime Vendors	A	B	C	D
ENVIRONMENTAL CONTROL				
Air flow measurement				
Analog variable control				
Boiler control				
Electrical energy control				
Chiller control				
Energy reporting				
Equipment monitoring				
Solar control				
Total this page				
Total preceding page(s)				
Total – Low Score indicates best vendor				

YES = 1,   QUALIFIED YES = 2,   NO = 4

Integrated System Evaluation Checklist

Area Being Rated Prime Vendors	A	B	C	D
SPECIAL REQUIREMENTS				
Dynamic color graphics				
Modular equipment				
Five-year equipment availability guarantee				
Ten-year modular replacement guarantee				
Ten-year modular compatability guarantee				
Total this page				
Total preceding page(s)				
Total – Low Score indicates best vendor				

YES - 1,   QUALIFIED YES - 2,   NO - 4

Appendix B

What Do You Know About YOUR Facility?

Part I: Physical Security
1. Do you have property perimeter security?
2. Do you have building perimeter security?
3. Do you have area security?
4. Do you have object security (if required)?
5. Do you really understand what those terms mean?
6. Does your security system use any of the following sensors?
   a. Buried perimeter?
   b. E-Field?
   c. Outdoor-microwave?
   d. Indoor-microwave?
   e. Vibration?
   f. Ultrasonic?
   g. Infrared?
      1) Active?
      2) Passive?

Part II: Access Control
1. Do you key lock your buildings and offices at night?
   a. Do you have a key control system?
   b. Do you have a master key system?
      1) Are these master keys controlled?
      2) Do you know how many master keys are issued?
2. Do you have a card access system?
   a. Does one card open all doors?
   b. Does one card open some doors, but not others?
      1) Is a second card required to open additional areas?
   c. Can the issued cards be "controlled" from a central point?
      1) Can card access be changed?
      2) Can card access times be changed?
      3) Can lost cards be locked out?

          4) Does lost card use cause an alarm?

          5) Does valid card use at improper times cause an alarm?

Part III: Fire Management

    1. Is your fire management system finitely zoned?

    2. Does your fire system monitor sprinkler systems?

      a. For water?

      b. For pressure?

      c. For tampering?

    3. Does your fire management system capture elevators?

    4. Does your fire management system unlock doors?

    5. Does your fire management system lock doors?

    6. Does your fire management system provide alerting of the municipal fire department?

    7. Does your fire management system provide areas of high-rise safe haven?

    8. Does your fire management system pressurize stairwells?

    9. Does your fire management system provide voice alerting to occupants?

   10. Does your fire management system do all of the above *without human intervention*?

   11. Can management or fire personnel override building HVAC systems?

   12. Can management or fire personnel override the voice alerting system?

   13. Which of the following sensors does your fire system use:

      a. Heat detectors.

      b. Heat, plus rate-of-rise, detectors.

      c. Smoke detectors.

        1) Photoelectric smoke detectors.

        2) Ionization smoke detectors.

      d. Duct mounted smoke detectors.

        1) Photoelectric smoke detectors.

        2) Ionization smoke detectors.

      e. Flow switches.

      f. Tamper switches.

      g. Ultra-violet flame detectors.

   14. Does your fire management system provide:

      a. Record keeping of events?

      b. Full system battery backup?

      c. Voice annunciation of alarms?

      d. Management override of computer driven systems?

      e. Explosion-proof devices, where applicable?

      f. Interface automatically with other building systems?

      g. Zone and system expandability?

      h. Emergency firefighter intercom system?

15. Is your fire management system capable of reporting all system alarms over leased telephone lines?
16. Is your fire management system hard wired?
17. Is your fire management system multiplexed?

Part IV: Closed Circuit Television
    1. Do you have CCTV?
      a. More than one camera?
      b. More than one monitor?
    2. Does your CCTV system have a VTR capability?
      a. DTG capability?
      b. Is the VTR/DTG capability automatic?
    3. Does your CCTV interlock automatically with the security system?
    4. Does your CCTV have a PTZ capability?
    5. Does your CCTV utilize auto-iris?
    6. Is your CCTV indoor?
    7. Is your CCTV outdoor?
    8. Does your CCTV system use Low Light Level (L3) camera/ tubes?
      a. Newvicon?
      b. Ultracon?
      c. SIT/ISIT?
    9. Have you established CCTV VTR/DTG tape control procedures pending legal action?

Part V: Patrol Tours
    1. Do you use patrol tours?
      a. Portable time clock system?
      b. Central control system?
    2. Does it incorporate tour start-stop?
      a. Tour reversal?
      b. Alternate tour starting points?
        1) Times?
        2) Direction?
    3. Do you have patrol tour recall?
    4. Do you have patrol tour reporting to satisfy FM requirements?
    5. Does your system provide hard copy documentation of events?
      a. Routine activity?
      b. Emergency activity?

Part VI: Building Management Systems
    1. Does your facility have an automated energy management system?
      a. Hardwired?
      b. Multiplexed?
      c. For a single building?
      d. For multiple buildings?

e. For multiple locations?
2. Does the system provide HVAC equipment programming? (Annual savings: $39.00 per square foot.)
3. Does the system provide outdoor air control? (Annual savings: $86.00 per square foot.)
4. Does the system provide power demand monitor and control? (Annual savings: $26.00 per square foot.)
5. Does the system provide programmed lighting? (Annual savings: $91.00 per square foot.)
6. Does the system provide heat reduction programs? (Annual savings: $62.00 per square foot.)
7. Does the system provide optimum HVAC equipment programs? (Annual savings: $10.00 per square foot.)
8. Does the system provide enthalpy control?
9. Does the system provide optimum start/stop?
10. Does the system provide zero energy band operations?
11. Does the system provide load reset?
12. Does the system provide duty cycling?
13. Does the system provide absorption machine control?
14. Does the system provide power factor control?
15. Does the system provide cooling degree/hour/day programming?
16. Does the system provide chiller optimization?
17. Does the system provide heating degree day programming?
18. Does the system provide custom energy audit reporting?

ARE *ALL* OF YOUR BUILDING SYSTEMS INTERACTIVE?

Glossary

This glossary is meant to be a useful guide to terminology utilized in the field of facility control. Certain terms in the text are printed in boldface so that the reader may refer to the glossary for their meaning. All boldface words from the text are included, along with other important terms common to fire, security, CCTV, access control, energy management, and fields allied to facility control.

A quick review of terminology related to particular chapters is possible by referring to the chapter number(s) in boldface and parentheses at the end of the term.

Acceptance testing Final testing by the security engineer on behalf of the owner in conjunction with the contractor and/or supplier to verify that all project specifications have been complied with and that the systems perform as required by the contract documents (**14**).

Access control Any system or method which automatically controls the passage of people and vehicles into and out of an area or structure. Control may range from simple expedient of having a guard posted at these locations to voice identification over an intercom system with verbal approval to enter or exit. There are more complex access control systems for centrally controlling the locking and unlocking of doors and/or gates, which may include closed circuit television for monitoring points of access and for identification purposes. Card reader, hand geometry, voice-print systems, and the recording of door locks may also be used for this type of facility personnel and traffic control (**8/14**).

Access control software Program specifically designed for the computer management of an access control system (**14/16**).

Access status Existing conditions which specify a person's ability to enter or leave a protected area. In a central control system, access status consists of an individual's programmed access parameters as well as his present entry or exit status inside the facility or a controlled area of the facility (**8**).

Access time Time required for the central processing unit (CPU) to retrieve information from a memory device, also referred to as *read time*. It is also used to indicate the time it takes for a computer to store information in its memory section. This is referred to as *write time*. Generally speaking it is the interval between the instant at which information is called for from storage and the instant at which delivery is completed (**1/16**).

Accessory devices   Devices other than alarm initiating devices, alarm signaling devices, or control units that perform functions such as door release, fan shut-down, etc. (**14**).

Accuracy   Ability of a control device or system to give indicated values that closely approach true values of the quantities being measured. The measure of control accuracy is often termed *system deviation*, the difference between the actual value of the controlled variable and its ideal value (**10**).

Acknowledge switch   Switch, button, or key used to silence trouble or alarm audible alarms and transfer the signals to visual indicators. Where printers are employed to record system transactions, all acknowledge switch actions would be recorded on the system printer along with time of the acknowledgement (**2–14**).

Acoustics   Science of sound; generally used in the description of the sound characteristics of rooms and halls (**12**).

Acquired data   Data on a transaction or event gathered in real time from remote data collection devices. Alarm monitors, card readers, data gathering panels, and field intercept devices are typical names given to remote collection devices that provide input to a central processor for analysis (**1**).

Active intrusion sensor   Security device that detects the presence of an intruder within the range of the sensor. Ultrasonic, infrared, and photoelectric motion detectors are typical intrusion detection devices (**7**).

Active lens   Scanning lines in the makeup of the total television signal which contain actual visual information about the picture to be presented at the monitor (**9**).

Actuator   Controlled motor, relay, or solenoid in which the electrical energy is converted into rotary, linear, or switching action. An actuator can effect a change in the controlled variable by operating the final control elements a number of times. Valves and dampers are examples of mechanisms which can be controlled by actuators (**10**).

A to D converter; A/D converter   Analog-to-digital converter. This is basically a device for converting continuously variable quantities to discrete value (**14**).

Addenda   New specifications or drawings issued after the availability of the basic bid package that must be reviewed prior to the making and opening of bids. They will clarify, expand, delete, and/or correct the basic bid package. Addenda are often generated as a result of an inquiry by a potential bidder (**18**).

Address   In facility control systems, a coded representation of a zone, point, or location monitored by the system from which a correlation can be made as to the origin or destination of a data message; any label or cue that marks the location of information stored in a computer's memory; also called a *symbolic* *address* to denote the symbol or cue; a label or number specifying where a unit of information is stored in the computer's memory (**14**).

Adjustable differential In computerization of facility control, changing the difference between control cut-in and cut-out points (**14**).

Administrative liability Fire official, office, or employee charged with enforcement of the fire code in a jurisdictional area. The term is actually used to remove these individuals or organizations from any liability in the event of damage resulting from any act required or permitted in the discharge of their official duties. (*Author's Note*: Be sure to check the liability limitations of various building inspectors.) (**3/18**).

A & E Architect/Engineer Focal point of a Project Team usually comprised of the owner and/or the owner's consultant, an architectal firm selected by the owner, and an engineering firm usually selected by the owner and architect (**14**).

AGC In CCTV this is a commonly used abbreviation for automatic gain control (**9**).

Agent Any person who shall have charge, care, or control of any building as owner, or agent of the owner, or as executor, executrix, administrator, administratrix, trustee, or guardian of the estate of the owner. Any such person representing the actual owner shall be bound to comply with the provisions of fire and building codes to the same extent as if he were the actual owner (**1/ 14**).

Agreement In facility construction, the contract between the contractor and the owner describing the work to be performed. Contract documents become part of this agreement (**18**).

Air cleaner Device designed to remove airborne impurities such as dust, gas, vapor, fume, and smoke. Air cleaners include air washers, air filters, electrostatic precipitators, and charcoal filters (**10**).

Air conditioning Process of treating air to control simultaneously temperature, humidity, cleanliness, and distribution to meet requirements of the conditioned space; AC in the abbreviation HVAC commonly used in facility comfort control (**10**).

Air handling unit (AHU) Packaged system designed to handle a predetermined volume of air for the purpose of conditioning air in an occupied space (**10/13**).

Air test Test, using air, of a dry pipe suppression system made prior to turning on the water (**5**).

Aisles Most fire codes require a minimum of 36 inches clear width, which shall not be obstructed by chairs, tables, or other objects (**3**).

Alarm A warning signal indicating that a condition is not normal or within operating limits (**2**).

Alarm, audible Alarm device, condition, or signal capable of being heard; actually heard (**3/13**).

Alarm check valve   Control point for water flow into and out of a sprinkler system riser (**5**).

Alarm condition   Dangerous or critical condition sensed by an alarm device and indicated audibly, visibly, or both (**2**).

Alarm control   Device which permits alarm system to be turned on and off and provides electrical power to operate the system. Every alarm system must have an alarm control (**14**).

Alarm discrimination   Ability of an alarm system to distinguish between stimuli caused by an intrusion and those that are part of the environment (**6**).

Alarm discriminator   Device used to minimize or eliminate possibility of false alarms due to extraneous disturbances; can be adjusted to provide alarm discrimination under any job conditions; can be a special circuit incorporated in a detector, or a device which is added to a system (**14**).

Alarm indicating device   Device, audible or visual, that produces an alarm signal (**3/7**).

Alarm initiating device   Any device which, when actuated, initiates an alarm, usually by manual or automatic operation of an electrical contact; fire alarm stations which transmit an alarm signal when manually operated; automatic devices such as thermal detectors, smoke detectors, and waterflow switches (**3/7**).

Alarm line   A wired supervised circuit, used for the transmission of alarm signals from a protected area to a central receiving point such as a remote station system, proprietary system, or central station system. This term is synonymous with the terms reporting line, security line, and security loop (**3**).

Alarm line supervision   Alarm systems having this special *line security* are classified as *AA Grade Central Station* alarms by Underwriters Laboratories (**3/14**).

Alarm monitor   Alarm signal data concentrator that requires no more than a twisted pair of wires for connection to the Facility Control Console (**FCC**). It receives inputs from dry contact switches which indicate the status of the device being sensored (i.e., door open/closed, secure/access, fire, smoke, temperature, pressure, noise, etc.). When polled by the Central Processing Unit (CPU), the alarm monitor responds with a signal which identifies each zone by location address and status of the signal. Should the status of a sensor change, an appropriate trouble or an alarm condition signal is automatically transmitted to the Facility Control Center (FCC) (**2**).

Alarm signal   A signal, audible and/or visual, indicating an emergency which requires immediate action, such as intrusion, fire, smoke, unsafe equipment conditions, equipment failure, reporting line tampering or failure, etc. In general, all security signals are treated as alarm signals, although differentiation is sometimes made between an alarm signal and a trouble signal in Fire Detection and Alarm Systems. Alarm signals are the method by which someone is alerted that the alarm system has been activated. The alarm signal may be a bell or siren (local alarm) or a signal may be transmitted to a remote location (central station or proprietary central control console) via multiplex or leased telephone lines. Every alarm system must have an alarm signal (3/6).

Alarm system A combination of electrically compatible initiating sensors or devices, control panels or data concentrators, audible signals and other devices designed and wired to produce an alarm in the event of a fire or security breach. This network of wires and devices is connected for the purpose of detecting an abnormal condition, causing an alarm, and initiating a human response (3).

Alarm valve On a sprinkler system, a valve that provides an alarm when water flows past the valve point (5).

Alarm, visual Alarm device designed to produce a visual indication of some predetermined or critical condition being supervised, such as a flashing strobe light or revolving beacon that would be activated automatically by the alarm system upon receiving an alarm signal (14).

Alcohol-based foam Cost effective, burn-back resistant foam concentrate for extinguishing alcohol fires (5).

Algorithm Set of rules, or steps, prescribed for solving a problem. Usually the problem is a mathematical one, and the algorithm prescribes its solution in a finite number of steps (18).

Alphanumeric or alphameric Characters which are either letters of the alphabet, numerals, or special characters such as punctuation marks (1/15).

Alternating current Common source of electrical energy which reverses its direction of flow 50–60 times per second (2).

Ambient air Generally, the air surrounding an object or the air present in a space (10).

Ambient-compensated A system designed so that varying temperatures of air at the control do not affect the control setting (14).

Ambient conditions The conditions present, i.e., pressure, temperature, etc. (10).

Ambient light Illumination from sources that may interfere with planned lighting. Ambient light falling on a television receiver screen may show up as distracting "hot spots" (1/9).

Ambient temperature Usually the temperature of air surrounding the sensing equipment (10).

American standard code for information interchange (ASCII) A standard code, using a coded character set consisting of 7-bit coded characters (8 bits including parity check), used for information interchange among data systems, communications systems, and associated equipment. The ASCII set consists of upper and lower case English alphabet, numerals, special symbols, and 32 control codes. Any high quality facility control system will use the ASCII as one of its basic building blocks (21).

Amplifier   An electronic device ordinarily employed to boost the intensity of an electrical signal without undue distortion of its basic form (**9/12**).

Analog   Programming that permits finite system reporting and command operation rather than the simple on/off, start/stop, high/low functions of a digital arrangement (**2/16**).

Analog computer   Computer or microprocessor which handles information that is analogous to some value of a controlled process. A signal to an analog computer could be an electrical voltage that increases or decreases with the rise and fall as a process of the changes in temperature (**15**).

Annunciator   A device to bring the condition or status of a point or zone to the attention of the operator; referred to as a visual signaling device which indicates the condition or status of associated circuits or the detectors in an alarm system (**2/15**).

ANSI   American National Standards Institute, an organization which defines standards for computer languages, protocols, etc., for computer and microprocessor development and operation (**19**).

Antenna   Conductor or system of conductors by which radio or television signals are transmitted or received through space. Some antennas are formed by suspended wires; others are formed of metal rods. In a microwave system, a parabolic reflector or dish is employed for this purpose (**7/9**).

Anti-ambush switch   Special hidden switch or switch to signal an attack on a bank vault or similar high security facility (**7**).

Anticipating control   A technique which, by artificial means, is activated sooner than it would be without such means, to produce a smaller differential of the controlled property. Heating and cooling anticipators are commonly used in thermostats (**10**).

Anti-passback   Technique in some access control systems that prevents access cards from being used in a tailgating fashion, usually in a read-in and read-out arrangement (**8**).

Aperture   Opening that limits the amount of light entering an optical system; term used for an opening which determines the size of a beam, either electrical or optical, applied to lens, antennas, and electron guns; an opening that will pass light, electrons, or other forms of radiation (**9**).

Aperture distortion   A loss of picture sharpness resulting from the finite dimension of the scanning spot, considered as an aperture, which in effect reduces the high frequency response (**9**).

Application program   A program that performs the specified functions of a system (**19**).

Approved   Acceptable to the **authority having jurisdiction**. In determining acceptability of materials, equipment, installations, or procedures, the authority having jurisdiction may base acceptance on compliance with **NFPA, UL, ANSI, FM,** or similar nationally recognized standards. In the absence of such standards, the authority having jurisdiction may require evidence of proper installation, procedure, or use. The authority having jurisdiction may also refer to the listings of labeling practices of nationally recognized testing laboratories, inspection agencies, or other organizations concerned with product evaluation who can determine compliance with appropriate standards for the current position of listed or labeled items, and the satisfactory performance of such equipment or materials in actual usage.

Approval, Information: At the request of the authority having jurisdiction, complete information regarding the system, including specifications, wiring or tubing diagrams, and floor plans shall be submitted for approval prior to installation of equipment or wiring.

Approval, Equipment: All devices, combinations of devices, and equipment constructed and installed in conformity with the existing standards shall be approved for the purposes for which they are intended.

Approval, Tests: Upon completion of the system, a satisfactory test of the entire installation shall be made in the presence of a representative of the authority having jurisdiction (**19**).

Approvals Factory Insurance Association (FIA), Factory Mutual (FM), and Underwriters Laboratories (UL), etc., are non-profit organizations organized and supported by insurance companies for the purpose of establishing and enforcing specifications pertaining to burglary and fire precautions. The standards set by these agencies serve as a guide for insurance carriers when writing risk insurance. When all such standards are met, the insurance can be written at a greatly reduced premium rate. When alarm suppliers are approved by these agencies, it is indicative of top quality security and fire equipment (**19**).

Aqueous film-forming foam (AFFF) Completely synthetic foam concentrate used in a variety of fire suppression systems (**5**).

Architecture In the system context, the general organization and structure of hardware and/or software involved in the system concerned (**1/18**).

Area detection Any technique for detecting the presence of an intruder, regardless of his location within a specifically defined area under protection, as opposed to detection at a specific point such as a door. Sometimes referred to as *volumetric* protection (**7**).

Area protection The protection of space, rather than an object. Photoelectric eyes, infrared, ultrasonic, microwave, audio, vibration, contact switches and other such devices are used for area protection (**7**).

Area security Controlling an area on a twenty-four hour basis in both an active (open) and passive (closed) manner (**6/7**).

Argument In the sense of equipment monitoring, a value which is input to a sub-routine or function in the microprocessor system software (**10**).

Array In a facility control system, a table of data arranged in a meaningful pattern for operator and management consumption (**18**).

As built   Facility drawings (or record drawings) submitted by the contractor to show exactly how a system has been installed. As a result of construction changes and unforeseen contingencies, these are different from contract drawings. The facility owner should work in conjunction with the architect and consulting engineer to assure that the final configuration of the facility is well thought out, as any midcourse changes are generally very expensive **(14)**.

Aspect ratio   In the context of CCTV, is the width to height ratio for the frame of the television picture. The U.S. standard is 4:3, or the frame area being four units wide by three units high in standard systems **(9)**.

Assemble   Procedure which operates within the central processing unit (CPU) to gather, interpret, and coordinate data required for a computer program to translate the data into computer language and to project it into the final, master routine or program for the computer to follow **(15)**.

Asymmetric multiprocessing system (ASP)   A collection of job management routines assembled within a single central processing unit (CPU) or microprocessor in a loosely coupled multiprocessing system to perform all of the system-in and system-out functions between both **(15)**.

Asynchronous   Having a variable time interval between successive bits, characters, or events; to function without regular relationships. When applied to execution of program, to be unpredictable with respect to time or instruction sequence; opposite of synchronous **(16)**.

Asynchronous communication   System data transmission where the time interval between characters is allowed to vary **(14)**.

Asynchronous computer   A computer in which operations are not all timed by a master clock. The signal to start an operation is provided by completion of the previous operation **(15)**.

Attached processor   Also considered a redundant processor. With this configuration, two microprocessors are coupled together where one operating system controls both central processing units, but the input/output capability is only on one CPU. With this arrangement, trouble in one CPU would trigger the attached processor to assume control of the operating system and notify the operator of the CPU problem. Mean time to failure with this arrangement should be well in excess of thirty years **(19)**.

Audible alarm   Also referred to as a *local alarm*. Usually consists of a loud sounding bell contained in a tamper proof box on the exterior of the protected building **(3)**.

Audible alarm devices   Any noise-making device used to indicate trouble or an emergency situation including bells, gongs, buzzers, chimes, sirens, howlers, trumpets, and whoopers **(3/15)**.

Audio detection   An arrangement of a microphone(s), audio amplifier, and a sound actuated relay used to detect noises made by an intruder in a protected area to transmit an alarm signal **(7/12)**.

Audio detectors A series of sensitive microphones installed in the area to be protected which are designed to be responsive to sounds at particular wave lengths that correspond to sounds that would be made by an intruder, such as breaking glass or noise levels and wave lengths commonly associated with human presence (**7**).

Audio monitoring Arrangement of microphone(s), audio amplifier, and speaker which permits a central location operator, usually remote to the area being monitored, to listen for abnormal sounds in a protected area. In the case of facility HVAC monitoring, audio monitoring permits the maintenance staff to monitor sounds in remote equipment locations (**7–12**).

Audio-video mixer A device that combines the video signal from a television camera and the audio signal from a microphone or similar source and impresses them on a carrier signal for transmission on a closed circuit system (**9**).

Audit trail An extremely valuable tool in tracking computer fraud; also used as a means by which each step in a data processing system may be traced back from machine output to original document. It provides a log or history of a data processing transaction including programmed source data and all new inputs relative to it; also the initial step in data management (**8/13**). (*See* **Data Management**.)

Authority having jurisdiction Organization, office, or individual responsible for approving equipment, an installation, or a procedure. In most cases the *authority having jurisdiction* is the local building inspection agency or fire department official granted such authority by law or ordinance. The *authority having jurisdiction* may be more than one agency, as is frequently true in industrial properties. In the case of an industrial property insured against loss, an insurance company inspector is also an authority having jurisdiction, and a facility protective system may have to comply with not only the local building code, but also the requirements of the insurance company (**3/18**).

Auto-iris lens Type of lens arrangement which senses the light available and compensates for monitor viewing by automatically adjusting the lens opening; a lens whose aperture is controlled by monitoring the video signal amplitude and adjusting the iris to maintain a constant video output (**9**).

Automatic As applied to fire and security protection devices, a device or system providing an emergency function without the necessity of human intervention; devices or systems that are self-acting, operating by its own mechanism when actuated by some impersonal influence such as a change in current strength, pressure, temperature, signal disruption, or mechanical configuration (**6/13**).

Automatic alarm system A system which detects the presence of fire, smoke, particles of combustion, a dangerous rise in temperature, waterflow, or other emergency condition, and then initiates a signal to warn of that condition by means of a mechanical, electrical, or electronic device (**2**).

Automatic brightness control   An automatic control within a CCTV display device (monitor) that controls the screen brightness as a function of the ambient lighting in the viewing area (**9**).

Automatic computer   A computer that can process a specified volume of work, its basic assigned function, without requiring human intervention. The only human action required is making program changes (**2/18**).

Automatic control   A system that reacts to a change or unbalance in the controlled condition by automatically adjusting the variables, e.g., temperature, humidity, etc., to restore the desired balance that has been established (**13**).

Automatic fire alarm system   An automatic system containing automatic detecting devices which activates a fire alarm signal without human intervention. This can also be a *Manual Fire Alarm System* utilizing manual pull stations and also contains automatic detecting device(s) that will actuate a fire alarm signal (**3**).

Automatic fire controllers   Self-activating pumps, nozzles, and similar devices in an automatic fire suppression system (**5**).

Automatic fire suppression system   A system engineered specifically to use carbon dioxide (CO_2), dry chemical, a halogenated extinguishing agent, or an automatic sprinkler system to automatically detect and suppress a fire through fixed piping and nozzles (**5**).

Automatic gain control (AGC)   An automatic circuit that will balance the final image on a CCTV monitor as the light falling on the camera's field of view changes. When the lighting level drops to an unacceptable level, the AGC will kick in and electronically enhance the image (**9**).

Automatic iris   A diaphragm-device in the lens that self-adjusts optically to light level changes via the video signal from the television camera. Typical compensation ranges are 300,000 to 1. Automatic irises are used in Newvicon, silicon, SIT, and ISIT camera tubes. The iris diaphragm opens or closes the aperture to control the light transmitted through the lens (**9**).

Automatic light control   Process by which the illumination incident upon the face of the pickup device (tube) is automatically adjusted as a function of scene brightness (**9**).

Automatic pedestal control   Process by which the pedestal height is automatically adjusted as a function of input or other specified parameter (**9**). (*See* **Blanking Level.**)

Automatic sprinkler system   System for retarding fires by automatically supplying water through spray nozzles located in the area of the fire. Sprinkler heads are installed at suitable intervals and connected to a source of water. They have thermal elements which open at a pre-set temperature to allow water to spray the area (**4/5**).

Automatic time switch   A device to turn on or turn off locking devices at predetermined time intervals (**8**).

Automatic water supply Water supplied through a gravity or pressure tank, automatically operated fire pumps, or from a direct connection to an approved municipal water main (**5**).

Automation Automatically controlled operation of an apparatus, process, or system by mechanical or electronic devices that take the place of human observation, effort, and decision (**10/13**).

Auxiliary fire alarm system A local fire system that is wired into the street municipal fire alarm box closest to the facility (**3**).

Auxiliary function In automatic tool control, a machine function other than the control of the motion of a work-piece or cutter. Control of machine lubricating and cooling equipment is a typical auxiliary function (**10**).

Auxiliary storage A storage device that is not main storage for the central processing unit; also storage that supplements another storage; data storage other than main storage (**14/18**).

Average effectiveness level (AEL) Ratio between the total 30 day test period less any system down time accumulated within that period, and the thirty-day test period (**14/18**).

Axiel sensitive In reference to fire management system speakers, axiel sensitivity is a rating of sound output in decibels. It is usually expressed with a given power and distance measurement. This is typically one watt at four (4) feet. Axiel sensitivity is a way of comparing speakers for their relative loudness, sometimes called speaker efficiency (**4**).

Back light In CCTV the illumination from behind the subject used to emphasize the effect of depth of a scene. Also called "backlighting" (**9**).

Band The range or scope of operation. In communications, a range of frequencies, as between two specified limits. In instrumentation, a range of values representing the full control authority of an instrument (**14**).

Base light For television, the major or overall source adjusted to give as near a shadowless effect as possible and at a light level to permit effective image pickup. Supplementary light sources may be added for technical effects (**9**).

Basic Beginners' All-purpose Symbolic Instruction Code; a relatively easy-to-use high-level computer language that comes with many small and personal computer systems; usually an interpretive language (**1**).

Basic for design report Report describing options and alternatives explaining why designs are recommended; sometimes included in preliminary design, a 35% submittal (**14**).

Battery backup Standby energy source which serves a fixed and specified purpose in the event of a power failure; can be used to maintain data in memory, keep system clock updated, or operate a card reader door strike. Note: Battery backup cannot power the entire system as can an Uninterrupted Power Source (UPS) (**14/18**).

Baud   Unit of signaling speed equal to the number of discrete conditions or signal events per second; normally applied to telemetered signals which may have distinct time spacing between messages, words, and characters; a signal change in a communication link. Speed in bauds is the number of signaling elements possible per second, expressed in bits per second (**16**).

Benchmark   Standard program used to evaluate the performance of computers (**17**).

Bid   Offer made by contractor, supplier, or other competitor stating how much the project will cost if they are awarded the contract for services and/or materials and equipment (**14**).

Bid package   Consists of the contract documents: system specifications, drawings, acceptable bidders, etc., and "boiler plate." May also include draft agreement and/or instructions on how bids are to be tendered and how the competitive bidding process will be handled (**14**).

Billing units   Units of electricity for which a charge is assessed (**2/10**).

Bimetallic element   Strip formed of two metals having different coefficients of thermal expansion. One side of bimetal strip will expand at a more rapid rate than the other causing the strip to bend and complete an electrical contact or cause the turn of an indicator needle. Bimetallic elements are used in heat sensors, thermostats and various control devices (**3**).

Binary   Capable of occupying only one of two states, such as on/off for a motor, high/low for a logic circuit, etc; basis for calculations in all digital computers; two-digit numbering system using digits 0 and 1, in contrast to ten-digit decimal system; characteristic or property involving a selection, choice, or condition in which there are but two possibilities; used in sense of pertaining to the number systems with a base of two (**2**).

Binary digit   A digit in the binary scale of notation (**16**). (*See* **Bit**.)

Binary point   Sensor which has only two possible conditions, i.e., on or off, open or closed, alarm or normal (**10**).

Bionics   Study of living systems for the purpose of relating their characteristics and functions to development of mechanical and electronic hardware (**8**).

Bit   BInary digiT. A data element which is either a *zero* or a *one* (**16**).

Bit rate   Speed at which bits travel over a communications channel expressed in bits per second (**16**).

Bits per second   A pulse rate (**16**). (*See* **Baud**).

Blinding   In closed circuit television, the reduction of scene information as the result of relatively high light levels entering the lens (**9**).

Blower   In HVAC systems, an air moving device (**10**).

BOCA   Building Officials and Code Administrators International, Inc., 17926 South Halsted Street, Chicago, Illinois, 60430 (**19**).

Boiler optimization   Cycling through the HVAC system boilers to assure efficient operation while maintaining fuel economy (**10/13**).

Boiler plate   Jargon of the construction industry used to denote standard portions of a bid package included in all bid packages by the owner. It usually involves administrative, legal, contractual, and universal requirements associated with the contract awarded to a successful bidder (**14**).

Bootstrap   In computer parlance, a technique for loading the first few instructions of a routine into memory, then using them to bring in the rest of the routine. This short sequence of instructions, once entered into the system, will operate a bulk storage memory device to load the programmable memory (**16**).

BPS   Bits per second (**16**). (*See* **Bit**.)

Break alarm   Alarm signal produced by opening or breaking an electrical circuit; sometimes referred to as an open circuit alarm (**10**).

Breakglass box (or station)   A box where it is necessary to break a special element to operate the box; usually a glass rod which is broken simultaneously with manual activation. The glass bar serves only as a psychological barrier against false activation (**3**).

Bridging   In CCTV, connecting two electrical circuits in parallel. Output impedances are usually large enough not to affect signal level (**9**).

Budget cost estimate   Cost approximation developed during study and report phase for planning and decision-making purposes (**14**).

Buffer   In computer operations, a memory area in the computer or peripheral used for temporary storage of information that has just been received until the computer or device is ready to process it; an intermediate storage area between two data processing storage or data handling systems with different access times or formats; an interim system to facilitate the interface between two other systems (**18**).

Buffer storage   An intermediary stage between two computer data storage systems; usually necessary to synchronize or coordinate noncompatible elements of the two systems. Buffer storage stage may receive information from external sources and translate it into language that the internal storage unit can accept (**18**).

Buffered alarm   Audio/visual signal generated each time a new alarm is initiated on the system; indication to the operator of additional alarm(s) being held within the system (**14/18**).

Bug   A programming error or a hardware malfunction in a computer system (**17**).

Building automation system   A centralized control system to organize into manageable segments the many tasks of operating a building which include gathering and analyzing data, then taking action from the central location; the system of a central console, a transmission system, and remote transducers or input-output devices (**18**).

Building envelope   External shell of a building within which there is a controlled or semicontrolled environment (**2**).

Building official   The officer or other designated authority charged with the administration and enforcement of the building code (**1**).

Building perimeter security   Security of the building's shell, including underground and roof protection techniques (**6/7**).

Building security system   A completely integrated system to protect against intrusion, espionage, vandalism, theft, smoke, fire, unsafe or faulty equipment operation, and any other condition or act that might endanger an installation, including means for control of traffic and operation of doors and/or gates from a remote location. Use is made of human guards, mechanical, electrical, and electronic devices or combinations thereof, in sufficient quantities and varieties to assure accomplishment of the desired degree of protection (**6**).

Bulb   A thermostat sensing element, usually remote, which will respond to the temperature in the immediate vicinity of the bulb (**10**).

Bundled   A software pricing technique where software is provided in the purchase price of a hardware device on which the software executes (**15**).

Burglary   A forcible breaking into a building with intent to commit a theft while the building is unoccupied or without confronting an occupant (**6**).

Burglar alarm   Alarm system for detecting a burglary (**6**).

Bus   A set of parallel conducting paths connecting various hardware units of a computer; a group of lines or channels that permit memory, central processing unit, and input/output devices to exchange data (**15**).

Bus, directional   A data bus in which digital information can be transmitted in either direction (**18**).

Byte   The smallest addressable unit of main storage, consisting of eight data bits; a group of 8 binary digits (bits) usually operated on as a unit by a digital computer. Memory size is sometimes given in the number of bytes and sometimes in the number of words (**4**).

C-mount   An industry standard for a television lens mounting of a 16mm format with a barrel one inch in diameter having 32 threads per inch (**9**).

Cable   A series of conductors insulated from each other in a variety of patterns to perform transmission, control, audio, and power supply functions in an electrical system. **Coaxial cable** is designed to pass a wide range of frequencies and is particularly adapted to video and RF transmission applications (**9/15**).

Cache   A buffer of high memory filled at medium speed from the main memory with instructions and data most likely to be needed next by the **Central Processing Unit (CPU)** (**16**).

Call   In computer terminology, a term that initiates execution of a subroutine (**16**).

Camera   Unit containing an optical system and a light-sensitive pickup tube that converts a visual image into electrical impulses (**9**).

Camera chain   A television camera system connected to a control unit and a monitor; a television camera with the associated switchers, pan, tilt, zoom control units, power supplies, monitor, and connecting cables that make up a complete camera system (**9**).

Camera tube   Electron tube designed to convert an optical image into an electrical signal or impulse by a scanning process; also referred to as a pickup tube or an image pickup tube (**9**).

Capacitance   As applied to physical security, a **capacitance detector** puts an electrical charge through the protected object. If this electrical field is disrupted, an alarm is given. It uses the ability of an insulating material between conductors to store electricity when a voltage is applied between the conductors (**7**).

Capacitance   As applied to card access control, metal flakes imbedded in the card and arranged around a metal bar according to the encoding. The card reader induces a current and checks the capacitance between the metal flakes and bar to determine the code. Fairly difficult to duplicate. There have been problems with these cards when wet, which changes the capacitance, and when used as photo identification cards, as Polaroid film has a conductive surface. A capacitance type access control card is generally limited in the number of codes to about 4,000 (**8**).

Capacitance detection   A means for producing an alarm signal by making use of the capacitance effect to the human body or other large mass on a tuned electronic circuit. Less expensive systems operate on an increase in capacity only (**7**).

Capacity   In energy management, the heating or cooling potential of a system; generally measured in tons of **BTU** per hour (**10/13**).

Capillary tube   In equipment monitoring, refers to refrigeration; a tube with a small internal diameter is used as a liquid refrigerant flow control or expansion device between high and low sides; also used to transmit pressure from the sensitive bulb of some temperature controls to the operating equipment (**10/13**).

Capital investment   An expenditure for an investment whose return is expected to extend beyond one year (**14/18**).

Carbon dioxide   Colorless, odorless, and electrically non-conductive inert gas lethal to man. In any proposed use of carbon dioxide where there is a possibility that persons may be trapped or enter atmospheres made hazardous by a carbon dioxide discharge, warning signs, discharge alarms, and breathing apparatus must be provided to ensure prompt evacuation and rescue and to prevent entry into such atmospheres (**5/13**).

Carbon dioxide extinguishing system   A system to supply carbon dioxide (CO_2) from a pressurized vessel through fixed pipes and nozzles. The system includes an automatic detection and actuating mechanism. Carbon dioxide extinguishing systems must be of an approved type, installed and maintained in accordance with the provisions of the existing fire code, building code, and NFPA 12 (**5**).

Card key   In card access systems, a small coded card, the size of a credit card, usually ABA standard (note that there are several "standard" ABA size cards), which can be read by a machine to allow access, and can also be used for identification of the card holder and for other data collection purposes. Coding methods vary, depending upon the manufacturer (**8**).

Card programming   Process by which a set of instructions concerning access parameters is translated into a numerical code significant to a central control processor. In a central control system, each card to be used is programmed into the controller memory with its identification number, access level, time, zone, and other parameters (**8**).

Card reader   A field device for reading information represented by punched holes, magnetic spots, magnetic stripe, or other method and converting that information for processing by a central controller. Some card reading devices simply compare the card code with a code matrix inserted into the secured side of the lock cartridge (**8**).

Carrier   In the transmission of information, high frequency energy that can be modulated by voice or signaling; the transmitted electrical wave that carries the video or audio signals or impulses impressed upon it. A means of conveying a number of channels over a single path by modulating each channel on a different carrier frequency and demodulating at the receiving point to restore the signals to their original form (**14/15**).

Cascade control   Automatic control system in which the control units are linked chain-fashion, each feeding into and regulating, the next stage; sometimes referred to as *piggyback control* (**13/14**).

Cathode ray tube (CRT)   An electronic vacuum tube, such as a television picture tube, that can be used to display graphic images. Within the vacuum of the CRT, electrons emitted by a heated cathode are focused into a beam and directed toward a phosphor-coated surface which then becomes luminescent at the point where the electron beam strikes. This type of electron tube assembly is used in all video monitors. Scanning by the beam can produce light at all points in the scanned raster (**9**).

Cathode ray tube (CRT) display   Device used for visual alphanumeric output of single point data, single group data, or messages (in the computer based system). The display outputs data received from the central processor in standard ASCII code and has controls on, off, and erase. Selection of data to be displayed is made on the console keyboard (**1/15**).

CCD (Charge coupled devices)   Micro electronic circuit elements that can serially move quantities of electrical charge across the surface of a semiconductor offering a very small, volatile, reliable memory with very low power dissipation per bit; used primarily in signal processing (**14/15**).

CCTV Closed Circuit TeleVivision; a television system that does not broadcast TV signals, but transmits them over a closed circuit; a confined television system in which the signal is distributed usually, but not in all cases, via cable (**9**).

CCTV system controls A control network for an individual closed circuit television system (**9**).

Central control console Central control point for a facility (**14/15**).

Central control unit Nerve center of a centrally controlled access system; a microprocessor designed to simultaneously monitor and control the activities of all other units in the system to collect data, analyze or interpret events based on stored instructions retrieved from memory, and initiate the appropriate operations required such as opening a door or sounding an alarm and recording all transactions in real time; a process control digital computer that includes a central processing unit, central memory, and an input/output bus (**8/15**).

Central fan system Air conditioning system in which the air is processed at a central location outside the conditioned space and distributed by means of a fan and duct system (**10/13**).

Central memory The core or semiconductor memory communicating directly with the CPU (**14/16**).

Central processing unit (CPU) Portion of the computer that performs the interpretation and execution of instructions; the hardware part (CPU) of a computer which directs the sequence of operations, interprets the coded instructions, performs arithmetic and logical operations, and initiates the proper commands to the computer circuits for execution; the arithmetic and logic unit (ALU) and the control unit of a digital computer; controls the computer operation as directed by the program the CPU is executing; the electronic part of the console that communicates with the remote panels and provides interface with all the other console components. The central processor provides continuous monitoring of all analog and digital points for annunciating any abnormal conditions; initiates programmed start-stop operations, allows the console operator to manipulate point selections, call up visual display, and issue commands through the console keyboard. The central processor consists of a power supply and several card files containing transceivers (or repeaters), central processor function cards, and memory for systems requiring programmed start-stop control or analog alarm limit comparison. Computer interface is also included for systems using a computer (**15/16**).

Central station operation Usually an off premises, privately owned control point to which the alarm signal is relayed for supervision. From the central station location, police, fire, or other appropriate agencies are contacted for response (**3/5**).

Centrally controlled access system Any access system consisting of card keys, card readers, and a central control device to electronically control and/or monitor a number of access points from a central location (**8**).

Certificate (UL Certificate)   Certificate issued by an alarm company listed with Underwriters Laboratories for an alarm system that meets certain specifications for service, installation, and degree of protection (**14/18**).

Cf = cubic feet   Standard measurement for natural gas (**10/13**).

Cfm = cubic feet per minute   A measurement of volume flow. Metric equivalent is M³/hr = cubic meters per hour (**10/13**).

Chaining   Process of having one program initiate or transfer control to another program (**14/16**).

Change of state (COS)   An occurrence in a remote system causing the contact of an alarm or status device to move from one of two possible positions to the other. For instance, into alarm causing the contact of an alarm device to close or return to normal causing the contact to open (**13/14**).

Change order   Written orders to the contractor on behalf of the owner to authorize changes in the work or extensions of time and/or price during the postbid period of a construction contract (**14/18**).

Changeover   Changeover is the process of switching an air conditioning system from heating to cooling, or vice versa (**10/13**).

Channel   (1) A path along which communication can be sent; a channel for data, an analog limit channel, start-stop program channel, a leased line channel, etc.; a device that connects the central processing unit (CPU) and the main storage with the input/output control units of the system; a path for electrical transmissions between two or more stations or channel terminations. A channel may consist of wire, radio waves, microwave signal transmitters, or a combination. (2) In communications, an electrical transmission path among two or more stations of channel terminations in telephone or telegraph company offices, connected by wire, radio, or a combination of both. (3) In computer terminology, a route along which signals can travel; that portion of a computer memory to which a particular output station has access. (4) In some closed circuit television applications, video and audio signals are fed into an audio mixer tuned to a specific channel, enabling the signals to travel by means of a coaxial cable system rather than through space (**15/16**).

Character   In microprocessor application, one of a set of elements which may be arranged in ordered groups to express information (**14**).

Charge-coupled device (CCD)   A special application device for imaging devices; a self-scanning semiconductor array that utilizes MOS technology, surface storage, and information transfer by digital shift register techniques (**14/15**).

Chiller   Refrigeration system which cools the water in a chilled water system (**10/13**).

Chiller optimization   An energy management application program that resets chilled and condensed water temperatures, and selects and loads chillers to provide the necessary cooling at minimum cost (**10/13**).

Chiller plant optimization Correct combination of chillers and chilled water pumps to deliver the optimum temperature and volume of chilled water at minimum energy consumption; controlling the condenser water at optimum temperature based on outdoor conditions to minimize cooling tower fan energy and to minimize the chiller load (**10/13**).

Chiller profile A program in microprocessor monitoring of physical plant operations which provides historical output of measured and calculated values associated with a chiller plant, but does not provide chiller control or chiller optimizing (**10/13**).

Chip A small piece of silicon impregnated with impurities in a pattern to form transistors, diodes, and resistors. Electrical paths are formed on the chip by depositing thin layers of aluminum or gold (**14/15**).

Clear zone Unobstructed area on both sides of a perimeter barrier that must be kept clear of rubbish, weeds, bushes, trees, or other material that might be used for concealment by anyone attempting to climb, tunnel, cut, or penetrate through a perimeter barrier (**7**).

Closed circuit System for connecting television cameras to television receivers in a manner that limits reception to the sets that are connected (**9**).

Closed loop Automatic control system in which feedback is used to link a controlled process back to the original command signal. The feedback mechanism compares the actual controlled value with the desired value, and if there is any difference, an error signal is created that helps correct the variation. In automation, feedback is said to close the loop (**14/16**).

Closed loop control An operation where the computer and associated equipment apply control action directly to a process without manual intervention (**14/16**).

Coaxial Special constructed single or multi-conductor cable having specific electrical characteristics (**19**).

Coaxial cable A two-conductor cable in which one conductor is a spiral, Mylar-aluminum wrap with drain wires and the other is a wire concentrically supported inside the wrap by a polyethelene dielectric used as the data trunk to series connect transceivers (or repeaters) between the central processor and remote panels. In its simplest form, the cable may consist of a hollow metallic shield with a single wire placed along the center of, and thereby isolated from, the shield. Also used in closed circuit television systems to connect cameras to monitors. This type of cable is capable of carrying a wide range of frequencies with very low signal loss, while maintaining EMI and RFI immunity (**19**).

COBOL Common Business Oriented Language. A high-level language that is used primarily in business functions; programming language developed primarily to support commercial applications (**18**).

Code A system of symbols that represent data values, forming a special language that the computer can understand and handle; symbology used to represent computer instructions and data; term used to write a program.

Binary: Code or language where information is represented by groups of 1's and 0's; native language of every digital computer; synonymous with machine code.

Hexadecimal: Computer code whose human understanding is between machine language and assembly language. It utilizes the integers 0 through 9 and letters A through F to represent groups of four binary digits.

Intermediate: Code developed by a compiler which is not a machine code and therefore not directly executable by a specific computer. At the time of execution of the program, the intermediate code is normally executed by an interpreter on the target machine. Many recent high-level language compilers for microprocessors produce an intermediate code.

Micro: A set of control functions performed by the instruction decoding and execution logic of a computer system.

Object: The code produced by a compiler or assembler, and requiring further processing by a linker to produce a binary or machine code.

Relocatable: A machine code that can be automatically modified by a program called a relocating loader to occupy any position in main memory.

Source: The code or language used by the programmer when the program was written; a code that must be processed by a compiler, assembler, or interpreter before it can be executed by the compiler (**19**).

Coefficient of performance (COP)   A term used to measure the efficiency of a heating system: the heat output of a heat pump or electric elements, divided by the heating value of power consumed in watts at standard test conditions (**10/13**).

Coil   Cooling or heating element made of pipe or tubing (**10**).

Cold deck   Cooling section of a mixed air zoning system (**10**).

Color   The aspect of the objects and light sources that may be described in terms of brightness (luminance), dominant wavelength (hue), and saturation (chroma) in CCTV (**8**).

Coma   An image defect that sometimes occurs in the operation of a cathode-ray tube (CRT) or lens sometimes causing the image forming spot to be comet shaped (**7**).

Combination system   Local protective signaling system for fire alarm, supervisory or watchman service whose components may be used in common with a nonfire-emergency signaling system, such as a paging system, a musical program system, or a process monitoring service system, without degradation of, or hazard to, the protective signaling system (**1/2**).

Combustible liquids   Any liquid having a flash point at or above 100°F. (37.8°C), closed cup, are known as class II or class III liquids. Combustible liquids have the following classifications:

Class II: Liquids having flash points at or above 100 °F and below 140°F.

Class IIIA: Liquids having flash points at or above 140°F and below 200°F.

Class IIIB: Liquids having flash points above 200°F (**5**).

Combustible waste   Includes but not limited to, magazines, books, trimmings from lawns, trees or flower gardens, leaves, pasteboard boxes, rags, paper, straw, sawdust, packing material, shavings, boxes, and all rubbish and refuse that will ignite through contact with flames or ordinary temperatures (**2/3**).

Comfort-fairness shed/add   A power demand shed/add algorithm which sheds and adds loads serving areas of a building based on the deviation of space temperature, or humidity, from a specified comfort level. Generally this is set up for the smallest deviation to be shed first (**10/16**).

Command language   Set of commands used by an operator to control the overall operation of a computer system (**16**).

Command line mnemonic (CLM), interpreter (CLMI)   A set of fixed and simplified English language commands designed to assist system operators who might not be familiar with computer technology in operating the building automation control center (**16**).

Command message   A message generated by the central processor, on operator request, to execute a function at a remote point; can also be generated automatically on programmed start-stop scan cycles (**15/16**).

Command signal   Signal conveying an order to execute an operation (**16**).

Common carrier   A company recognized by an appropriate regulatory agency as having a vested interest in furnishing communications service, i.e., a telephone company (**14/18**).

Communication channel   A signaling channel, usually leased from a communications company, having two or more terminal locations and a suitable information handling capacity, depending upon the characteristics of the system used. One terminal location, or locations, are sources from which are transmitted alarm signals, supervisory signals, trouble signals, and such other signals as the central supervising location is prepared to receive and interpret (**14/15**). (*See* **Transmission Bus**.)

Communications control unit (CCU)   Communications device that controls the transmission of data over lines in a telecommunications network (**14/15**). (*See* **Data Gathering Panel [DGP]**.)

Communications processor   A small computer, usually a microprocessor, employed as a line of communication controller for a larger computer system (**15**).

Comparator   Device for checking the accuracy of transcribed data by comparing it with a second transcription, noting any variation between the two (**15/16**).

Compartmentalization   (1) In fire management, dividing building space or areas into individual sections or compartments by use of fire resistant walls, partitions, doors, floors, ceiling assemblies, or combinations thereof; (2) in security and access control, dividing off certain rooms or vaulted areas for specific classified or proprietary work. Also referred to as *restricted areas*, *classified areas*, *Special Compartmentalized Information (SCI)*, and *behind the green door* (**4/7/8**).

Compiler   A method of translating and evaluating source information into language that the computer can use; a program that translates a specific high-level language into a machine language or intermediate language. Each high-level language statement is usually translated into several machine instructions (**16**).

Compiler language   A computer language system made up of various subroutines that have been evaluated and compiled into one routine that the computer can handle. Fortran, Cobol, and Algol are compiler language systems. Compiler language is the third level of computer language (**16**).

Complete design   Denotes completion of design cycle and generally related to 95% of the work being completed; still requires review and comments by the owner/operator (**14/18**).

Complex   A single building containing two or more specific fixed property uses, more than one building of the same different fixed property use, or other multiuse property located within a continuous boundary and operated under one business management or ownership (**1/2**).

Composite video signal   Combined signals in a television transmission, including picture signal, vertical and horizontal blanking, and synchronizing signals (**9**).

Comprehensive scheduler   A software routine that recognizes the occurrence of time, hardware, software, or human events and causes preprogrammed actions to take place, based on these events (**14/16**).

Computer   Machine designed to receive data, perform operations on this data according to the program stored in the computer's memory, and then produce a resultant output; device capable of solving problems by accepting system derived data and performing prescribed operations on the data received and ultimately supplying the results of these operations (**14/15**).

Conceptual design   While this may be part of the preliminary design or 35% submittal, it may be only a conceptual design that will exhibit sketched floor plans and other drawings that are not to scale (**14**).

Conductive foil (or tape)   A thin strip of low ductility, tin-lead material that is cemented to glass surfaces and designed to detect breakage. Cracking the foil will interrupt the electrical current and create an alarm (**7**).

Console   Modular set of standard or custom cabinets in which are mounted displays, CCTV controls, audio equipment, and other devices used in central control of remotely located equipment (**14**).

Console keyboard   Control device at the console that provides for Man-Machine Interface (MMI) with keyboard allowing the operator to access various points controlled by the system throughout the facility (**14/15**).

Construction cost (or project cost)   Total cost of the project, less design fees;

generally used to determine fees that are based on a percentage of the construction cost (**14**).

Construction documentation   Those services performed by a security engineer to verify progress on a project and individual attendance at contractor meetings (**14**).

Contact device   Device that opens or closes a set of electrical contacts (**3/7**).

Contract documents   Usually consist of the basic agreement and addenda, contractor's bid, contract drawings, specifications, modifications, and administrative materials (**14**).

Control cabinet (or panel)   An enclosure for centrally and remotely locating the electrical devices, modules, and connectors associated with the system (**15**).

Control cascade   A computerized method of control in which various control units are linked in sequence with each control unit regulating the operation of the next control unit (**13**).

Control center   A centralized location within the complex for the monitoring and control of the facility's systems (**15**).

Control interpreter language (CIL)   An interpretive language in software offered in some systems that permits the operator to independently modify existing software applications or write entirely new control sequences (**16**).

Control loop   (**2**). (*See* **Loop**.)

Control point   A device, such as a thermometer, door control, or the position of a robot arm, which is controllable from a central location (**15**).

Control sequence   Standard equipment operating order that is established upon a correlated set of data environment conditions or variables managed by the facility control computer (**2**).

Control unit   Part of the CPU that directs a sequence of operations, interprets coded instructions, and initiates proper commands via the computer circuits to execute these instructions (**15**).

Controlled space   Space controlled for temperature, access, or security reasons (**2/8**).

Controller   A device or group of devices that serve to govern points throughout the control system in a predetermined manner (**15**).

Controls   Various devices that govern the performance of a system (**14**).

Core memory   Area in the main computer commonly used for storage of programs or data (**16**).

CPS   Characters per second or cycles per second (**15/19**).

Crash   Unwanted and ungraceful shutdown of the control system caused by a hardware or software malfunction. CPU redundance minimizes this problem (**15/16**).

Critical loads   Those building loads that are very important to the normal operation of the facility (**2/13**).

Critical time programmer   The clock within the facility control system CPU that programs loads to bypass their normal cycling schedule during critical times (**2/15**).

Cross zoned   A computer room fire zoning technique to preclude a single zone from accidentally discharging; requires detectors from two different zones to initiate an alarm before the suppressing agent will discharge (**7**).

CRT   Cathode Ray Tube terminal that displays system output on a television-like tube (**15**).

Cybernetics   Study of the control and communication that takes place within man, animals, and computer type machines (**14**).

Cycle time   The minimum time elapsed between the starts of two successive accesses to any one storage location (**15**).

Cycling   A rhythmic change of the factor under control at or near the desired value (**10**).

Cycling rate   The number of complete cycles, including both on and off times, that a system goes through in one hour (**10**).

Data   Collection of facts, numeric and alphabetical characters which is processed or produced by a computer (**1/16**).

Data base   Nonredundant collection of interrelated information and items; any organized and structured collection of data in memory (**14/16**).

Data communications equipment   Communications interface device for converting digital information to and from a communicable form (**15**).

Data entry   Communications system application in which information normally flows only in one direction, in this case from the operator's terminal to the computer memory (**13/14**).

Data file   File of raw data in a format understood and used by a program (**16**).

Data integrity   Data that cannot be inadvertently modified. If for any reason the data file is damaged or destroyed, it can be recreated (**16**).

Data security   Protection of data from unauthorized disclosure, modification, or destruction (**7/16**).

Date-time-generator   Device to superimpose the date and time of an event on video tape; used to document CCTV surveillance (**9/13**).

Debug   A procedure of running a program to detect and correct errors in a program. It is designed to detect, locate, and remove mistakes from a routine or malfunction from a computer (**17**).

Dedicated minicomputer   A minicomputer or microprocessor containing all elements of a true computer that has been designed specifically to perform one general function under a particular set of software programs (**14/15**).

Degradation System operations will continue, but at a reduced level, in the event of main power loss **(8/18)**.

Delinquency signal Signal indicating a response requirement in connection with the supervision of patrolling protection officers or system attendants **(11)**.

Demand charge That part of the electrical billing format based on kW demand and the demand interval, generally expressed in dollars per kilowatt; charges are to offset the utility's need for a larger generating capacity **(10/13)**.

Demand control Computer based technique that controls the kW demand level by shedding loads when the kW demand exceeds a predetermined set point **(2/10)**.

Demand interval Period of time on which kilowatt demand is monitored and billed by a utility, usually 15 or 30 minutes in length **(10)**.

Demand peak The greatest amount of kilowatts needed during a demand interval **(2)**.

Demand rate Term used by public utilities to describe the maximum rate of use of electrical energy averaged over a time interval and expressed in kilowatts **(10)**.

Depth of field In-focus range of a lens or optical system; latitude of range at which a lens will keep an object in sharp focus at a given lens setting **(9)**.

Depth of focus Range of film-to-lens distance for which the image formed by the lens is clearly focused **(9)**.

Design review meeting A meeting with the owner, architect, and other pertinent design team members which usually takes place at the end of each project submittal phase, i.e. 35%, 60%, and 95% of design completion **(14/18)**.

Design team Usually consists of an architect, mechanical engineer, electrical engineer, civil or structural engineer, and specialty consultants in the field of fire, security, CCTV, access control, and energy management **(14/18)**.

Detailed cost estimate At the 95% design submittal meeting, a fairly accurate cost estimate is usually presented. This estimate is normally calculated to the chronological midpoint of the installation and includes escalation factors **(14/18)**.

Detailed design Level of design that will eventually result in a complete design which includes drawings, specifications, and cost estimates **(14/18)**.

Detector Device designed to detect or perform a single act of initiating a signal **(3/7)**.

Detector, thermal fire Heat responsive devices such as tubing, cable, or thermostats **(3/5)**.

Device, computer A computer peripheral or an electronic component **(2/15)**.

Device, sensor A unit of an electrical system which is intended to carry, but not utilize electrical energy **(2)**.

Diagnostic program   Machine executable instructions that are used to detect and isolate the various system component malfunctions (**16**).

Diagnostics, on-line   Diagnostic messages that the system provides to the console operator while normal system functions continue (**16**).

Digital   Data expressed in numerical format; a noncontinuous or pulsed signal that is either "on" or "off" (**2/14**).

Direct access storage device   A storage device that provides direct access to data. The access time is effectively independent of the location of the data (**15**).

Direct digital control (DDC)   A control loop in which a digital controller periodically updates the process as a function of a set of measured control variables and a given set of control algorithms (**16**).

Disc memory   A bulk storage, random access device for storing digitally coded information (**15**).

Distortion   An undesired change in the signal waveform from that of the original signal (**9**).

Distributed control system   A distributed system of the highest order; distributed control usually implies distributed processing and distributed data; little functionability is lost in any processor on the network if communication is lost with other processors (**18**).

Distributed processing system   A system of multiple, programmable processors each performing its own task, yet working together as a complete system to solve still other tasks (**18**).

Documentated system software   Written documentation of how the software is assembled and exactly what functions it will perform. Essential for a valid and successful facility control system (**14/16**).

Door release, magnetic   Device that holds doors in an open position by means of an electromagnet. In event of a fire alarm, the electrical current is released by the alarm system and the spring loaded door swings closed (**4**).

Door switches   Usually magnetic contact switches which may be surface-mounted or recessed, exposed or concealed on or within normal openings such as doors or windows. When the door or window is opened, the magnetic field is broken and an alarm activated (**7**).

Dry bulb temperature   Air temperature as read by an ordinary dry bulb thermometer (**2/10**).

Dry chemical extinguishing system   A system consisting of dry chemicals and expellant gas storage tanks, fixed piping, and nozzles used to assure proper distribution of the approved extinguishing agent (**4/15**).

Dry pipe system   In water-fire suppression systems the piping is filled with air under pressure and a permanent water supply; normally used in situations where a standard wet pipe system might freeze and the pipes burst. An approved automatic valve releases the water by either the release of the air or thermostatic electric control in the event of fire (**4/5**).

Dual infrared detector (IR/IR) Twin device designed to detect body heat. Effective at reducing false alarms **(5/13)**.

Dual infrared and ultrasonic detector (IR/US) Intrusion detection device; detects body heat (IR) and movement (US) **(7/13)**.

Dual infrared and ultraviolet detector (IR/UV) Designed to detect both heat and flame **(5/13)**.

Dual sensored devices Designed to reduce false alarms by requiring both sensors to be in alarm before an indicating signal is generated **(2/13)**.

Dual track tape Specially designed tape for alerting building occupants of fire or other emergency situations; part of an emergency alerting system **(4/13)**.

Duplex Simultaneous two-way independent transmission of data signals **(14)**.

Duress alarm An emergency alarm that permits a silent signal to be given while all other activity appears perfectly normal **(7/8)**.

Duty cycling Energy management application program which reduces the consumption of electrical energy by cycling equipment so that minimum operating time is used to maintain comfortable, environmental conditions **(10/16)**.

Economizer System of dampers, temperature and humidity sensors, and motors which maximize the use of outdoor air for cooling **(2/10)**.

Economizer control System of ventilation control in which outdoor and return air dampers are controlled to maintain proper mixed air temperature for the most economical operation **(2/10)**.

EDP Electronic Data Processing Transformation of raw data into useful information by electronic equipment **(1/13)**.

E-field sensor Passive sensor that detects changes in the earth's ambient electric field caused by the movement of an intruder **(7)**.

Electric door strike Electromechanical device used to unlock or release a door when energized by a reader terminal interface on command from an on-line central controller **(8)**.

Electrical capacitance fence sensor A technique where an electrical aura is sent through and developed around the fence; when an intruder disrupts the aura or touches the fence an alarm signal is generated **(7)**.

Electromagnetic locking device Two piece locking device consisting of an armature and electromagnet. When energized, the magnetic attraction bonds the two together with holding power up to 3,000 pounds. The magnetic bond is immediately broken when de-energized **(7/8)**.

Electromechanical Controls which contain both electrical and mechanical components **(2/14)**.

Electronic vibration detector Extremely sensitive detection device which utilizes a contact microphone to protect safes, walls, ceilings, floors, filing cabinets, and works of art **(7)**.

Emergency eye wash   Safety device designed to simultaneously flood both eyes with water by means of a foot trip **(11/13)**.

Emulator   A program that allows one processor to simulate the instruction set of another processor, as in the case of a redundant processor **(14)**.

Energy consumption charge   Part of the electric utility bill that is based on kilowatt hour (kWh) consumption; covers the cost of utility fuel, general operating costs, and part of the amortization of the utility's equipment **(2/10)**.

Energy management   Efficient control of the use of energy within a given facility **(2/10)**.

Energy management software   Programs specifically designed to reduce energy consumption in a building. These programs range from very simple to extremely complex **(16)**.

Energy management system   A set of devices, plans, or techniques which control the use of energy (electrical, gas, solar, etc.) within a given environment or facility **(14)**.

Enthalpy   A measure of the total heat content of the air including the sensible heat or air temperature as well as the latent heat or relative humidity **(2/10)**.

Enthalpy control   An energy management application program which reduces cooling cost by selecting either the outside air or return air stream to be cooled, depending upon which has the least enthalpy **(10/16)**.

Environmental control system   Process of controlling the environment by heating, cooling, humidifying, dehumidifying, or cleaning the air **(14/18)**.

Environmental systems   Instrumentation and control devices which affect or indicate the environment inside the facility **(10/13)**.

Event initiated program (EIP)   A program which issues specified commands to any number of system points based on a system event, such as a change of status, absolute or lapsed time, operator command, or command from another program **(14/18)**.

Execute   Command given to the system by the operator to perform a computer instruction or run a program **(2/13)**.

Executive   A routine designed to organize and regulate the flow of work in a computer system by initiating and controlling the execution of other programs; a principal component of most operating systems; also referred to as *Operating System* or *OS*, *Supervisory Routine*, *Executive Routine*, and *Supervisor* **(14/16)**.

Exhaust air   Air removed from the conditioned space by the ventilation system and discharged outdoors **(2/10)**.

Exit device   A lock on the door which can be opened from inside by applying pressure to the bar or handle; also called a crash bar **(1/7)**.

Explosion-proof   A device constructed in a manner to prevent the surrounding atmosphere from being exploded by the operation of, or the results from, operating the item so classified **(5/14)**.

Externally operable   Capable of being operated without the operator being exposed or being in contact with live parts; also covers remote control **(5/14)**.

Extinguishment   Stopping a fire by removing fuel, heat, or oxygen; usually accomplished by flooding or smothering the burning object with water or man-made suppression agent **(4/5)**.

Facility control center (FCC)   Master control center for all building systems; designed so that the various building systems are mutually supportive in an emergency **(7/15)**.

Factory mutual (FM)   Independent approval service; recognized authority in sprinkler and other building protection systems; FM tests and approves a wide variety of fire and safety related equipment **(5/15)**.

Fade   Gradual lowering in amplitude of a signal **(19)**.

Fail safe   In electrical load management, the return of all controlled devices to conventional control in case of a load management panel failure. In protection system electrically locked doors, it is the automatic unlocking of the secured doors **(7/10)**.

Fail safe solenoid   A device that automatically unlocks a door when power is cut off **(14)**.

Fail secure   In protection systems, electrical locking devices will automatically go to the locked condition in the event of a power failure **(7/8)**.

Failsoft   In the event of a hardware failure, falling back to a degraded mode of operation rather than letting the system fail completely with no response for the user; implemented by a system program; also called *graceful degradation* **(14/16)**.

Fallback   A mode of operation where manual or special program procedures are used to maintain some level of performance **(16)**.

False alarm   Receiving an alarm signal without the presence of the hazard indicated; may be caused by equipment failure, line failure, mischief, or human error **(3/7)**.

Far remote   A facility belonging to the parent company, but located many miles from the primary facility control center (FCC) **(14/18)**.

Fast track   The almost concurrent conduct of design and construction/installation services with the objective of completing the project in the shortest time possible or in less time than a typical project of similar nature **(14/18)**.

Fault   An open or ground condition on any line extending from a control unit **(1/13)**.

Fault-tolerant   Software or systems which still execute commands properly, even though certain parts may fail **(14/16)**.

FCC audio system   An audio control system that has been integrated with other building control systems; automated audio monitoring; supervised voice communications system, automatically responsive to facility alarm systems **(12/14)**.

Feedback   The signal or signals that are fed back to the facility control center from a controlled process to denote that it has received the command and has acted upon it **(14/18)**.

Fiber optics   A communication technique where information is transmitted in the form of light over a transparent material, such as a fiber of glass; providing noise free communication and nonsusceptibility to electromagnetic interference **(13/14)**.

Fiberoptic bundle   An assembly of many thousands of hair-sized fibers that are designed to carry light impulses arranged so that an image is transmitted from one end to the other **(9/14)**.

Field expandable   A system designed to permit functions and capabilities to be increased in the field rather than at the factory; normally accomplished by insertion of plug-in modular subassemblies **(1/18)**.

Field of view   Maximum angle of view that can be seen by an individual or an optical system **(9/11)**.

Field order   A written order issued by the security engineer, owner's authorized representative, or architect which requests minor changes which do not change price or timing of a project **(14/18)**.

Fifty-percent submittal   A report associated with an intermediate design phase and submittal; sometimes referred to as a sixty-percent submittal **(14/18)**.

Final design   Follows the incorporation of all final changes covered in the review of the 95% design meeting **(14/18)**.

Fire   Any instance of destructive and uncontrolled burning to include combustible solids, explosions, and liquids or gases that ignite **(3/4)**.

Fire alarm   An alarm system designed to detect and report a fire **(3/13)**.

Fire alarm monitoring   Central monitoring of fire alarm systems by trained personnel **(3/4/5)**.

Fire command station   An area set aside to provide fire personnel and building management a protected and convenient location for coordinating emergency actions in a crisis situation; capable of direct and overriding control of building management systems; focal point for emergency audio announcements to building occupants and for firefighter communication **(14/15)**.

Fire damper   Special HVAC dampers designed and installed to prevent fire and smoke from propagating from one area of the building to another; system controlled to automatically open or close during fire emergencies; may be manually controlled from the Fire Command Station **(3/4/5)**.

Fire division wall   A *fire rated wall* which has a fire rating of two hours or longer **(4)**.

Fire door   A door and its assembly constructed and assembled in place to give protection against the passage of fire. Such doors require an inspection label affixed by the testing or inspecting agency **(3/7)**.

Fire protection system An automatic system including stand-alone systems, devices and equipment to detect fire, actuate an alarm or suppress a fire, or any combination thereof (**3/4**).

Fire retardant material Material that has been tested, evaluated, and rated by nationally recognized testing laboratories as being fire retardant in a set or series of fire environments (**3**).

Fire suppression system A mechanical system designed and equipped to detect a fire, actuate an alarm, and to suppress a fire (**3/4**).

Fire wall A physical barrier constructed to retard the spread of fire; rated according to its ability to withstand fire (**3/4/5**).

First priority In emergency situations, real-time voice announcements will automatically override pretaped information (second priority) or audible signals (third priority) (**12**).

Fixed data Data which remains constant; source data; programmed instructions entered by the system user (**14/16**).

Fixed lens In closed circuit television, a camera lens with a set focal length; a lens incapable of zoom function (**9**).

Fixed rate In energy management, an energy consumer that is either on or off; one incapable of consuming energy at reduced or varying levels (**10/13**).

Fixed temperature, heat-activated device Device designed to initiate an alarm when the ambient temperature reaches its predetermined heat tolerance level (**3**).

Fixed temperature, rate-of-rise detector Device designed to initiate an alarm at a fixed ambient temperature, but will initiate an alarm earlier if the temperature in the area rises at a designed unacceptable rate, as in the case of hot gases from a fire (**3**).

Flame detector A device designed to sense the radiant energy produced by heat or flame; may range from ultraviolet through the visible and infrared spectrums. These detectors are line of sight and react instantly to flame (**4/5**).

Flame stage The point at which a flame has reached sufficient quantity of heat and is available to ignite the gases of unburned particles that have been liberated by thermal decomposition (**3**).

Flash point The minimum temperature in degrees Fahrenheit at which a flammable liquid will give off sufficient vapors to form an ignitable mixture with air near the surface or in the container, but will not sustain combustion (**4/10**).

Flattened rate design Where all energy used will cost the same, regardless of the quantity used (**10/14**).

Floroprotine Foam concentrate; an oil resistant, water-bearing, burnback resistant, sealable self-sealing, noncorrosive and dry chemical compatible firefighting suppression agent; compatible with subsurface injection for tank farm and shipboard applications (**5**).

Foam concentrates   Fire-fighting foam agents used against liquid fires and for mitigation of hazardous liquid spills; may be mixed with salt or fresh water during application; works well at low temperatures; also known as **Aqueous Film-Forming Foam (AFFF)**, **Light Water (trade name)**, and **high expansion foams (5)**.

Foam extinguishing system   A special system to mechanically or automatically discharge a foam made of concentrates, over the area to be protected **(1/5)**.

Focal length   Distance from the optical center of a lens to the camera tube target; indicative of the image size produced **(9)**.

Foil   A ribbon of metallic material that is wired as part of an alarm circuit and is typically attached to glass windows and doors **(7)**.

Foot rail   A special foot-operated manual holdup signaling device **(7)**.

Frangible bulb   Control element in a sprinkler head designed to melt at a set temperature **(4/5)**.

f-stop   Refers to the speed or ability of the lens to pass light. The lower the f-stop number the faster the lens **(9)**.

Fuel loading   Building contents that are subject to burning; not a part of the building construction; items within a structure which will burn and/or give off toxic fumes when subjected to excessive heat **(4)**.

Function keys   Operator terminal keys which, when depressed, are interpreted by the computer as a specific command **(14/18)**.

Fusible element   A metal element in a sprinkler head or other similar device designed to melt at predetermined temperatures to release a flow of water or suppressing agent **(3/4/5)**.

Fusible link   A metal element designed to melt at a predetermined temperature; normally used on weighted fire doors mounted on sloping tracks; when the set temperature is reached, the link melts and, in theory, the fire door rolls closed **(3/4/5)**.

Gain   The increase or amplification achieved in an amplifier circuit; expressed in decibels (dB) **(12/14)**.

Gate valve   A valve for shutting off the water supply to a sprinkler system. This value should only be turned off in emergencies and for repairs **(4/5)**.

General alarm   Term usually applied to the operation of all audible alarms calling for the evacuation of a building **(3)**.

Generator   In computer terminology, a program that creates another program or set of data **(16)**.

Ghost   In CCTV, a spurious image resulting from an echo within the system **(9)**.

Glass break detectors   Sensors that are activated by the sound of breaking glass **(7)**.

Globe valve Fast and silent shut-off valve for a sprinkler system; suitable for clean water only; will handle velocities up to 10 feet per second; valve plug closes against the head of the pump; may be installed in any position; also called a *check valve* (**4/5**).

Graphic CRT terminal A CRT terminal capable of displaying user programmed graphics (**14/18**).

Graphic, full A CRT display unit, usually in color, where each individual pixel of a graphic is controllable with software (**14/18**).

Graphics The use of diagrams or other graphic means to present operating data, curve plots, answers to inquiries, and other computer output (**14/18**).

Ground A conducting connection, whether intentional or accidental, between an electrical circuit or equipment and the earth, or to some conducting body that serves as a ground in place of the earth (**10/14**).

Ground loop The path taken by a circuit including two or more ground reference points intended to be at the same voltage (zero), but which are not because of ground resistance. It can result in hum and other undesirable disturbances in circuits, particularly where relative signal strength is low (**10**).

Grounded Connected to the earth or to some conducting body that serves in place of the earth (**10/14**).

Grounds perimeter protection Any means, whether human, electronic, or a physical barrier, used for protection starting at the property line and working inward toward the buildings (**7/13**).

Group, logical A collection of points whose number and order are established by software and hence are not constrained by the hardware configuration (**14/18**).

Group, physical A collection of points controlled by a single control panel whose number and order are determined by the hardware configuration of the control panel (**14/18**).

Guard tour The patrol of a plant or area by a protection officer who may not make fixed or established rounds, but will vary his daily routine (**11**).

Half duplex operation Operation of a signal transmission system in either direction over a single channel, but not in both directions simultaneously (**1/14**).

Halogenated extinguishing systems A system of pipes, nozzles, an actuating mechanism, and a container of halogenated agent under pressure (**5**).

Halon 1301 An extinguishment agent used in closed environment suppression systems. The generic chemical name for Halon 1301 is bromotrifluoromethane, $CBrF_3$. The other extinguishment agent in this class is Halon 1211, bromotrifloromethane, $CBrClF_2$ (**5**).

Handling of doors The direction the door swings when it is opened. (1) Left Hand Door—swings inward and to the left; (2) Left Hand Reverse Door—

swings outward to the left; (3) Right Hand Door—swings inward and to the right; (4) Right Hand Reverse Door—swings outward and to the right (**1/14**).

Handshaking   A preliminary procedure performed by modems and/or terminals and computers to verify that communication has been established and work on the computer can proceed (**15/16**).

Hard copy record   An output printed on a permanent medium, such as paper, which can be produced at the same time that information is produced in machine language (**14/15**).

Hardware   In computer driven systems, the physical components of the computer processing system; the mechanical, magnetic, electrical, and electronic devices of which a computer is built, including similar components of peripheral devices (**15**).

Hardwired   Pertains to wiring systems in which conductor pairs for each signal are run between the control center and the signal source or destination; non-multiplexing; a wiring arrangement connecting sensors and devices with Intelligent Control Panels in a multiplexed system (**2/14**).

Hard wiring   Making a permanent connection by wiring between devices. Also used in referring to permanent line voltage (120 or 240VAC) wiring (**2/14**).

Heat-detecting cable   Heat-detecting wire installed in direct contact or near the equipment to be protected; effective for a wide variety of heat detecting applications; tested and listed by U.L. (**3/4/5**).

Heat reclaim   The process of reusing discharged heat from such sources as exhaust fans, condenser coils, and hot water drains to do useful work (**2/10**).

Hidden demand charge   Utility billing for electricity that contains a hidden charge for a low load factor for a building, which penalizes the energy user through this hidden charge (**2/10**).

High coercivity   Technical term for a magnetic stripe access control card where the stripe has a magnetic measurement of 4,000 oersteds (**8**).

High expansion foam   One of many types of foam concentrates available (**5**).

High limit control   A device which normally monitors the condition of the controlled medium and interrupts system operation if the monitored condition becomes excessive (**10/14**).

High line security   A highly specialized transmission bus supervision that precludes the possibility of line bridging or signal substitution; very effective for security on extremely sensitive communication channels (**7/14**).

High rate discharge HRD extinguisher   A highly specialized piece of equipment primarily used in explosion suppression and advance inerting of adjacent areas (**5**).

High security   Term used when discussing sensitive security problems; entails specialized equipment, high line security, skilled monitoring and effective response; designed to provide the ultimate in physical security for a high priority area **(7/15)**.

Holdup alarm Silent alarm system to indicate a holdup in progress **(7)**.

Homing A closed circuit television system where one or more CCTV cameras send their pictures directly (homing) to a single monitor for viewing **(9)**.

Horns In general, horns can be used in place of vibrating bells to provide a more distinctive sound **(3)**.

Host computer The primary or controlling computer in a data communications system; also the computer which executes the control systems programs **(14/18)**.

Humidification The process of increasing the water vapor content of the conditioned air **(10/14)**.

Humidistat A regulatory device, actuated by changes in humidity, used for the automatic control of relative humidity **(10/14)**.

Humidity control Controlling the water vapor within a given space **(10/14)**.

HVAC Industry and trade terminology for **H**eating **V**entilating and **A**ir-Conditioning **(2/10)**.

HVAC economizer Computerized control of building temperature, humidity, dampers, and motors; programmed to sense inside and outside temperature and humidity with the object of controlling dampers and motors to make maximum use of outdoor air for building cooling **(10/16)**.

Hygrometer An instrument responsive to humidity conditions of the atmosphere **(10/14)**.

Hysteresis The lag in an instrument's or process's response when a force acting on it is abruptly changed. Hysteresis may be caused by various mechanical, electrical, or physical conditions and may or may not be desirable **(10/14)**.

Ideal curve A method of determining when load shedding should occur. Actual energy usage is compared to an ideal curve which is based on the maximum allowed kilowatt level during the utility's demand interval **(14/18)**.

Immediate access Ability of a computer to put data into or remove it from storage without delay **(14/18)**.

Incident light Light that falls on an object **(9)**.

Incipient smoke detectors Senses particles of combustion smaller than one micron (one millionth of a meter), too small for the eye to see, and initiates an alarm. Ideal for detecting fire at the very earliest stage **(3)**.

Incipient stage First stage of a normally developing fire. In the development of a fire, thermal decomposition of combustible material produces large quantities of minute particles of combustion which can normally be sensed by **ionization smoke detectors** **(3)**.

Indicating device   Any audible or visual signal employed to indicate fire, intrusion, supervisory or trouble condition. Horns, bells, sirens, electronic horns, buzzers, speakers, and chimes are audible indicating devices. Lights, beacons, strobes, target and meter deflection are examples of visual indicators (**3/7**).

Indicating device circuit   A circuit to which automatic or manual signal initiating devices are connected, including circuits which connect such devices directly to the facility control center (**3/7**).

Industrial process   Central monitoring of systems other than fire, security, and holdup devices; includes water levels, boiler pressures, temperatures, humidity, etc. Monitoring is accomplished with special sensors, and the system operator is notified for corrective action when an alarm is initiated (**10/18**).

Information retrieval   The techniques employed for recovering certain desired information from a computer's memory (**14/16**).

Infrared, active   A system consisting of an infrared transmitter and receiver that is actuated by an object passing between the two units (**7/13**).

Infrared beam sensor   A system consisting of an infrared transmitter and receiver. When the IR beam is broken an alarm is initiated (**7**).

Infrared (IR) heat detector   A device designed to sense stabilized radiation within an area, causing an alarm when there is a change in the radiation pattern (**3**).

Infrared illuminator   An infrared lens on a powerful searchlight used to illuminate scenes under surveillance of an IR equipped CCTV camera; also used by security personnel equipped with special IR glasses (**9**).

Infrared motion detector   A sensor that detetcts changes in the infrared light radiation from parts of the protected area (**7/13**).

Infrared, passive   A device that is actuated by a change in the amount of infrared energy being received by it from the area it is viewing (**7/13**).

Infrared radiation detection   Detection units designed to sense stabilized radiation within an area and cause an alarm when a change of radiation occurs (**7/13**).

Initiating device   A manually or automatically operated device designed to initiate a signal to a control center from which an *indicating* alarm signal is activated (**3/7**).

Initiating device circuit   A circuit to which automatic or manual initiating devices are connected (**3/7**).

Inside perimeter   A line of protection adjacent to a protected area and passing through those points where entry into the area can be effected, such as doors, windows, skylights, tunnels, or other points of access (**6/7**).

Instantaneous rate   A method for determining when load shedding should occur. Actual energy usage is measured and compared to a preset kilowatt level. If the actual kilowatt level is exceeded, loads will be shed until the actual consumption rate drops below the set point (**10/13**).

Instruction set The repertoire of operations that a CPU can execute (**14/16**).

Insulation A material having good dielectric properties and suitable for separating adjacent conductors in a circuit (**14**).

Integrated system evaluation checklist A method of evaluating vendors during the system selection process. (A suggested checklist is in Appendix B.) (**14/18**).

Intelligent control panel (ICP) A microprocessor based control panel that provides basic data gathering functions as well as additional functions, such as lockout control, run-time accumulation, local point control, and local execution of application software such as duty cycling, load reset, optimum start/stop, and event initiated programs. Also known as *Intelligent Gathering Panels*, *Field Interface Devices* (*FID*), and *Data Gathering Panels* (*DGP*) (**14/15**).

Intelligent device A device that contains a microprocessor (**14/15**).

Intense heat Where vapor temperatures and pressure are directly related. This type of superheat is measured by comparing the temperature of the vapor to what the vapor temperature would ordinarily be at the measured pressure. Also referred to as the fourth or *High Heat Stage* of a fire (**3/4**).

Intensified vidicon (IV) A standard vidicon TV image pickup tube of the direct readout type coupled with fiber optics to an intensifier to increase tube sensitivity (**9**).

Interactive Computer functions which include operation, control, and programming performed on an inquiry-response dialog basis between operator and machine (**14/16**).

Interactive dialog Direct communication between a computer and the operator without the use of punched cards, magnetic tape, or similar medium. A CRT terminal or printer terminal serves as a means for the operator and computer to communicate in real time by a question and answer dialog (**14/16**).

Interface A shared boundary; the bringing together, in an organized manner, of hardware, software, and human operators; channels or parallel paths and associated control circuitry that provide the connection between the central processor and its peripherial units; the connection that allows two separate items to be tied together (**14/18**).

Interference Extraneous energy which interferes with the reception of desired signals in a signal transmission path (**13/14**).

Intermediate design Though not usually listed as a basic engineering phase, it may signify 50% to 60% submittal level on large projects (**14/18**).

Interrupt The initiation, by hardware, of a routine intended to respond to an external, device originated, or internal, software originated, event that is either unrelated, or asynchronous with, the executing program (**15/16**).

Interstage differential In a multi-stage HVAC system, the change in temperature at the thermostat needed to turn on additional heating or cooling equipment (**2/10**).

Intrascene dynamic range   In television, the useful camera operating light range, from highlight to shadow, in which detail can be observed in a static scene when both highlights and shadows are present (**9**).

Intrusion alarm   Alarm signal generated by an intrusion detection device or system (**7**).

Intrusion detector   A sensor used to detect the entry or attempted entry of a person into the area being protected including infrared (heat sensing), ultrasonic (motion sensing), microwave (motion) sensors and other alarms and electronic devices (**7**).

I/O (input/output)   A general term for the equipment used to communicate with a computer and the data involved in the communication (**14/18**).

Ionization smoke detector   A dectector designed to sense particles of combustion at the earliest stage of development, usually before the outbreak of smoke or visible flame (**3**).

ISIT (intensifier silicon intensifier target)   Trade name of a TV image pickup tube of the direct readout type designed for extremely low level light (L^3) applications. This is essentially an SIT tube with an additional intensifier fiber optically coupled to provide increased sensitivity (**9**).

Isolated   An area or point not readily accessible to persons unless special means of access are used (**2/13**).

Jump   A computer instruction that causes the processor to get its next instruction from a specified address in memory (**16**).

K   A unit for measuring the capacity of a computer memory. 1K is equal to 2^{10} or 1,024 units. 4K is 4,096 units. Memory size is usually measured in words or bytes (**19**).

Key lock system   Any system in which a metal key instead of a coded card is inserted into the locking device to gain entry (**8**).

Kilowatt   1,000 watts. Abbreviated: **kW** (**19**).

Kilowatt hour   A measure of electrical energy consumption, 1,000 watts being consumed per hour. Abbreviated: **kWh** (**10/13**).

kW demand   The maximum rate of electrical power usage for a 15 or 30 minute interval in commercial buildings for each billing period. A utility meter records this maximum rate and customers are billed for this peak rate, usually once per month (**10**).

kWh consumption   The amount of electrical energy used over a period of time; the number of kWh used per month. Often called *Consumption* (**19**).

Lace paneling   Surfaces of walls, door panels, and safes are often protected against entry by lacing or weaving a close lace-like pattern of metallic foil or a fine brittle wire on the surface. Entry cannot be made without first breaking the foil or wire, thus setting off an alarm (**7**).

Lag   In a television pickup tube, persistence of the electrical charge image for two or more frames after excitation is removed (**9**).

Lag   Preferred engineering term for delay in the response of a control system to a change in the variable being controlled (**10**).

Large scale integration (LSI)   Manufacturing technology in microminiaturization in which many thousands of components are packaged into one small *chip* (**14/18**).

Leased line   A conductor rented from a common carrier for purposes of interconnecting data modems between a central processor and those at distant, remote stations or at any remote station where it is not feasible to run coaxial cable for purpose of data transmission; ordinarily, a pair of voice-grade channel conductors for data transmission (**14/18**).

Life safety   National Fire Protection Association Standard 101 (**4**).

Light emitting diode (LED)   Low current and voltage light used as an indicator (**10/14**).

Light water   Trade name for a synthetic **aqueous film-forming foam**; also referred to as **AFFF** (**5**).

Lighting control   Technique for limiting energy consumption by reducing the on-time of building lighting systems (**14**).

Limit control   Temperature, pressure, humidity, dew-point, or other control that is used as an override to prevent undesirable or unsafe conditions in a controlled system (**2/13**).

Limit shutdown   Condition in which the system has been stopped because the value of the temperature or pressure has exceeded a preestablished limit (**10/13**).

Limited water supply system   The least amount of water allowed by standards and codes; generally a 20 minute supply of water or 15,000 gallons available on site are required (**5**).

Line amplifier   Amplifier for audio or video signals that feeds a transmission line; also called a *program amplifier* (**9/12**).

Line printer   The most common type of output unit which converts data into printed form that can be visually examined and understood by the user; generally, an electromechanical device which types out complete lines of print (**14/18**).

Line supervision   An electrical method of monitoring power, wiring, and/or devices to insure that they are in proper operating order at all times (**14/15**).

Listed   Equipment or materials included in a list published by a nationally recognized testing laboratory, inspection agency, or other organization concerned with product evaluation that maintains periodic inspection of production of the listed equipment or materials, and whose listing states either that the equipment or materials meet nationally recognized standards, or has been tested and found suitable for use in a specified manner (**14/19**).

LLTV Also LLLTV and L³TV. Abbreviation for low light television which is the name given to CCTV systems capable of operating with scene illumination less than 0.5 lumens/ft² (**9**).

Load That part of an electrical circuit in which useful work is performed; in a heating or cooling system, the heat transfer that the system will be called upon to provide; any equipment that can be connected to a load management system; in programming, to enter data into storage or working registers; to bring a program out of storage for execution (**10**).

Load factor A comparison of kilowatt hours of electricity consumed to the peak rate at which power was consumed. Load factor is always a number between zero and one and is expressed as the kilowatt hours consumed over a specified period divided by the product of the kilowatt peak demand registered, times the number of hours in the period (**10**).

Load leveling An algorithm that distributes the on/off cycles of equipment in each cycle period of a duty cycling program (**10**).

Load management The control of electrical loads to reduce kW demand and kWh consumption; computer controlled devices which effectively reduce kW and kWh consumption (**10**).

Load programmer Any device which turns loads on and off on a real time, time interval, or kW demand basis (**10/14**).

Load relay A relay that directly switches a load (**10/14**).

Load reset An energy management application program which reduces the amount of energy used for heating and cooling by resetting the setpoint of the discharge temperature of the primary conditioner based on the load of greatest demand (**10/14**).

Load shedding Manual and computer manipulation of energy consuming devices to prevent exceeding the demand limit set for the facility (**10/13**).

Local alarm A local system that produces a signal at the premises protected; an alarm that originates from a local building system as a result of an automatic or a manual initiating device. Such systems range from simple bell systems to elaborately zoned buildings and presignal systems (**3**).

Loop (1) In electronics, a complete electrical circuit. (2) In computer terminology, a series of instructions being performed repeatedly until a terminal condition prevails. (3) In automatic control, loop is the path followed by command signals, which direct the work to be done, and feedback signals, which flow back to the command point to indicate what is actually being done (**14/18**).

Looping-bridging Camera input connections have corresponding output connections which allow for video input signals to be bridged to a second switcher where two monitors will act in a like manner until manually switched elsewhere **(9)**.

Looping-homing   All camera input connections have a corresponding, one-on-one, output connection which allows each independent video signal to be inputed at a second switcher **(9)**.

Low limit control   A device which normally monitors the condition of the controlled medium and interrupts system operation if the monitored condition drops below the desired minimum value **(10/14)**.

Machine   A computer or CPU **(1)**.

Machine language   Language that can be directly used by a computer; a series of **bits** written as such to instruct computers; the first level of computer language, with *assembly language* and *compiler language* being the second and third computer languages **(1/16)**.

Magnetic buried line sensor   A buried system designed to detect the movement of ferrous material across the magnetic field that is produced both above and below the ground; not influenced by seismic or acoustic effects; cosmetically invisible **(7)**.

Magnetic card   (1) Where metal shims are embedded in the card and sensors detect the presence or absence of material to determine the code; (2) where magnetic material is embedded in the card and the encoding is done via the placement, polarity, and strength of the applied field; (3) where a strip of magnetic tape is applied to the card, allowing a large amount of information to be stored on the card and read by a compatible card reader. Cards can be demagnetized by exposure to strong electric fields such as generators in power plants **(8)**.

Magnetic switches   Switches consisting of two parts, a magnet, usually mounted on a door or window, and a switch assembly, mounted on the frame of the door or window. Also called *magnetic contact devices* **(7)**.

Mainframe   The central processing unit, main memory, and input/output (I/O) interfaces of a computer **(14/18)**.

Main storage   Program-addressable storage in a computer system, where computer instructions are executed and data is processed, incorporating both real storage and virtual storage **(14/18)**.

Manual   Systems in which an emergency must be discovered and the signaling device activated by human action **(1–11)**.

Manual station, break glass   A manual break glass station is a fire alarm station in which it is necessary to break a glass plate or rod in order to activate the station alarm sequence. Also called a *manual fire alarm box* and a *manual pull station* **(5)**.

Manual video switcher   Video switcher which requires human manipulation to move monitoring from one video camera to another **(9)**.

Manufacturer's specifications   The engineering and architectual specifications found in a manufacturer's technical literature (**14/18**).

Mass storage system   A system that extends the virtual storage concept to direct access storage and extends the user's on-line data storage capacity to as much as 472 billion characters of information (**14/18**).

Master key system   See chapter 8, Movement Control, for detailed explanation of Master Key System, Grand Master Key, Operational Key, and Sub-Master Key arrangements (**8**).

Matrix   In an automation system, an arrangement of circuit elements such as wires, relays and diodes which performs logic functions in data handling; a device to route, distribute, or decode data signals; a group of numbers organized on a rectangular grid and treated as a unit. The numbers can be referenced by their location on the grid (**16**).

Maximum off-time   The greatest period of time a load can remain de-energized before it must be restored (**10/16**).

McCulloh system   In a central station operation, special circuits permitting several alarm subscribers to share the same leased line, helping to reduce telephone costs (**2**).

McCulloh type system   An arrangement of apparatus and wiring which enables an alarm initiating circuit to function despite an open and/or ground at the same point. Called *Manual McCulloh* if manual switching is required or *Automatic McCulloh* if the switching is automatic (**14**).

Media   In computer systems, the physical material on which data is recorded, such as paper tape, cards, magnetic disk, magnetic tape, and bubble memory (**15/16**).

Medical alert   A signal activated by an injured person or bystander where medical assistance is required. The signal is transmitted to a remote receiving station or facility control center for action. In some cases the type and location of the signal will indicate the type of medical response required (**2/13**).

Mega   When measuring computer memory, *mega* is equal to 1,048,576 units; otherwise one million and abbreviated *M* (**16**).

Memory   A device or media used to store information in forms that can be understood by the computer hardware; usually used to denote data retention inside the computer; synonymous with internal computer storage available retrieval (**15/16**).

Memory, bubble   Bubble memories are made from magnetic materials called *garnets*. Bubble memory access time is slower than semiconductor memory, but offers nonvolatility, low power dissipation, and no moving parts (**18**).

Memory capacity   The maximum number of storage positions in the main memory of a computer (**14/16**).

Memory modules   Individual devices or memory boards that may be added as increments of memory; usually 4K, 8K, 16K, or 32K words in length depending upon individual systems (**14/15**).

Memory, non-volatile   Memory which does not lose its stored information or data when power to the system is lost (**14/16**).

Memory, off-line   Memory not under control of the central processing unit (**14/16**).

Memory, on-line   Memory under the control of the central processing unit (**14/16**).

Memory, programmable   Memory that can be both read from and written into by the processor, synonymous with **RAM (random access memory)** (**14/16**).

Memory, protected   Programmable memory that cannot be written into, usually on a temporary basis (**14/16**).

Memory, read-write   Computer memory which can be both read from and written into by the system operator (**14/16**).

Memory, volatile   Memory which loses its stored instructions and data when power to the system is lost (**14/16**).

Menu penetration   A man-machine interface technique in which operator control of the system is accomplished by the selection of desired actions from tables or lists of alternatives (menus) presented on the system CRT (**11/14**).

Menu selection   A method of presenting the system using an alpha numeric English language listing of possible alternatives for the operator to select from. In a user friendly system, operator selection is implemented with a limited number of keyboard entries, usually one, two, or three (**15/16**).

Mercury switch   A drop of mercury contained within a glass vial triggers an alarm when the device is tipped; the seesaw movement of the vial in reaction to the mercury's movement causes an alarm to be initiated (**7**).

Message   A physical quality of transmitted information that is physically continuous and processed as a unit (**14/16**).

Metallic foil   Thin strips of lead/tin foil affixed to a glass surface. If the glass is cracked, the current flowing through the foil is disrupted and an alarm results. Economical protection, but requires frequent maintenance, especially on glass doors (**7**).

Microphone   In security, a device employed to pick up discrete sound frequencies and convert them into electrical variations for transmission on electrical cables. In audio control, a technique for monitoring closed or remote areas for unusual sounds in response to a signal from another system, usually mechanical equipment rooms, stairwells, or potential holdup areas (**7/12**).

Microprocessor   An exceedingly small digital computing device; any device, small in size, that processes data and is claimed to be a microprocessor by its manufacturer; often used to describe any new process control product that embodies a microprocessor, i.e., a microprocessor based data acquisition system. The central processing unit (CPU) of a microprocessor is usually constructed with semiconductor technology **(14/15)**.

Microprocessor based controls   Computer based controls that are designed to effectively manage a large number of CCTV cameras; facilitates handling as many as 64 cameras by a single operator **(9)**.

Microprocessor-LSI   Central processing unit (CPU) of a digital computer placed on a Large Scale Integration (LSI) chip that contains the arithmetic, logic unit, and control unit of a computer. Microprocessors are in building blocks of 880 and 770 microprocessors which have additional interfacing to operate displays, printers, annunciators, etc. **(14/15)**.

Microprogram   A program of subcommands to be handled by a computer to provide data for a higher level program that has been constructed from precomputed subcommands. The execution of a microprogram is usually initiated by computer software instruction **(16)**.

Microwave   In security, very short radio waves that readily pass through rain, snow, and fog. These waves are not affected by lightning, neon lights, auto ignitions, or other man-made electrical noises and may be beamed like a spotlight, and can be reflected from or scattered by striking solid objects **(7/14)**.

Microwave motion detection   A means of detecting the presence of an intruder through the use of radio frequency generating and receiving equipment **(7)**.

Minicomputer   A digital computing device, larger in size than a microcomputer and having a typical word length of 16 or 32 bits. An addressable main memory is typically from 64K to over 1M. Compared with a microcomputer, the minicomputer is typically characterized by higher performance, a richer instruction set, a variety of high level computer languages, several operating systems, and networking software **(15/16)**.

Minimum off-time   Amount of time that a load must remain de-energized once it has been shed **(10/14)**.

Minimum on-time   Shortest period of time that a load can be energized when it is being duty cycled **(10/14)**.

MMI   Man-machine interface; a program which provides the human interface functions for a computer system; the driver for the primary operator terminals of the system **(14/16)**.

Mnemonic   A symbolic representation or abbreviation designed to aid operators in identifying the full name. *JSR* may be the mnemonic for *Jump to SubRoutine* **(11/14)**.

Modem   A MODulation/DEModulation device that permits computers and terminals to communicate over telephone lines and enables digital data to be transmitted on analog-type networks; also called a *data set* **(14/15)**.

Modification   A written change to contract documents, signed by the owner and the contractor, resulting in a field order or a change order **(14/18)**.

Modular expansion System hardware and software design technique which permits system growth based on an original set of central equipment; modular increments are added in both hardware and software to meet system growth requirements (**13/14**).

Modular peripheral hardware A term that includes input, output and storage devices, card readers, magnetic disks, paper tape printers, etc., all of which are operated under computer control and constructed as standard compatible units which can be used to easily expand a system or to build a wide range of system configurations (**15/18**).

Modularity (1) Modular hardware that allows a user to start a system modestly and easily add additional hardware components, memory capacity, and terminals as future requirements dictate. (2) Modular software has the ability to easily add new software to the system without scrapping existing software operating system applications and without major system reconfigurations (**15/16**).

Module A system module that contains circuitry to provide a distinct function and usually plugs into a base panel. Equipment assembled with modules is said to be of modularized construction (**14/15**).

Money clip Robbery alarm device, usually found in a cash drawer; a contact is closed and a silent alarm actuated when money is removed from that segment of the cash drawer (**7/12**).

Monitor (1) In CCTV, a device for viewing the television camera directly to the camera output. A true monitor does not incorporate channel selector or audio components. (2) In computer terminology, a program that exercises primary control of the routines that comprise the operating system; a program that controls I/O and related functions; also called a *supervisor* (**9/15**).

Monitoring station Physical location where human activity interfaces with control system annunciators and/or alarm receivers (**11/14**).

Morning warmup A control system which keeps outside air dampers closed, after night setback, until desired space temperature has been achieved (**10/13**).

Motion detection A system designed to generate an alarm by sensing the movement of an intruder within the protected area usually accomplished by ultrasonic, microwave, or infrared detectors (**7/13**).

Motion detectors Devices that detect movement of an intruder within a protected area and activate an alarm. These units operate by filling a space with energy patterns that are observed by the sensor. When an intruder disrupts the invisible pattern, an alarm is triggered (**7/13**).

Multiplexer (1) In television, a specialized optical device that makes it possible to use a single television camera in conjunction with one or more motion picture projectors and/or slide projectors in a film chain. (2) In computers, a unit used for combining signals, thus reducing the required number of transmission paths (**9/14**).

Multi-programming   A technique for executing numerous programs simultaneously by overlapping or interweaving their execution. This permits more than one program to time-share machine operations (**14/16**).

Multizone system   (1) A centralized HVAC system that controls several zones with each zone having its own thermostat. (2) A fire detection zoning arrangement that provides the system operator with finite information concerning the location of the zone in alarm and the type of initiation device, manual or automatic. (3) In security zoning, specific location for the initial alarm followed by additional alarm, in sequence, as the intruder moves through additional security zones within the protected facility (**10/13**).

Municipal trip   Device within a fire alarm panel which automatically alerts the local (municipal) fire department of the alarm (**3/4**).

N.C.   Term referring to *normally closed* contacts of a relay. Contacts are close-circuited when the relay is de-energized (**2/13**).

Near remote   A facility located near the prime location, yet separated geographically by a short distance or physical barrier such as a freeway or river (**14/18**).

Neutral zone   Range in the total control zone where the controller does not respond to changes in the controlled process. A dead zone, usually at the midpoint of the control range (**10/13**).

Newvicon   Trade name for a TV image pickup tube of the direct readout type designed for low light applications. The photoconductive target is a heterojunction structure characterized by high sensitivity, about 20 times that of a sulfide target, nonblooming of high brightness details, relative freedom from burn-in, and good resolution. The newvicon tube, in most cases, must be equipped with an auto iris lens system (**9**).

NFPA   National Fire Protection Association; primary source for standards for fire protection equipment and installation. NFPA standards should always be checked by competent authority before the purchase, installation, or construction of any item pertaining to fire systems; especially NFPA No. 70, National Electric Code, and NFPA No. 72D, Proprietary Protective Signaling Systems (**3/19**).

Night cycle   Energy management application program which maintains specified levels of temperature in the controlled space during unoccupied periods (**10/16**).

Night purge   Energy management application program which causes the cool night air to be used to reduce the temperature in a building thereby reducing energy requirements during morning occupancy cool down (**10/16**).

Night setback   Ability to reduce heating expense during unoccupied hours by lowering temperature, closing outside air dampers, and intermittently operating blowers (**10/16**).

N.O. Term referring to *normally open* contacts of a relay. The contacts are open-circuited when the relay is de-energized **(2/13)**.

Noise (1) In television systems, an undesirable voltage originating in television equipment or from some external source, which produces an interfering signal in the received picture. (2) In electronic systems, the undesirable background signals that clutter the control signal; also the sum of all unwanted signals such as hum, hiss, rumble, interference, distortion, etc. **(9/14)**.

Numerical control Method of controlling a process, machine tool, or assembly line by means of digital instruction carried on punched tape, magnetic tape, or other such transmission system **(10/16)**.

Object protection A security technique for direct protection of *things*; often the final stage of an in-depth protection system utilizing property line, building and area protection devices; generally used to protect safes, filing cabinets, desks, models, art work, and expensive equipment; also called *object security* **(7)**.

Oersted A measurement of magnetic data holding power for the information contained on a magnetic stripe card; 400 oersteds being typical and 4,000 oersteds on a high coercivity card **(7)**.

Off-line Term used to describe the state of peripheral equipment or user activity that is not under the control of the central processing unit (CPU) **(15/16)**.

Off-line locks/systems (1) Equipment not under the control of a central processor; (2) access equipment at entrances and exits which makes independent access decisions **(15/16)**.

On-line Term used to describe the state of peripheral equipment or user activity that is under the control of a central processing unit (CPU) **(15/16)**.

On-line operation In control terminology, the operation in which data is fed directly from the controlled process into the computer that exercises direct control based on this data. Since the computer's reaction is moment-to-moment without appreciable time lag, the resulting actions are said to be on a *real time* basis **(15/16)**.

On-off control A simple control system, consisting basically of a switch, in which the device being controlled is either fully on or fully off and no intermediate positions are available **(10/14)**.

Open loop Method of control in which there is no self-correcting action for an error in the desired operational condition **(10/13)**.

Open loop control Computer-evaluated control action is applied by an operator **(10/13)**.

Operating system (O/S) A main program that schedules and controls the execution of all other programs used by the computer; an organized collection of routines and procedures for operating a computerized system, the software which controls execution of computer programs (**14/18**).

Operating system functions   Routines and procedures normally performed by the operating system (O/S) include: (1) scheduling, loading, initiating, and supervising the execution of programs; (2) allocating storage, input/output units, and other facilities of the computer system; (3) initiating and controlling input/output operations; (4) handling errors and restarts; (5) coordinating communications between the human operator and the computer system; (6) maintaining a log of system operations; and (7) controlling operations in a multi-programming, multi-processing, or time-sharing mode (**14/18**).

Operational security   Control of process and personnel primarily by administrative means to include security procedures for all nonsecurity personnel, as well as the administration of security systems, processes, and personnel (**6/13**).

Operations research   Method used to solve large scale or complicated problems arising from any operation, i.e., production, distribution process, etc., where a major decision must be based on solving a large number of variables (**14/18**).

Operator's console   Input/output device or group of devices used to communicate with the control system (**13/14**).

Optical cards   Access control cards with a pattern of light spots that are read by special illumination, frequently infrared (**8**).

Optimization   Process of operating an environmental system at maximum efficiency to obtain the desired environmental conditions at all times with the least consumption of energy (**10/14**).

Optimum start/stop   Energy management application program which forecasts the optimum start time and stop time of the controlled plant or fan system in order to reduce equipment run-time while maintaining building comfort conditions at times of human occupancy (**10/13**).

"Or equal" specifications   Term describing equipment on the basis of an actual manufacturer and the manufacturer's model numbers and requiring any purchased equipment to be no less than equal in quality and performance capabilities (**14/18**).

OS&Y   Term used to describe **Open**, **Stem**, and **Yoke** valve found in most sprinkler systems (**3**).

Outline specification   A draft specification that gives a level of detail comparable to the 35% submittal; usually provides only rudimentary and generic descriptions and general locations of equipment installation (**14/18**).

Output   (1) The signal level at the output of an amplifier or other device; (2) in electronics, the power, energy, or signal delivered by a device or system; (3) in computer terminology, the processed information being delivered by a computer or a device used to accomplish this data delivery (**13/14**).

Outside air Air brought into the ventilation system from outside the building not previously circulated through the system (**10/13**).

Outside perimeter Line of protection surrounding the protected building, but somewhat removed from the structure itself. A perimeter fence surrounding a building is a typical example of outside perimeter protection. Also called *outdoor protection* (**7/13**).

Overhead suppression systems Industrial application for carbon dioxide or other type suppression systems (**5**).

Override Manual or automatic action taken to bypass the normal operation of a device or system (**13/18**).

Overshoot An excessive response to a undirectional signal change. Sharp overshoots are sometimes referred to as *spikes* (**2/10**).

Owner In contractual agreements, any person who alone, or jointly or severally with others, has the legal title to any building, structure, or premises; a person having a vested or contingent interest in the property in question (**14/18**).

Owner's authorized representative (OAR) The individual selected by the owner and designated in writing to act in the owner's behalf, generally in matters concerning a specific project (**14/17**).

Paging systems System intended to page one or more persons by means of voice over loudspeaker stations located throughout the premises (**12/14**).

Pan Technique for achieving a panoramic effect by pivoting a television camera back and forth across the area to be viewed (**9**).

Pan and tilt Device upon which a camera can be mounted that allows movement in both azimuth (pan) and in a vertical plane (tilt); the dual capability of being able to pan and/or tilt a camera (**9**).

Panel An electrical cabinet that provides basic control circuitry for the function required; space may be provided for inserting modules (**14/15**).

Panic alarm A signal, usually silent, that is sent to a remote receiving location where a response may be generated (**7/13**).

Passive A non-powered component which generally presents some loss to a system; also incapable of generating power or amplification (**3/7**).

Passive infrared detectors Devices that sense a change in infrared energy levels caused when a human body moves through a protected area; not subject to false alarms due to noise, vibration, etc. These units are essentially line of sight sensors (**7**).

Patrol tour management Technique for controlling and supervising protection personnel as they move about the facility. The system provides safety for the patrolling personnel and hard copy documentation of the tour. Also called a **patrol tour system** (**11/13**).

Patrol tour station   Device located at divergent points throughout the facility used as check-in points for protection officers on tour; may also serve as an emergency call station. Also called a *watch tour box* (**11**).

Patrol tour system   Computer supervised patrol tour management arrangement; automatically provides a record of tour activity; monitors movement of the officer while on tour; also called **patrol tour management** (**11/13**).

Payback   The total project investment divided by one year's savings. This gives the number of years it will take to recover the investment with no regard to interest or taxes (**14/18**).

PC Board   A **P**rinted **C**ircuit **B**oard; a circuit board whose electrical connections are made through conductive material that is contained on the board itself, rather than with individual wires (**15/16**).

Peak demand   Greatest amount of kilowatts needed during a demand interval (**10/14**).

Performance specification   A document that describes in detail how equipment should function and may also include quality and manufacturing requirements. This type of specification lets the owner know what the end product will do and puts the owner in the position of not having to determine whether or not a manufacturer's piece of equipment will function as required (**14/18**).

Perimeter barrier   Any physical barrier used to supplement the protection of an inside or outside perimeter (**7**).

Perimeter protection   Condition in building security resulting in the use of devices which detect intrusion through doors, windows, and other access points. Also called *perimeter security* (**7**).

Peripheral   Devices used for storing, entering, or retrieving data from the computer system (**15**).

Peripheral control unit   Intermediary control device that links an item of peripheral equipment to the central processing unit (**CPU**) (**15**).

Peripheral equipment   Any console device that is not part of the central processor, but is connected to the CPU via function cards, console cabling, or other input/output means; includes, but is not limited to keyboard, visual display, teletypewriter, projector, CRT display, pilot lights, tape reader, etc. Does not include the trunk system and remote panels (**15**).

Photoelectric beams   An instrument consisting of two elements, one that transmits a beam of light and one that receives the light beam. Usually the transmitting beam is infrared, making it almost invisible to the naked eye. The devices are used in conjunction with a security alarm system for alerting purposes. Mirrors may be used to crisscross an area or bend around corners and obstacles; however, each mirror reduces the total light path (**7**).

Photoelectric smoke detector   Device designed to detect ambient smoke through photoelectric beam obscuration (**3/4/5**).

Physical barrier   Any physical means to impede, delay, or prevent intrusion into a protected area. Barriers may be natural, like rivers, cliffs, or other natural features, or structural, like fences, walls, floors, grilles, roofs, barbed wire, or combinations thereof (**7**).

Physical record   In computer terminology, a record that is stored, retrieved, and moved within the system. A physical record may contain all or part of one or more logical records (**14/18**).

Physical security   Control of the physical environment by physical means, to include barriers, locking systems, mechanical systems, signs, design and layout of the facility, and protective lighting; in order to deny, delay, or discourage unauthorized or illegal intrusion (**6/7**).

Picture signal   That portion of the composite video signal which lies above the blanking level and contains the picture information (**9**).

Pilot light display   A matrix of lights designed to display selected, digital alarm or trouble points (**2/13**).

PIV   Term used when referring to a Post Indicator Valve; a valve for shutting off the water supply to a sprinkler system (**3**).

Pixel   A single point or dot in the grid of dots that forms the image on CRT display units. Also called a *picture element* (**14**).

Plenum chamber   An air compartment connected to one or more distributing ducts (**13/14**).

Plunging   Tendency of a foam or other suppressing agent to move beneath a burning fluid; negative aspect of some foam concentrates; failure of a foam concentrate to control a fire (**5**).

Point   A finite address of a field input/output device which may be either analog of digital (**14/16**).

Point, physical   A hardware device, sensor or actuator, that provides a discrete value or status as input to and/or output from a controller (**14/15**).

Poke-through construction   Holes or gaps in original construction created during remodeling or repair of structure which permit propagation of smoke and flame during the remodeling phase, if not properly covered (**4**).

Polar solvent   Alcohol based aqueous film-forming foam concentrate that resists de-stabilization that occurs when used in contact with some solvents (**5**).

Polling   In data communication, a method used in multiprocessing to identify the source of interrupt requests; the interrogation of the devices on a system by the processor to determine if and where any I/O operations are pending (**14/16**).

Port   Communications channel between a computer and another device (**14/15**).

Portable detector system   A complete detector system which is easily transportable. The system normally has devices for sensing, alarm lines, local alarm generating devices, and automatic or manual resetting switches (**7**).

Portal control   Entry and exit points managed by an access control system; usually consists of a two door cubicle with an interlocking arrangement where only one door is actually locked at any one time. Not to be confused with a man trap where both doors will lock with an unauthorized access attempt (**8**).

Position sensor   A device which measures position and converts the information into a signal that can be used by a control system (**13/15**).

Post indicator valve   (**3/4/5**) (See **PIV**).

Power demand control   An energy management application program which controls electrical equipment in buildings in order to level the demand peaks that cause expensive surcharges (**10/16**).

Power factor   A ratio, sometimes expressed as a percent, of actual power (watts) in an AC circuit to apparent power (volt-amperes); a measure of power loss in an inductive circuit. When the power factor is less than 0.9, the utility may impose a penalty (**10/13**).

Power factor charge   A utility charge for a poor power factor. It is more expensive to provide power to a facility with a poor power factor (usually less than 0.8) (**10/13**).

Power factor correction   The act of installing capacitors on a utility service's supply line to improve the power factor of the building (**10/13**).

Power fail/restart   The capability that enables a computer to return to normal operation after a power failure (**10/13**).

Power supply   Voltage and current source for an electrical circuit. A battery, a utility service, and a transformer are power sources (**10/13**).

Preaction system   A supplementary fire detection system which senses the presence of fire and initiates a flow of water into pipes of a dry system (**5**).

Predesign services   May include many activities such as site visits, field investigations, studies, and surveys (**14/18**).

Predicting method   Method for determining when load shedding should occur. Formula used to arrive at a preset kilowatt limit (**10/13**).

Preheat   A process of raising the temperature of outdoor air before incorporating it into the rest of the ventilating system when very large amounts of outside air must be used (**10/13**).

Preliminary cost estimate   Initial estimate of potential project costs for all equipment, materials, labor, overhead, and profit usually developed during preliminary design services and associated with the 35% or 50% submittals. Does not include consulting and engineering fees (**14/18**).

Presignal alarm   An arrangement where the activation of an automatic or manual initiating device will subtly alert key personnel who then have the option of initiating a general alarm; also referred to as a *dual alarm* (**3**).

Pressure controls   Normally limit controls used as protectors in the cooling system to establish pressure control limits which protect the system from extremes in refrigeration suction and discharge line pressures (**10/13**).

Pressure detection device　Device designed to sense pressure, manual or ambient, and initiate an alarm (**7**).

Pressure sensitive buried line sensor　System of buried sensors, usually oil filled tubes, sensitive to pressure. Pressure on the line hydraulically causes a contact to close at the end of the tube which activates a signal to generate an alarm at the facility control center (**7**).

Pressure sensitive mats　Security devices typically used under carpeting; flat switches that activate an alarm when pressure is applied (**7/13**).

Prevention　In high-rise buildings, the training, equipment, drills, and housekeeping conducted to prevent fires from starting or to hold any fire problem to a minimum (**4**).

Preventive maintenance program　A computer driven technique designed to provide prevention maintenance scheduling based on manufacturer's recommendations and equipment/system/device use and/or time. Program monitors individual equipment run-time and automatically publishes work orders that detail preventive maintenance actions to be taken. Work orders include inspections, texts, repair tools required, expendable supplies (and quantity) needed, class of maintenance, technician and time required to complete the task (**13/14**).

Primary control　A device which directly or indirectly activates the controlled piece of equipment in response to specific needs indicated by the controller; typically a motor, relay, valve, or other primary control unit (**10/13**).

Primary trunk facility　That part of a system's communications channel that connects all outlying facilities to a central supervising or satellite station; also referred to as a **transmission bus** (**14/15**).

Printer　An output mechanism which prints characters; a teletypewriter or line printer, used to provide hard copy reports of alarm data and/or selected system logs (**14/15**).

Printer, character　A device that prints a single character at a time. Speed is specified in characters per second (**14/15**).

Printer, line　An output device that prints an entire line of information at a time. Speed is specified in lines per second (**14/15**).

Priority　In computer terminology, an order of precedence established for competing events (**14/16**).

Priority, command　Priority level associated with a command sent to a system point. The command is executed if the command priority is greater than the residual priority of the last command executed on the controlled point (**14/16**).

Priority, residual　A priority level associated with a command sent to a point and which remains associated with that point if the command is executed (**14/16**).

Priority, scheduling　Scheduling of programs and routines based on priority rather than position in the queue (**14/16**).

Priority shedding   Ordering of loads in a shed schedule in such a manner that noncritical loads are shed first and more critical loads are shed last, should that become a requirement (**10/13**).

Procedure   (1) In facility control planning, the course of action taken for solving a problem. (2) In computer terminology, a collection of related job steps that have been recorded in a special Partitioned Data Set (**14/18**).

Process control   In computer parlance, control of a series of correlated operations or procedures designed to achieve a goal or purpose (**10/14**).

Process monitoring alarm system   An alarm system used to supervise the functioning of a commercial process, such as manufacturing operations, heating or refrigerating systems temperature control, etc., when failure of the supervised process would result in fire or explosion endangering life or property (**5/10**).

Process monitoring service system   System used to supervise the normal functioning of a commercial process, where abnormal condition does not constitute a fire or explosion emergency (**10/13**).

Processor   Device capable of receiving data, manipulating it, and supplying results, usually of an internally stored program; a program that assembles, compiles, interprets, or translates; used synonymously with CPU (**14/15**).

Products of combustion   First stage of a fire; precedes the smoke stage; microscopic particles of burned material too small for the human eye to see (**5**).

Programmer   An individual who prepares programs for a computer (**11/14**).

Project cost   Signifies the total cost, excluding design fees, of a project; often used to determine fees or the basis of percentage of project cost; also called *construction cost* (**1/14**).

PROM   Programmable Read-Only Memory; a type of semiconductor memory that is not programmed or encoded during fabrication. Programming requires a later physical operation often performed by a PROM burner. Some PROMs can be erased after programming (**14/16**).

Proprietary fire alarm system   Fire system owned and operated by the primary user; supervised by trained and competent personnel (**2**).

Proprietary protective signaling   Centralized alarm termination point within a facility that is owned and operated by the primary user; may include alarms originating from fire, security, robbery, burglary, safety, process manufacturing, and any other alerting system for the protection of life or property (**3**).

Proprietary specification   Specifications written with the explicit understanding that a certain manufacturer will be selected. The owner must interpret the manufacturer's terminology and trust that the end result of the installation will satisfy specific requirements. Not to be confused with a *performance specification*. Generally not used under federal or military contracts since it is a noncompetitive process (**14/18**).

Proprietary system   Systems that are owned and monitored by the building owner or his agents. Generally used in large building complexes where there is a 24-hour, 7-day protection service available to monitor the alarm receiving console. Noncontiguous properties under a single ownership may be considered as *the property* and be connected to a single central supervising console (**14/ 18**).

Protected area   Term used to indicate the specific area being protected by an alarm system; (1) an area specifically zoned for fire detection and alarm; (2) a secured area monitored and controlled by a manned or electronic security system or enclosed by barriers; indicates an area under surveillance (**3/6**).

Protective rings   Concentric lines of protection for a facility. (1) Grounds protection starts at the property line. (2) Building perimeter protection includes the entire building shell. (3) Space or area protection includes controlled or security compartmentalized areas. (4) Object protection provides specific protection for individual items or groups of items (**6**).

Protective signaling system   Electrically operated circuits, devices, and instruments, together with the necessary electrical energy, which are designed to transmit alarm, supervisory, and trouble signals necessary for the protection of life and property (**3/6**).

Protective systems, equipment or apparatus   (1) In fire systems, automatic sprinklers, standpipes, carbon dioxide, and halon systems, automatic covers, and other devices used for initiating alarms, indicating the problem and location and otherwise controlling conditions dangerous to life or property; (2) in security systems, those security devices designed to detect and alert response forces to intrusion activity (**3/6**).

Protocol   In computer terminology, a set of conventions between communicating processor covering the format and content of messages to be exchanged (**14/16**).

Proximity alarm   A detection unit designed to protect metal objects. If the metal object is touched or the unit's aura penetrated, an alarm sounds (**7/13**).

Proximity card reader   A card reader designed to sense a number of passively tuned circuits which have been embedded in a high grade fiberglass-epoxy card; activates when an authorized card is held two to four inches from the reader; relatively immune to vandalism (**8**).

Psychometer   An instrument with wet and dry bulb thermometers, for measuring the amount of moisture in the air (**10/13**).

Queue   Computer approach to sequencing instructions within the CPU for designating the sequence of actions on the system by priority (**14/16**).

Queuing theory   Research technique concerned with the correct sequential orders of moving units; may include sequence assignments for bits of information, whole messages, assembly line products, or automobiles in traffic (**16**).

Raceway   Any channel for holding wires, cables, or busbars that is designed expressly for, and used solely for, this purpose (**10/14**).

Radio-frequency interference (RFI)   An electrical signal propagated into and interfering with the proper operation of electrical or electronic equipment. This may be any frequency in the electromagnetic spectrum, 0 Hz to above 10^{22} Hz. **(13/14)**.

Radio frequency motion detection   A means for detecting the presence of an intruder through use of radio frequency generating and receiving equipment **(7)**.

Random access   Technique for storing information so that its recovery time will not be influenced by how recently it was stored. Permits information recovery at will **(14/16)**.

Random access memory (RAM)   Data stored in RAM can be electrically altered or erased; a type of memory whose access time is not significantly affected by the location of the data to the access point. Usually implies volatile, semiconductor memory in modern microprocessor-based systems **(14/16)**.

Rate base   The utility's property, used and useful in producing electricity for its customers in a specified period, on which the utility is permitted to make profits **(10/14)**.

Rate level   Actual dollar amounts a utility is authorized to collect **(10/14)**.

Rate-of-rise detector   Type of thermal detector which responds to rate of temperature change rather than to a fixed temperature. Usually activated when the ambient temperature rises approximately 15° per minute **(3/4)**.

Read only memory (ROM)   Memory whose preprogrammed contents cannot be altered by the computer: nonvolatile, semiconductor memory; almost all computers have some ROM in which instructions and data are stored to initialize the system after power has been lost. Also called *ROM* **(15/16)**.

Recall lamp   Light or LED on a patrol tour watch station; indicates to the patrolling officers they should return to a predetermined point or call in to a central location **(11)**.

Receiver controller   A device that accepts the signal produced by a transmitter and converts it for suitable operation of the controller **(14/15)**.

Record documents   Copies of submittals at each design phase kept by the architect or engineer as a record copy to verify changes requested and/or made **(14/18)**.

Redundancy   In general instrumentation, redundancy is the duplication of functions deliberately designed into a system to provide immediate substitution in case of component failure **(14/18)**.

Register   (1) In HVAC, a combination grille and damper assembly covering an air opening. (2) In computers, a memory location in the arithmetic and logic unit or in RAM used for the temporary storage of one or more words to facilitate arithmetic, logic, or transfer operations. Special purpose registers are called accumulator, address, index, and instruction registers **(10/16)**.

Reheat Process of adding heat to air to maintain the correct temperature after it has previously been cooled to some specified dew point to control humidity (**10/13**).

Relative humidity Ration of existing vapor pressure of the water in the air to the vapor pressure of water in saturated air at the same dry bulb temperature (**10/13**).

Relay An electromechanical switch that opens or closes contacts in response to some controlled action. Relay contacts are normally open (N.O.) and normally closed (N.C.) (**10/13**).

Remote control Mechanical and electrical installations that make it possible to control, operate, regulate, and adjust equipment located some distance from the facility control center (**13/14**).

Remote control panel An electrical box specially designed to serve as a remotely controlled junction box; designed to support multiplexed control over building control functions; may be modularily expanded to meet future requirements; some are specifically designed, listed, and/or approved for fire, security, access control, and/or access control functions. Also called *field intercept devices (FID), data gathering panels (DGP)* (**15**).

Remote controlled camera A television camera equipped with accessories permitting it to be manipulated and adjusted by means of electronic controls (**9/13**).

Remote monitoring Use of sensors, devices, and equipment to monitor remote or inaccessible equipment from a strategically located, but remote, central control point (**13/14**).

Remote-station system System of electrically supervised devices employing a direct private or leased line connection between the alarm signal actuating devices at the protected premises and the signal indicating equipment in a remote station (**3/6**).

Remote temperature set point Ability to set the temperature control point of a space from outside the space; often used in public areas (**10/13**).

Repeater A transceiver used to receive, amplify, reshape, and retransmit signals; normally used to increase the range of a system beyond the normal function range (**14/15**).

Repeater facility Equipment needed and location required to relay signals between a central station, satellite station, and/or the protected premises (**14/15**).

Replacement theory Mathematics of determination and failure, used to estimate replacement time and costs and to determine optimum replacement policies (**14/15**).

Reset Process of automatically adjusting the control point of a given controller to compensate for changes in outdoor temperature. A hot deck control point is normally reset upward as the outdoor temperature drops. The cold deck control point is normally reset downward as the outdoor temperature increases (**10/13**).

Resolution   The ability of a television system to distinguish and reproduce fine detail in the subject picked up by the camera (**9**).

Restart, automatic   Capability of a computer to perform automatically the initialization functions necessary to resume operation following an equipment or power failure (**10/13**).

Retarding chamber   Used in dry pipe systems to actuate electric or water motor alarms (**5**).

Retrofit   To upgrade an existing system; replacement of an existing system (**3**).

Return air   Air which is drawn back into the ventilation system from the controlled space (**10/13**).

Return-on-investment (ROI)   One year savings divided by the total investment times 100%. Also termed a "rough ROI" because it ignores such factors as depreciation, time value of money, taxes, and rising energy costs (**1/14**).

Riser   A vertical water pipe used to carry water for fire protection to elevations above or below grade as a standpipe riser, sprinkler riser, etc. (**4/5**).

ROM, PROM, EPROM, EAROM   Read Only Memory. Memory whose pre-programmed contents cannot be altered by the computer: a nonvolatile, semiconductor memory; also *Programmable Read Only Memory, Erasable Programmable Read Only Memory, Electrically Alterable Read Only Memory* (**16**).

Roof venting   Manual and automatic means of releasing buildup of vapor, gas, smoke, or other potentially dangerous fumes from within a structure; designed to release internal pressure from a burning building (**4/14**).

Rooftop unit   HVAC unit/system placed on a roof and connected to ducts which supply conditioned air to the area below its location (**10/13**).

Rotating loads   Alternately shedding and restoring loads assigned to a specific channel so that they will not be shed continuously. Also called *Alternating Channels* (**10/13**).

Rotational shed/add   A power demand shed/add algorithm where loads are shed and added in a rotational order. Usually applied to loads of equal priority in the building complex (**13/16**).

Routine, diagnostic   A utility routine which checks out a hardware device or helps locate a malfunction in the device (**14/16**).

Routine, error   A program which automatically initiates corrective action when a hardware or software error is detected (**14/16**).

RS-232 & RS-422   Technical specifications published by the Electronics Industry Association establishing the interface requirements between modems and terminals or computers (**13/14**).

Runner   A central station employee or protection response force who responds to alarms at the client's premises when an alarm signal has been received (**1/13**).

Running Current   The current that flows through a load after inrush current; usually called *full load current* (**10/13**).

Satellite station   Normally an unattended location, remote from the primary facility, and connected with the facility control center by a communications link (**13/14**).

Scan, active   To interrogate stored information on a continuous basis; to examine point by point in a logical sequence (**14/16**).

Scan, passive   To interrogate stored information by exception and only when the point scanned changes state (**14/16**).

Scanner   Device for moving a CCTV camera back and forth over a designated area (**9**).

Scanning   Moving electron beam of an image pickup tube or a picture tube diagonally across the target or the screen area of the tube (**9**).

Screen   Intrusion detection device made by constructing a frame of interwoven dowels which have been grooved and laced with fine copper wire for use inside air-conditioning ducts and ventilation shafts as well as other openings through which the building might be entered. Any attempt to cut or remove the screen usually results in an alarm (**7**).

Screens   Specially designed window screens containing inconspicuous alarm wire to protect against entry through the screen material (**7**).

Seasonal peak   Maximum demand placed on a utility's capacity resulting from seasonal factors; some utilities have summer peaks, some winter peaks, and some both (**10/13**).

Second priority   In fire alarms, a signal priority for alerting occupants; preceded only by a live voice announcement; they may be a prerecorded tape announcement or simply a fire alarm (**4/5**).

Second source   A manufacturer who makes a product that is interchangeable with the product of another manufacturer (**14/17**).

Security engineering   An engineering discipline that involves security system design services based upon the application of the principles of physical sciences (**6/14**).

Security level   Degree of protection provided by an access control device or system access codeword arrangement (**8/13**).

Seismic sensor   A sensor, usually buried underground, which is designed for grounds perimeter protection to sense pressure, vibration, ferrous metal or a combination, and to initiate an intrusion alarm (**7/13**).

Self-closing   Normally closed and equipped with an approved device to insure closing after having been opened for use; more effective when sensors report an abnormal (open) state (**3/4**).

Sensible heat   Heat that changes the temperature of the air without a change in moisture content. Changes in dry bulb thermometer readings are indicative of changes in sensible heat (**10/13**).

Sensing devices   Sensors which detect the hazard being protected against, i.e., the presence of an intruder or fire (**3/7**).

Set point   The required or ideal value of a controlled variable, usually preset into the computer or system controller; also a value on the controller scale at which the controller indicator is set (**10/13**).

Shall   The term *shall*, when used in a code or standard, indicates a mandatory requirement (**14/18**).

Shed   To de-energize a load in order to maintain a kW demand set point (**10/13**).

Shop drawings   All drawings, sketches, and similar materials developed by the contractor to illustrate how contract work is to be accomplished. Shop drawings are usually required by specifications (**14/18**).

Short list   A term used in project bidding; a list made up by the owner/operator/design team; a process for selecting final bidders; short listed bidders will usually be asked to submit technical proposals prior to the final selection process; a device for reducing the field of bidders to those most capable of providing the end product desired (**14/17**).

Should   The term *should*, when used in a code or standard, indicates a recommendation or that which is advised, but not required (**14/18**).

Siamese   A hose fitting for combining the flow from two or more lines into a single stream, or vice versa (**3/4**).

Silencing switch   A manually operated switch which silences trouble signals and transfers the trouble indication to a lamp; also called an **acknowledge switch** (**13/15**).

Silent alarm   Alarms which do not sound a local alarm when activated (**6/7**).

Silicon intensifier target (SIT)   A TV image pickup tube of the direct readout type designed for low light applications. Has high sensitivity, low lag, and good resolution (**9**).

Silicon target   A high sensitivity TV image pickup tube of the direct readout type utilizing a silicon diode array photoconductive target (**9**).

Silicon tube   A camera tube with a silicon target made up of a mosaic of light-sensitive silicon material. Depending upon the light source, the silicon target tube is 10 to 100 times as sensitive as a sulfide vidicon tube, however, an auto-iris must be used (**9**).

Simplex switch   A method of operation in which communication between two stations takes place in only one direction (**14/18**).

Single entry access system   System designed to prevent the pass-back of access cards; used for parking lots, turnstiles, and sensitive areas where a read-in, read-out system is required (**8**).

Single point data   In multiplex systems, information about a single sensor, indicating an on/off, open/closed status (**13/14**).

Single zone system   HVAC system controlled by a single thermostat or an area protected by a single alarm loop (**10/13**).

Smart card   In access control, a special card packed with up to 4,000 bits of information; effective, but expensive; requires extensive programming and special card readers (**9**).

Smoke detector, visible   The two types of visible smoke detectors are beam detectors and spot detectors. Smoke in an area reduces the beam of light and initiates an alarm (**3/4**).

Smoldering   Self-sustaining combustion of material without any flame being evident (**3/4**).

Smoldering stage   As fire in a solid fuel develops, it reaches a smoke or smoldering stage. In this case the combustion has reached a point where the volume and collective mass of the particles of combustion are visible to the human eye (**3/4**).

Software   Term used to describe all programs whether in the machine, assembly, or high-level language; includes programs, routines, codes, and other written information used with digital computers, as distinguished from *hardware*, the equipment itself (**14/16**).

Software, application   Software which has value to a user in reducing operating costs or increasing system performance, but which is optional in that it is not required to make any hardware unit perform its basic function (**10/16**).

Software, canned   Off the shelf, proven and documented computer programs to perform one or more general or specific functions (**10/16**).

Software support   A service, usually offered for an annual fee, which entitles a software customer to assistance by telephone or mail, a subscription to software release bulletins, and information on new releases of follow-on software products; synonymous with *software maintenance* (**16/17**).

Software, system   Software which is required to make a hardware unit perform its basic function; also called *base software* (**14/16**).

Software tools   A collection of notations, programs, and management procedures which result in productive software development (**14/16**).

Software, utility   Software which facilitates the installation, start-up, checkout, trouble shooting, maintenance, and manipulation of other software (**14/16**).

Sole source   A contract awarded without competitive bidding; usually involves the submission of a proposal for services and/or equipment by the offerer. Bid terminology (**14/18**).

Solid state   Electronic components made of solid materials, as opposed to vacuum tube or electromechanical relays. Transistors and magnetic computer cores are examples of solid-state components (**14/15**).

Sonic motion detection   System using audible sound waves to detect the presence of an intruder or any other disturbance of the sound pattern in a protected area (**7/13**).

Source code   Term used to describe assembler and high level programmer developed code (**14/16**).

Source program   A computer program as written in source code by the programmer. It must be translated into an object program before execution by the computer (**14/16**).

Space security   An area protected by an active security system (**7**).

Space thermostat   Thermostat whose sensor is located in the controlled space (**10/13**).

Special permission   Written consent of the **authority having jurisdiction** (**14/16**).

Specification   The part of a bid package or contract that provides a precise written technical description of equipment, materials, performance, standards, quality of workmanship, installation details, locations, and other criteria that obligate a contractor to procure and install a system as intended by the owner's design team (**14/16**).

Spike   A transient interference of short duration, comprising part of a pulse, during which the amplitude considerably exceeds the average amplitude of the pulse. May create spurious signals or disruption in nearby communication lines (**10/13**).

Sprinkler alarm system   An alarm system activated by waterflow from a sprinkler system (**3/4**).

Sprinkler head   End device on a sprinkler system; designed to provide the most effective spray of water on the area to be protected (**4/5**).

Sprinkler system supervision   An alarm system used in conjunction with sprinkler systems. It increases the reliability of a sprinkler system by checking the valves and critical parts of the system to be sure they are ready to function in case of fire (**3/4**).

SPST switch   Single pole, single throw switch; a simple on-off switch. (**1/13**).

Stand-alone   Term used to designate a device or system which can perform its function independent of any other device or system (**5/13/15**).

Standard equipment   Equipment design, approved or listed for specific functions that is readily available; an item manufactured on a production basis; an item readily replaced by a like item; not equipment specially designed for a single project or function (**14/18**).

Standby power supply   Equipment that supplies power to a system when primary power is interrupted (**13/14**).

Standpipe   A wet or dry pipe line, extending from the lowest to the uppermost story of a structure; equipped with a shut-off valve with hose outlets on every floor (**3/4**).

Start/stop program   A special type of Event Initiated Program which automatically initiates a sequence of commands to building equipment or points at specified times or as a result of special events (**13/16**).

Startup   The process of loading and initializing an operating system (**15/16**).

Stay-behind   An individual who remains behind in a protected area after it has been closed for normal access (**7/13**).

Steel masking   Where the superstructure of a large building blocks the transmission of radio signals in and around the facility (**1/12**).

Stop action   Technique used with closed circuit television to freeze electronically a single image on the video monitor. Used for identifying intruders and photographing suspects captured on video by the CCTV system (**9**).

Storage, mass   Auxiliary or bulk memory as opposed to main memory. Disk drives and tape drives are common mass storage devices. Synonymous with *secondary memory* or *bulk memory* (**15/16**).

Stress sensitive device   A device designed to initiate an alarm when placed under stress; ideal for specialized space intrusion detection (**7**).

Study   Any research effort conducted on behalf of the owner, including feasibility, needs assessment, risk assessment, security surveys, etc. A predesign term (**14/16**).

Study and report phase   A basic engineering phase that includes predesign services by a series of professionals from fire, security, and energy management fields (**14/16**).

Subroutine   A collection of instructions that direct one or more specific program functions. A side-function in which the computer carries out a mathematical or logical portion of a complete routine (**14/16**).

Subsequent alarm   Feature which provides for resounding of alarm signals for any new alarm, after they have been silenced from a previous alarm (**3/13**).

Supervised   In fire systems, a technique for assuring the detection and alarm system is in operating order; in audio systems, line supervision is required to permit the audio system to serve as an emergency signal system; also a term used to indicate *supervised wiring* (**4/12**).

Supervised system   A system in which all component wiring and devices are supervised. Usually a separate source of power is necessary to operate the trouble signal (**13/14**).

Supervision   An electrical method of monitoring power, wiring, and/or devices to insure that they are in proper operating order at all times. In alarm systems, the electrical circuits are given single and double supervision to indicate any break or ground in the system (**13/14**).

Supply air reset   Manual or automatic technique for controlling the volume of outside air that is to be mixed with the system's return air (**10/13**).

Suppression system alarms   Alarm systems associated with life safety suppression systems. Codes and standards require that all flow, valve monitoring, and low pressure alarms must be tested and in service prior to acceptance approval by the authority having jurisdiction. Written records must be maintained covering the testing and inspection of most suppression systems (**4/5**).

Surveillance   Monitoring of building equipment conditions such as temperature, pressure, motor, or other equipment conditions that, if not correct or operating properly, could cause damage in a facility; a separate field of technology to insure safe and correct operation of all mechanical and/or electrical equipment associated with total control of a facility (**13/14**).

Survey   Generally refers to documentation of existing conditions only; usually the first step in the development of an improved facility control system (**1/14**).

Switcher, camera   A set of push buttons that allow the operator to select a specific television image from any of several cameras to be viewed (**9**).

System   The computer and all its related components; a collection of parts or devices making an organized whole, through some form of regular interaction or interdependence; often includes operational, physical, and technical aspects of the complete facility; generally understood as a design that considers man, machine, and facility (**14/18**).

System, forced-circulation   Heating, air-conditioning, or refrigeration system in which the heating or cooling fluid circulation is controlled by a fan or pump (**10/13**).

System, special   A nonstandard hardware and/or software configuration which is designed, developed, and installed for a unique customer request; usually not a good approach as future availability of parts, service, and special maintenance may become excessively expensive (**14/18**).

System, standard   A system configured and installed using off-the-shelf standard equipment with proven, well documented software (**14/18**).

System status   The condition of a particular point of a system such as Normal, Abnormal, On, Off, Alarm, and Overload (**13/14**).

Systems approach   Design of building controls into a single integrated operating system to be mutually supportive in event of an emergency; ability for different building systems to interact in an efficient manner (**6/14**).

Tailgate   In movement control, where one individual (or vehicle) follows another into a controlled area on the basis of the first individual's (or vehicle's) bonifide access; a problem controlled by *man-traps*, *portal control*, and an *anti-passback* card system (**8**).

Tamper device   A device, usually a switch, used to detect any attempt to gain access to intrusion alarm circuitry or sensitive control panels. If the panel has the cover pried off or if there is any attempt to remove the switch from its mounting, an alarm sounds at the facility control center (**7**).

Taut wire detector In security systems, a device consisting of a wire pulled to a set tension where an alarm will be sounded if the tension on the wire is increased or decreased beyond set limits (**7**).

Technical proposal A proposal, sometimes requested from short-listed bidders, requesting that they describe, in writing, how they intend to fulfill the requirements of the specifications; expensive for manufacturers to prepare so should be used sparingly (**14/18**).

Technical security Control and management of the facility security systems, usually by electronic means (**6/7**).

Telemetered Signals that are generated at a remote location by sensors and transmitted by radio or cable to a central location where they can be read out, displayed, and/or recorded (**14/18**).

Telephone lines Method of transmitting signals from a remote location to the primary facility control center. All such lines have no association whatever with the owner's existing voice lines (**13/14**).

Temperature compensated duty cycling Cycling electrical loads on a regular periodic basis to reduce overall kWh consumption. Comfort limits are defined in software to preclude the cycling of equipment from violating comfort limit conditions (**10/13**).

Temporal tone A loud monotone used in alerting systems which is designed to alert occupants to an emergency situation; used in lieu of a *slow whoop* (**3/4/5**).

Thermal detectors Heat detection devices with a thermostatic element used to detect excessive heat. Such devices will usually activate when the ambient temperature around the detector reaches approximately 135°F. While economical, they are not as sensitive as smoke or ionization detectors (**3/4**).

Thermostat Basic controller of the HVAC system which senses space temperature and signals a requirement for heating or cooling to maintain the temperature set point (**10/13**).

Third priority A third level of signaling priority; normally a horn, bell, or siren; to be superseded by a (first priority) live voice announcement and (second priority) pre-taped emergency announcement (**3/4/5**).

Thirty-five percent submittal Usually associated with the level of completion of design services equivalent to 35% of the work; called a preliminary design phase (**14/18**).

Title I services Used by federal and military contracting officers to designate design services up to the 35% or 50% level of completion; may include predesign services (**18**).

Title II services Used by federal and military contracting officers to designate design services up to complete/final design (**18**).

Ton of refrigeration　Refrigerating effect equal to 12,000 BTU per hour, or the amount of heat required to melt one ton of ice (**10/13**).

Tool function　In automatic machine tool control, a command which identifies a specific tool and calls for its use via the computer system (**10/13**).

Total facility control　(1) Complete control in the most efficient and effective manner over all systems within the confines of the owner's property; maximum efficiency of equipment and personnel while still maintaining all normal work functions and comfort control. Prime concern is the protection of life, property, and proprietary information. Safety of personnel is paramount. Facility systems normally operate in their design role, but through the master control center, interface with one another to provide mutual support in the event of any emergency. When properly designed, installed, and serviced, any such system should provide the owner with a return on investment in less than five years, regardless of how sophisticated the initial system (**14/18**).

Transformer　System power supply; an inductive stationary device which transfers electrical energy from one circuit to another (**14/18**).

Transistor　Small, solid-state electronic component employing a semiconductor such as germanium or silicon to perform the functions of amplifying, switching, or controlling small electrical signals (**14/15**).

Transmission　Any condition which interrupts communication between protected premises and the central supervising station (**2/13**).

Transmission line/bus　Conductor system designed to transmit electrical impulses from one location to another. This may be the line connecting the transmitter to the antenna or the coaxial cable linking separate locations (**14/18**).

Transmitter　A system component to which initiating devices or groups of initiating devices are connected. The component transmits the signals to the facility control center CPU indicating the status of each, as well as their transmission circuitry (**13/15**).

Transponder　Multiplex alarm transmission system functional assembly located within the protected premises. It is capable of receiving interrogation signals from another location by way of a communication channel and then supplying response signals indicative of the status of the signal encoding devices connected to it (**7/15**).

Trap　Device installed within a perimeter-protected area that serves as a secondary protection (**7**).

Trouble signal　Visual or audible signal indicating a fault condition of any nature, such as a circuit break or ground or other trouble condition occurring in the device or wiring association with a protective signaling system (**3/4/5**).

Turn-key　A product, equipment, system that is delivered, installed, checked out, debugged, and turned over to the owner/operator ready to run (**14/18**).

Twin agent　In fire/explosion suppression, a dual discharge of agents to assist in assuring extinguishment or suppression; where two suppression agents are discharged simultaneously to suppress a fire (**5/13**).

Ultrasonic motion detector   Device that uses inaudible sound waves to detect the presence of an intruder; consists of a transmitter and receiver placed in the area to be protected. When the sound waves are disturbed, the normally stable ultrasonic wave pattern is distorted and an alarm is generated **(7)**.

Ultraviolet (UV) flame detectors   Particularly suitable for rapidly developing fires that emit flame, such as hydrocarbons and munitions materials. Designed to provide high speed detection where fires are anticipated to develop almost instantaneously with little or no incipient or smoldering stage **(3/4/5)**.

Underwater intrusion detection   Devices designed to detect undesirable underwater activity; standard equipment designed to detect the presence of submersibles or underwater swimmers **(7/13)**.

Underwriters Laboratories Inc. (UL)   Founded in 1894, Underwriters Laboratories is chartered as a not-for-profit organization. UL maintains and operates laboratories for the examination and testing of devices, systems, and materials to determine their relation to hazards to life and property. A *published standard* is a UL Standard that has cleared UL's standards development procedures, adopted and published as a UL Standard for Safety **(19)**.

Uninterrupted power source/supply (UPS)   A complete power backup system that supplies power to a central controller in the event of a power failure **(14/18)**.

Ustulate metal   Heat sensitive metal designed to melt at predetermined temperatures; used as a semiactive door closing device in fire emergencies **(4/5)**.

Utilization equipment   Items which utilize electric energy for mechanical, chemical, heating, lighting, or similar purposes **(10/13)**.

Variable air volume system   Centralized HVAC system that supplies conditioned air to zones where a regulator and a thermostat determine the volume of air delivered to the space **(10/13)**.

Variable rate   An energy consumer suitable for system monitoring; equipment that lends itself to energy consumption control **(2/10)**.

Vehicle detector   Usually a buried sensor designed to pick up vehicle movement. Detectors may give only a signal or cause supplementary action such as automatic activation of a vehicle barrier **(7/8)**.

Vibration detector   A device that can be used on walls, doors, and windows. The sensor is set to react to vibrations of the surface on which it is mounted and to initiate an alarm when this occurs **(7)**.

Video cassette recorder (VCR)   Device tied to the CCTV system for manually or automatically recording scenes viewed by selected cameras of the system; also called a *video tape recorder (VTR)* **(9)**.

Video control console   Section of the facility control center which is devoted to manipulation of CCTV cameras; location of monitors and video recording systems **(9)**.

Video motion detection   Specialized use of CCTV to monitor controlled areas or objects. Intrusion into an area under this type of surveillance will generate an alarm and permit the operator immediate viewing of the act causing the alarm (**9**).

Video signal equipment   Refers to all equipment required by or ancillary to collecting, transporting, controlling, viewing, and recording a video signal (**9**).

Vidicon   Television image pick up tube in which a charge-density pattern is formed on a photoconductive surface scanned by a beam of low-velocity electrons for transmission as signals; generally requires more light than other video pickup tubes (**9**).

Visible flame   That point in combustion where flame becomes visible to the human eye or detectable by ultraviolet flame detectors (**3/4/5**).

Visual alarm signals   Visual devices that range from very small pilot lights and Light Emitting Diodes (LED) to alarm activated strobe lights for alerting occupants to emergency beacons in high noise areas and for indicating to arriving fire personnel where to enter a facility for best access to the area in alarm (**3/4/5**).

Voice communication and alarm speakers   Supervised speakers, UL listed for audio and emergency alarm annunciation; normally used in conjunction with a fire alarm system and may include a prerecorded voice message to inform occupants of specific courses of action (**3/4/5**).

Voice-grade channel   A leased telephone line with band width sufficient to carry voice communication between 300 and 3,000 Hertz (**2/14**).

Voltage peak-to-peak (VPP)   Total voltage from the most positive point to the most negative point of one cycle of a signal (**10/13**).

Walkthrough   (1) In computer parlance, a meeting during system program development, at which time a programmer explains the logic of a new program to peers. The purpose is to expose logic faults before the system program is written (coded). (2) In project development, an opportunity for potential bidders to physically view an existing facility and hear the basic requirements of the owner; usually accompanied by a *pre-bid meeting* (**14/18**).

Waterflow alarm   Water system arrangement that initiates an alarm as a result of water flowing through the piping system. This may initiate a straight manual action or activation of an electronic switch by the flow of water in the sprinkler system (**3/4/5**).

Water flow detector   Device used on a sprinkler system to detect the flow of water in the system which would occur when a sprinkler head activates or a pipe has been broken (**3/4/5**).

Water gong   Mechanical device attached into the sprinkler system piping that causes a bell or gong to sound by only the flow of water through the system; requires no electricity or electronic connection to sound a local alarm (**3/4/5**).

Waterproof So constructed or protected that water or weather will not interfere with successful operation; does not imply the ability to withstand submersion to any depth or pressure **(14/18)**.

Waterside intrusion detection Collection of sophisticated detection devices designed for surface and subsurface detection of intruders; requires very little in the way of operator training and can be exceptionally effective against surface craft as well as small submersibles and SCUBA swimmers **(6/7)**.

Weatherproof So constructed or protected that exposure to the elements will not interfere with successful operation **(14/18)**.

Weather-resistant So constructed or treated that exposure to a moist atmosphere will not readily cause malfunction **(14/18)**.

Weather-tight So constructed or protected that exposure to weather will not result in the entrance of moisture **(14/18)**.

Weigand effect In access control, use of a coded pattern of magnetic wires to generate a code number **(8)**.

Weight sensing mats (1) In intrusion detection, mats used either on or under a carpet to sense weight and generate an alarm. (2) In access control, a technique used to preclude tailgating by sensing floor weight at the controlled entrance point **(7/8)**.

Wet bulb temperature Air temperature measurement which can be used to determine the relative humidity of air. The term is derived from the fact that a thermometer bulb is encased in a wick soaked with water **(10/13)**.

Wet pipe sprinkler system A series of pipes, normally filled with water, that lead to spray nozzles. This system should not be exposed to freezing temperatures **(4/5)**.

Window bugs Small microphones, tuned to the frequency of breaking glass, used to monitor glass windows and doors against unauthorized entry **(7)**.

Winning Being awarded a contract for equipment, services, and/or supplies; usually awarded on the basis of best value received by the owner, but not necessarily on the basis of the lowest bid **(14/18)**.

Wire lacing A network of wires installed across door panels, floors, walls, and ceilings and connected into a supervised security circuit as a fixed protection device **(7)**.

Wooden screens Devices made of wooden dowels with very fine, brittle wire running through each dowel. Dowels are assembled in a cage-like fashion, usually with no opening larger than four inches, to protect building openings. Wiring, connected to the security system, will generate an alarm if broken **(7)**.

Word In computer terminology, a group of characters that occupy one storage location. In most digital computers, a word is composed of bits (binary digits), or a combination of bits with letters; also a coded signal extracted from a memory unit **(14/16)**.

Word length   Number of bits in a computer word (**14/16**).

Work   Materials and equipment required and services performed under the terms described by the contract documents; may also describe services performed by the architect and engineer (**14/18**).

Work area   In computer terminology, an area of storage that is required by a routine for developing a result; after the result has been developed, the work area may be released for reallocation for another routine's use (**14/18**).

Zener diode   A semiconductor used as a constant voltage reference or control element in various electronic circuits, particularly power supplies (**14/15**).

Zero energy band   An extremely efficient energy management application program which allows space temperature to float between user-selected settings, thus eliminating the consumption of heating or cooling energy while temperature is in this comfort range. A Honeywell trademark for *dead band* (**10/16**).

Zero offset   In automatic machine tool control, the characteristic which allows the zero reference point of an axis to be located within a specified range, with the control remembering the location of the permanent zero (**10/13**).

Zone   An area within a structure designated as a fire, security, or comfort control zone. An operator can identify any emergency originating in this area by the system's zoning arrangement. The more zones there are, the more finitely each can be made, permitting a more rapid response (**2/13**).

Zoned system   Burglar and fire alarm systems designed to divide the protected property into separate reporting areas (**3/7**).

Zone-in-alarm   In a facility protected by a fire or security system, an area, designated a zone, that is in a state of alarm which can be identified by where the signal originates (**3/7**).

Zoning, mixed air   Hot and cold air mixed in just the right proportions to maintain the desired zone temperature. The air is channeled into a heating section (hot deck) and cooling section (cold deck) and then mixed (**10/13**).

Zoom   To enlarge or reduce, on a continuously variable basis, the size of a televised image; may be done electronically or optically (**9**).

Zoom lens   An optical system of continuously variable focal length in which the focal plane remains in a fixed position; special camera lens that always remains in focus on an object within its wide range (**9**).

Index

399